Pragmatics in English

Pragmatics – the study of language in context, and of how we understand what other people say – is a core subject in English language, linguistics, and communication studies. This textbook introduces the key topics in this fast-moving field, including metaphor, irony, politeness, disambiguation, and reference assignment. It walks the reader through the essential theories in pragmatics, including Grice, relevance theory, speech act theory, and politeness theory. Each chapter includes a range of illustrative examples, guiding readers from the basic principles to a thorough understanding of the topics. A dedicated chapter examines how research is conducted in pragmatics, providing students with resources and ideas for developing their own projects. Featuring exercises, a comprehensive glossary, and suggestions for further reading, this book is accessible to beginner undergraduates, including those with no prior knowledge of linguistics. It is an essential resource for courses in English language, English studies, and linguistics.

Kate Scott is an associate professor and school director of research at Kingston University, London, and has over ten years' experience of teaching English language, linguistics, and pragmatics at undergraduate and postgraduate levels. She is the author of *Pragmatics Online* (2022) and *Referring Expressions, Pragmatics, and Style* (2019), and co-editor of *Relevance, Pragmatics and Interpretation* (2019, with Robyn Carston and Billy Clark).

Cambridge Introductions to the English Language

Cambridge Introductions to the English Language is a series of accessible undergraduate textbooks on the key topics encountered in the study of the English language. Tailored to suit the needs of individual taught course modules, each book is written by an author with extensive experience of teaching the topic to undergraduates. The books assume no prior subject knowledge, and present the basic facts in a clear and straightforward manner, making them ideal for beginners. They are designed to be maximally reader-friendly, with chapter summaries, glossaries, and suggestions for further reading. Extensive exercises and discussion questions are included, encouraging students to consolidate and develop their learning, and providing essential homework material. A website accompanies each book, featuring solutions to the exercises and useful additional resources. Set to become the leading introductions to the field, books in this series provide the essential knowledge and skills for those embarking on English language studies.

Books in the series

The Sound Structure of English Chris McCully

Old English Jeremy J. Smith

English around the World (1st ed.) Edgar W. Schneider

English Words and Sentences Eva Duran Eppler and Gabriel Ozón

Meaning in English Javier Valenzuela

The Emergence and Development of English William A. Kretzschmar, Jr.

Linguistics and English Literature H. D. Adamson

English around the World (2nd ed.) Edgar W. Schneider

Pragmatics in English Kate Scott

Pragmatics in English

An Introduction

Kate Scott

Kingston University

CAMBRIDGE
UNIVERSITY PRESS

Shaftesbury Road, Cambridge CB2 8EA, United Kingdom

One Liberty Plaza, 20th Floor, New York, NY 10006, USA

477 Williamstown Road, Port Melbourne, VIC 3207, Australia

314–321, 3rd Floor, Plot 3, Splendor Forum, Jasola District Centre,
New Delhi – 110025, India

103 Penang Road, #05–06/07, Visioncrest Commercial, Singapore 238467

Cambridge University Press is part of Cambridge University Press & Assessment,
a department of the University of Cambridge.

We share the University's mission to contribute to society through the pursuit of
education, learning and research at the highest international levels of excellence.

www.cambridge.org
Information on this title: www.cambridge.org/highereducation/isbn/9781108836005

DOI: 10.1017/9781108870047

First published 2023

Printed in the United Kingdom by TJ Books Limited, Padstow Cornwall 2023

A catalogue record for this publication is available from the British Library.

Library of Congress Cataloging-in-Publication Data
Names: Scott, Kate, 1976– author.
Title: Pragmatics in English : an introduction / Kate Scott.
Description: Cambridge, United Kingdom ; New York, NY : Cambridge
University Press, 2023. | Series: Cambridge introductions to the English
language | Includes bibliographical references and index.
Identifiers: LCCN 2022027052 | ISBN 9781108836005 (hardback) |
ISBN 9781108870047 (ebook)
Subjects: LCSH: Pragmatics. | English language.
Classification: LCC P99.4.P72 S35 2023 | DDC 420.1/45–dc23/eng/20220822
LC record available at https://lccn.loc.gov/2022027052

ISBN 978-1-108-83600-5 Hardback
ISBN 978-1-108-79910-2 Paperback

Additional resources for this publication at www.cambridge.org/scott-pragmatics

For Deirdre

Contents

Figures

Tables

Preface

I was introduced to the field of pragmatics whilst studying for my MA in linguistics at University College London (UCL) in 2003. I have been learning and teaching pragmatics ever since. Over that time, I've taught pragmatics at undergraduate and postgraduate levels across three different institutions. My aim in writing this book has always been to create a learning and teaching resource that I would have found most helpful as a teacher. The explanations, discussions, and questions in this book have been developed out of my teaching experiences. I have done my best to pre-empt common misunderstandings and confusions, and I have used the analogies and examples that I have found to work most effectively in the classroom.

Pragmatics is a wide field, and no one textbook will ever be able to cover all the ideas that fall under the broad pragmatics umbrella. This book's focus on theoretical pragmatics reflects my background as a relevance-theorist. I have, however, tried to include a range of approaches that students and other interested readers can use to think about and analyse language in context. The book is designed to accompany a ten-to-twelve-week university module in pragmatics. I have presented the topics in the order that I would teach them, and many of the examples and exercises are taken directly from my own teaching materials. The chapters can be followed in the order in which they appear, and this should provide an overview of issues and approaches in theoretical pragmatics. However, I have also tried to make each chapter useful as a standalone discussion of a topic, and readers are encouraged to dip in and out, as they find most useful. The final chapter is designed to support students who are conducting projects in pragmatics.

Finally, following a convention from the pragmatics literature, I refer to speakers as 'she' and hearers as 'he'. This is simply to help track referents through a discussion, and no further significance is intended.

Acknowledgements

I have been incredibly lucky to have been taught pragmatics by some wonderful teachers over the years. My thanks go to Robyn Carston, Tim Wharton, and, of course, Deirdre Wilson for their knowledge, insights, and patience.

I also owe a huge debt of thanks to the students that I've taught over the years at UCL, Middlesex University, and Kingston University. Many of their names appear in the examples in this book. It may be a cliché to say that you don't really know a subject until you have taught it, but I find it to be true, and my students have been invaluable in helping me to truly know, understand, and love pragmatics.

I feel incredibly lucky to be part of a network of amazing linguists, researchers, and educators, many of whom have contributed, directly or indirectly, to the materials in this book. Particular thanks go to Ryoko Sasamoto and Billy Clark who have always been so generous with their ideas, time, and feedback.

Finally, thank you to Helen Barton from Cambridge University Press for her patience and enthusiasm for the project, and to an unknown number of anonymous reviewers who have provided invaluable feedback on the development of the chapters.

CHAPTER 1

What Is Pragmatics?

In This Chapter ...

In this chapter, we introduce the subject of pragmatics and cover some basic concepts, definitions, and topics that will be central to the ideas discussed in the rest of the book. We begin with some definitions of pragmatics, and a key distinction is made between those approaches which focus on social factors, and those which take a more theoretical approach. The latter will be the focus of this book. We suggest some questions that might be of interest to those working in theoretical pragmatics. Next, we move on to think about the role that context plays in interpretation. This leads us to a key distinction between sentences and utterances, with utterances as the focus of pragmatics. We then consider two different ways in which meaning may be communicated: via code and via inference. As we will see, inference plays a central role in the interpretation of utterances. Next, we discuss the idea that the identification of intention lies at the heart of utterance interpretation. This leads to a discussion of the cognitive abilities that are thought to underlie inferential processes of this sort: mindreading, metarepresentation, and theory of mind. We look at what it means to be able to have thoughts about other people's thoughts and why this is key for pragmatic processing. The chapter ends with a brief overview of the topics that will be covered in the rest of the book.

1.1 **What Is Pragmatics? Some Definitions**

Language is a uniquely human communicative tool. We use it in almost every aspect of our lives. From communicating basic survival needs, to expressing emotions, to discussing complex philosophical issues and abstract notions, we use language to convey meaning. Therefore, the study of language must involve the study of meaning. It is standard to recognise two subfields in the study of meaning: **semantics** and **pragmatics**. Where the line between the two is drawn is a matter of – often heated – debate, and we will explore some of the issues related to this debate in the chapters of this book. However, broadly speaking, we can understand the difference by thinking about the role that is played by **context**. Semantics is concerned with the meaning of a linguistic expression independent of the context in which it is used. Pragmatics, on the other hand, is the study of how meaning is produced and understood in context. Work in pragmatics focuses on what a particular speaker means when she utters a particular linguistic expression on a particular occasion.[1] Table 1.1 provides some further definitions from a selection of sources.

Table 1.1 *Definitions of pragmatics*

Pragmatics studies language in context and the influence of situation on meaning	Fromkin (2000, p. 4)
Pragmatics is concerned with the interpretation of linguistic meaning in context	Fromkin and Rodman (1998, p. 190)
Pragmatics: the study of speaker meaning and how more is communicated than is said	Yule (2010, p. 292)
Pragmatics is often described as the study of language use, as opposed to language structure	Wilson and Sperber (2012, p. 1)
[Pragmatics] is concerned with 'meaning in context'	Chapman (2011, p. 1)
Pragmatics is the study of the relations between language and context that are basic to an account of language understanding	Levinson (1983, p. 21)

[1] Throughout this book, as in other pragmatics literature, I will follow the convention of referring to the speaker as *she* and the hearer as *he*. This is for ease of explanation and has no further significance.

While there are some differences in these definitions, some commonalities also emerge, with the notion of context playing a central role. Pragmatics is concerned with the aspects of interpretation that are affected by context, and those working in pragmatics ask questions about the influence that context has on what a speaker is understood to have communicated. Another common theme that emerges from these definitions is a focus on language in use. Language, of course, is always used in a context.

When we consider pragmatics as a field of study, we find some differences of opinion with regard to how it fits into the wider picture of communication and linguistics. For some, pragmatics is a key area in the study of language, and without a theory of pragmatics, we cannot fully understand how language is used to convey meaning. For others, pragmatics sits outside of linguistics proper and, indeed, may even be thought of as a 'wastebasket' for anything that is not worthy of scientific study.

We find a wide range of phenomena and concerns discussed under the umbrella of pragmatics. Some of these align closely with issues from the philosophy of language, while others are, perhaps, more connected with sociolinguistics and intercultural communication. In this book, I follow Chapman (2011) in recognising a rough distinction between two broad areas of pragmatics. Chapman refers to these areas as 'theoretical pragmatics' and 'social pragmatics'. Both are concerned with the influence that context has on interpretation, and both focus on language in use. However, they approach the topic from different perspectives and focus on different data and different issues. Social pragmatics tends to focus on examples of naturally occurring discourse and seeks to analyse conversations and interactions in terms of social and cultural factors. Theoretical pragmatics, on the other hand, focuses on how words, expressions, and sentences are used to convey meaning in different discourse contexts, and on how hearers go about interpreting language in these contexts.

These two approaches are, of course, complementary. Work on naturally occurring data and interactions informs the development of theories, and theoretical work underpins the analysis of naturally occurring data. In this book, we focus on theoretical pragmatics, and we look at a range of frameworks and approaches for analysing how language is used and understood in context. While social and cultural factors inevitably play a role in the interpretation of specific utterances in specific contexts, the focus here will be on the general processes that underlie these interpretations. The following is a non-exhaustive list of the types of questions that those working in theoretical pragmatics might attempt to answer.

- Are we born with pragmatic abilities, or do we learn them?
- How do hearers disambiguate between ambiguous words?
- How do we assign reference?
- How does irony work?
- Why do we use figurative and non-literal language, and how do these convey meaning?
- Why do misunderstandings occur between people who speak the same language?
- Why are puns funny?
- How do words convey different meanings in different contexts?
- How do we use language to make promises, threats, and bets?
- What is the point of small talk?

We will return to many of these questions in later sections of this book, and we will discuss some possible answers that have been proposed. In the rest of this chapter, we lay the groundwork for what follows with an overview of the key ideas and concepts that underlie the field of pragmatics.

1.2 Communicating in a Context

When we communicate, we make choices. We make choices about the specific words that we use, the order in which we use them, and the way in which we say or write them. Some of these choices are constrained by the grammar of the language. For example, in English, subjects come before the verb, and objects come after it. However, many of the choices that we make are not driven by the grammar, but by subtle differences or nuances in what we want to communicate or how we want to communicate it.

There is very rarely, if ever, only one way in which we can convey any particular message to an intended audience. We usually have options. Consider, for example, the contrast between the use of the active and passive voice in (1) and (2), respectively.

(1) We made mistakes

(2) Mistakes were made

Both (1) and (2) conform to the grammar of English and both could be used to describe the same situation. However, a speaker's choice between the two will be driven by the context in which she is speaking and by subtleties in what she wants and intends to communicate.

When we speak, we also make decisions about how formal, how direct, and how polite our utterances will be. Consider the various ways in which you could ask someone to open a window, for example. Some possibilities are given in (3) to (5). There are, of course, many more.

(3)   Open the window!

(4)   Would you be so kind as to open the window?

(5)   It's getting a bit stuffy in here, isn't it?

The utterance in (3) is the most direct, and, perhaps, the least polite. The request in (4) does not directly ask the hearer to open the window, but rather queries his willingness to do so. As a consequence, it is likely to be perceived as more polite. The utterance in (5) makes no reference to the window at all. However, in certain contexts it is likely to be interpreted as an indirect request that a window be opened.

The choice between direct and indirect requests is not driven by requirements in the grammar of the language. All these examples are grammatical English sentences. Rather, the choice between them is driven by the speaker's communicative intentions and will have been influenced by the context in which she is speaking. The choices that we make often have a lot to do with the social context in which we are speaking, with our relationship with our interlocutors, and with the overall message that we are trying to communicate. This overall message will often go beyond the literal meaning of the words that we use, and it may include information about our emotions and attitudes. It will also include everything that we want to hint, imply, or suggest. Furthermore, successful interpretation of our message will usually depend on the hearer having access to specific contextual information. The overall message that is communicated depends on the context in which the utterance is produced.

Pragmatics is the study of the context-sensitive decisions that speakers make, and it is the study of the effects that these decisions have on what is communicated. Some studies in pragmatics, for example, ask questions about what drives a speaker to choose one possible option over another, and they consider what this reveals about the speaker's intended meaning. Other studies may focus more on the hearer's perspective and will ask questions about how a speaker's choices affect interpretation. Pragmatics, as a field, is concerned with everything that is communicated by an utterance beyond the literal, encoded meanings of the words that are used.

Speakers will often say one thing but **imply** something else or something extra. We have already seen this in the indirect request in (5). The speaker has said that the room is getting a bit stuffy, but she has implied that she would like the window to be opened. We can also see this indirect use of language in Zelda's reply to Celia's question in (6).

(6) Celia: Did you enjoy dinner last night?

Zelda: I don't like Italian food

Zelda has replied to Celia's question, not by stating whether she enjoyed dinner, but by making a statement about her dislike of Italian food. If we only have access to the information that Zelda gives directly in her reply, then we cannot know for sure whether the answer to Celia's question is yes or no. However, we can go beyond what she has stated and relate the contents of her utterance to the context in which she is speaking to work out what she means by what she has said. We are likely to conclude that Zelda did not enjoy dinner last night. Furthermore, we are likely to conclude that this was because the food at the dinner was Italian, which we now know Zelda does not like.

We can only work out these two conclusions by thinking about the context in which the utterance was produced. In this case, it was produced as an answer to a specific question. However, Zelda could have uttered the same words in any number of other contexts, and while the basic statement would have remained more or less the same, the implied meaning would be different. Consider, for example, that Celia had asked a different question, as in example (7).

(7) Celia: Shall we order a pizza for dinner?

Zelda: I don't like Italian food

Now Zelda is making the same statement, but because the context is different, her answer implies something else. In this case, she implies that she does not think they should order a pizza for dinner.

Next consider (8).

(8) Celia: What do you think of my new Christmas jumper?

Zelda: (Ironically) Oh it's lovely. Very understated!

Here Zelda answers Celia's question ironically. The statement that she makes is seemingly the opposite of what she really means to communicate. The jumper is anything but understated, and Zelda not only implies that she does not think much of Celia's jumper, but she also communicates something more about her general attitude towards it, and perhaps even about her attitude towards Celia herself. Again, we see that to understand what a speaker means, we must go beyond what they have said. We discuss irony in more detail in Chapter 8.

Pragmatics, as a field of enquiry, seeks to understand how we go beyond what has been literally and directly said by a speaker to work out what the speaker meant to communicate by producing a particular utterance in a particular context. Whenever we communicate with someone, we must take the context into consideration. When we study language and language use, whether we are focused on production or interpretation, we need to understand how speakers and hearers communicate in a context. Pragmatics is the study of the choices we make when we speak, write, or sign, and how these affect the interpretation of meaning. Without an understanding of pragmatic processes, we do not have a full understanding of how we communicate. In this book, we discuss some of the key topics in the study of pragmatics. To do this we first need to outline some underlying ideas and assumptions and define some key terms and vocabulary.

1.3 Sentences and Utterances

Outside the realms of linguistics and pragmatics, the term *sentence* is far more commonly used than the word *utterance*. For example, an exam paper might instruct us to provide our answers in full sentences, or a university student might be advised to use shorter sentences in their essays. While reading the previous section, you might, therefore, have been surprised to find the word *utterance* used where, perhaps, you might have expected to find the word *sentence*. In pragmatics, we make an important distinction between these two terms. Pragmatics is the study of utterance interpretation. What, then, do we mean by an utterance, and why do we need to distinguish between sentences and utterances in this way?

The grammar of a language generates sentences. The strings of words in (9) to (11) are grammatical sentences of English, as are, I hope, most of the sentences in this book.

(9)   She looked happy

(10)   I don't watch nonsense

(11)   It's too hot

Sentences have syntactic and semantic properties. For example, the sentence in (9) is formed of the feminine singular pronoun (*she*), followed by a verb in the past tense (*looked*) and an adjective (*happy*). These three lexical items have been put together in a way that obeys the syntactic rules of English. The syntactic properties of the sentence are specified by the grammar of English and are independent of any context. This gives us the **sentence meaning**.

Any competent speaker of English will have access to the sentence meaning of the linguistic sequences in (9) to (11). While the semantic and syntactic properties of a sentence determine the sentence meaning, a sentence itself does not express a **proposition**. A proposition can be thought of as a representation of a state of affairs, and a proposition can be either true or false. Notice, that, even though we understand the sentence meaning of the examples in (9) to (11), we cannot say whether they are true or false without further information. Sentences only express propositions when they are used by speakers in a particular discourse context and with a particular intended meaning. When a sentence is used by a speaker to communicate a proposition, we say that it is an utterance. We assess whether a speaker has said something true or false on the basis of what is known as the proposition expressed. The **proposition expressed** is the thought that has been explicitly communicated by the speaker. We return to this notion in more detail in Chapter 2.

Consider example (9) again. To work out the proposition that the speaker intended to express when she produced this string of words, we need to go beyond the context-independent sentence meaning. We need to consider a variety of contextual factors. Who is the speaker? When and where is she speaking, and perhaps, most crucially, what is she intending to communicate? Imagine that (9) is uttered by Pauline as an answer to Gemma's question in (12).

(12) Gemma: Did Luisa get the job?

Pauline: She looked happy

In (12) the sentence from (9) has been uttered by Pauline to express a particular proposition. In this case, it expresses the proposition that Luisa looked happy. Notice that, unlike the sentence in (9), Pauline's utterance in (12) can be either true or false. Her utterance is true if Luisa looked happy, and it is false if Luisa did not look happy. Also notice that the meaning of Pauline's utterance in (12) is not exhausted by the sentence meaning or by the proposition that it is used to express. It is reasonable to assume that Pauline intended her utterance in (12) to also communicate that she thinks that Luisa got the job. Again, this implied meaning depends on the context. It would be impossible to reach this conclusion about what Pauline means without knowledge of the context. However, if we do not reach this conclusion and we do not assume that Luisa (as far as Pauline knows) got the job, then we have not fully grasped Pauline's intended overall meaning.

Any one sentence may be used to express different propositions when used in different contexts and with different intended meanings. In each case, we have a different utterance. If, instead of asking about Luisa, Gemma had asked about Jessica in (12), the same sentence, uttered as a reply, would have expressed a different proposition (the proposition that Jessica looked happy) and it would also have implied something different (that Pauline thinks that Jessica got the job).

Pragmatics is concerned with the interpretation of utterances. The marks on this page are written utterances. When you speak or sign, in whatever language, you are producing utterances. Utterances happen. They are acts of communication. They are spoken, heard, written, or read. Sentences, on the other hand, are abstract. They are objects of study and analysis, rather than tools of communication. When a sentence is produced in a context, we create an utterance. It is utterances that are used to communicate meaning, and utterances are always context dependent.

Finally, while we usually talk about utterances as uses of sentences, they need not take the form of a full, grammatical sentence. The examples in (13) to (15) might not technically be sentences in a prescriptive, grammatical sense as they lack a verb. However, if they are used in a context to convey a particular meaning, we say that they are utterances.

(13) Over there

(14) Finally

(15) Of course

Accessing sentence meaning is a matter of decoding linguistic signals. However, to derive utterance meaning, we must also perform inferences. We consider the differences between these two processes in the next section.

1.4 Code and Inference

One way of communicating information is to use a **code**. A code is a system where a particular signal always communicates the same message. A particular input always results in the same output. Information can be transferred because the person (or the computer) transmitting the information has access to the same coding system as the person (or the computer) who is receiving it. Traffic signals are codes, for example. Everyone using the roads knows that a red light is the agreed signal for *stop* and a green light is the agreed signal for *go*. In coded systems, a particular signal always conveys the same meaning. Red always means *stop* in the traffic light system and green always means *go*. Anyone who has access to the code can interpret the signal.

Languages are codes. When we learn (or try to learn) a new language, we often spend a lot of time and effort learning the new code. For example, an English speaker learning Spanish must learn that the concept which, in English, is represented by the word *cat*, is represented in Spanish by the word *gato*. The concept is the same. A cat is still a cat whichever language you are speaking. The signal that is used to talk about that concept is, however, different. To learn the new code, we must learn which signal maps onto which concept, and if we have access to a code, then we have access to the encoded information.

Decoding the words of a language will, however, only get us so far in working out what a speaker intends to communicate. First, the way in which words encode meaning is not always as straightforward as the way in which traffic lights encode instructions to *stop* or *go*. One word often maps onto more than one meaning (**ambiguity**), while other words encode concepts that are vague or incomplete in some way. Consider the straightforward and everyday sentence of English in (16).

(16)   It is too hot

Any reasonably competent speaker of English will recognise the words in (16) and will be able to decode the lexical items and construct a syntactic representation of the sentence. However, if decoding were the only interpretation process available, we would not be able to determine what proposition the speaker is expressing. Remember that a proposition represents a state of affairs and can be true or false. The coded information in (16) does not, on its own, provide enough information for us to work out what state of affairs is being described. We cannot know what conditions would make (16) true or false based on the encoded information alone.

After decoding, we are left with various questions that need to be answered if we are to understand what the speaker of (16) means. We must, for example, decide what the pronoun *it* refers to. There are very many possibilities. If the speaker is talking about the weather, then *it* might refer to the ambient temperature. However, if she is talking about a cup of tea that she has just made, then it is likely that she is referring to the temperature of the liquid. There is nothing in the code to help us choose between these meanings.

In English, the word *hot* has at least two separate meanings. When talking about the weather or a cup of tea, it is likely to refer to temperature. However, it can also be used to talk about the taste of food, as a close synonym for *spicy*. Again, there is nothing in the code to help us choose between these meanings. Finally, the adverb *too* depends on the word that it modifies for part of the meaning that it conveys. We cannot fully understand what is being communicated by its use in (16) unless we can answer the question 'too hot for what?' Is the weather too hot for comfort? Is the weather too hot to do exercise? Is the cup of tea too hot to drink? Is the food too spicy for the speaker's taste? To move from the sentence meaning to the utterance meaning, we must answer these questions. In doing so we construct a proposition that can be evaluated as true or false. Two possible propositions that could be expressed by (16) (and there are many more) are paraphrased in (17) and (18).

(17) The food is too hot [spicy] for Alex's taste

(18) The weather is too hot [temperature] to go for a run

Propositions are abstract representations, and so the content in (17) and (18) is a rough approximation of the propositional content of the corresponding utterances. We could be more precise and specific by, for example, specifying that the temperature in (18) is the temperature at the current time and in the current location. However, for now, the key point to understand is that the same sentence can be used to express different propositions. To reach these propositions we must go beyond what is encoded. This process of using what we know about the world and what we know about the context to develop the encoded content into a proposition is a process of **inference.**

Next, imagine that the utterance in (16) is produced as the answer to the question in (19).

(19) Are you going to eat the rest of the chilli?

In the context of this discourse, the speaker of (16) is not only saying that the chilli is too hot. She is also implying that she is not going to eat the rest of it. Again, this extra meaning is not encoded anywhere. The hearer must work it out by considering the context in which the utterance has been produced. This is also a process of inference.

When a speaker intends to communicate something more than they literally say, they are implicating. When a hearer interprets an utterance as communicating more than it literally means, they are inferring. Some brief discussion of terminology is useful at this point. The terms *imply* and *infer* are often used loosely and interchangeably in everyday conversation. However, when we are talking about pragmatics, it is important to use them precisely. They describe opposite sides of the same relationship. Speakers imply. Hearers infer. For example, I might tell you that I have been smiling all day to imply that I am happy. If this part of the communication is successful, then you will infer that I am happy from the information that I have given you.

Propositions that are implied rather than stated are known as **implicatures.** If we imagine that Dan utters (16) ('It is too hot') as the answer to the question in (19) ('Are you going to eat the rest of the chilli?') then we can identify (at least) the implicature in (20).

(20) Dan is not going to eat the rest of the chilli (because it is too hot)

He has not said this, but his answer strongly implies this in this context.

It is also worth making a distinction between implicatures and **implications**. Implicatures are intended implications. While it is reasonable to assume that Dan intended to communicate (20) when he uttered (16), not everything that we may infer from somebody's utterance is necessarily intended. Utterances often lead to implications that the speaker did not intend. Imagine that Albert has very strong feelings about people who prefer cats to dogs. He thinks they tend to be less friendly and less loyal. On meeting him for the first time, Eileen tells Albert that she loves cats and that she is most definitely more of a cat person than a dog person. This information has implications for Albert. He will infer that Eileen is likely to be less friendly and less loyal than his other friends who prefer dogs. However, Eileen has not intended for him to draw this conclusion. It is not part of her intended meaning. Contrast this with their conversation in (21).

(21) Albert: Would you like another glass of wine?

       Eileen: I have to get up early in the morning

In this case, Albert is likely to infer that Eileen does not want another glass of wine and that the reason for her refusal is her early start the next day. However, crucially, these are inferences that she intends for him to draw. The assumption that Eileen does not want another glass of wine is not only an implication of her utterance; it is also an implicature.

We explore the notion and nature of implicatures further in Chapter 2, and we will also look more closely at the different processes of inference that are involved in working out a speaker's overall intended meaning.

1.5 Pragmatics and Intentions

Implicatures, as we have seen, are intended implications. Intentions are central to the field of pragmatics. An utterance only has meaning because it has been uttered by a particular person and because that particular person intended to communicate a particular message. To work out the overall intended meaning of an utterance, a hearer must form a hypothesis about what the speaker of the utterance intended to communicate by uttering it. Indeed, it is this aim of working out what a speaker intended to communicate that drives our pragmatic interpretation processes.

To illustrate the role played by speaker intentions, let us start by considering some examples of indirect requests and answers. We have already seen several cases in which yes/no questions have been answered indirectly, and, indeed, indirect utterances are very common in everyday conversation.

Imagine, for example, that Julia and Sam are at a party when the exchange in (22) takes place.

(22)   Sam: Do you want another drink?

        Julia: It's getting late

Sam has asked Julia a yes/no question and yet she has not stated *yes* or *no* in her answer. If Sam takes Julia's utterance at face value, he will not have an answer to his question. However, if he takes Julia's utterance as a clue to what she intends to communicate, he can infer whether she is likely to want another drink or not. He is, in very general terms, looking for what she could have intended to communicate by mentioning that it is getting late. Sam needs to make sense of her statement in terms of how she could have intended it to provide an answer to his question. He will probably find himself thinking about possible ways in which the time, and, in particular, Julia's opinion that it is now getting late, might be intended to help him infer either yes or no. He is likely to conclude, that if, in Julia's opinion, it is getting late, then she probably does not want another drink, and, indeed, he may conclude that she is ready to leave the party. He infers that this is what Julia intends to communicate when she utters her indirect answer in (22).

   In example (22), the inferences that Sam must make to work out Julia's intended meaning are straightforward. Indeed, we may hardly even notice that we are going beyond the encoded meaning when we interpret utterances of this sort. However, next we will look at some less straightforward cases, and we will consider the roles that intentions play in their interpretation. First, read the example in (23) and think about what Ryoko means when she utters it.

(23)   Ryoko: I miss not being in Seville

Most people agree that Ryoko is speaking nostalgically about Seville, and that she is expressing her feelings of missing her time there. Now look again at (23) and ask yourself what the actual encoded meaning of the words is. It is quite different to how most people, initially at least, interpret it. To make sense of the encoded meaning of (23), we must imagine that Ryoko is currently in Seville and that she misses being anywhere else. That is, she misses *not* being in Seville. Many people find it hard to accept that this is the meaning we logically end up with if we simply decode the words, assign reference to the pronoun *I*, and apply the syntactic rules of English. If you are struggling to see this interpretation, consider the sentence in (24).

(24)   I miss being in Seville

Most speakers of English can accept that (24) expresses the proposition that the speaker misses being in Seville. Ryoko's utterance in (23) adds a negation to the state of being that Ryoko describes. Therefore, it means that she misses the state of not being in Seville. Why, then, is this not the meaning that the hearer typically assumes Ryoko to have communicated in (23)? And why can it be so difficult to accept the encoded meaning?

Examples like (23) are sometimes referred to as **pragmatic illusions**. Even when we consciously know and accept the literal, logical meaning of the words and structures that make up Ryoko's utterance, we continue to have the illusion that it means the same as (24). We can begin to understand why these illusions might arise by once again returning to the notion of intentions. Communication is driven by intentions. A hearer's task is to work out what the speaker intends to communicate. We do not decode words and apply syntactic rules in a vacuum. We process an utterance in a context, and we seek out the speaker's intentions. While an utterance is a clue to this meaning, it does not determine it. When we process (23), a variety of factors push us to form the hypothesis that Ryoko intended to communicate nostalgia for being in Seville, rather than for her time not being in Seville. These might include the fact that she is not in Seville at the time of speaking but may also involve more general assumptions about the nature of nostalgia and the sort of things people feel nostalgic about.

In the case of pragmatic illusions, there is a good chance that neither the speaker nor the hearer even notices the discrepancy between what has been said and what is intended. We may, however, become more consciously aware of the role of intentions in the case of slips of the tongue or malapropisms. Consider, for example the line in (25) from Shakespeare's *Much Ado About Nothing* spoken by the bumbling, yet self-assured constable Dogberry (Act 3, Scene 5, Lines 43–4).

(25) Our watch, sir, have indeed comprehended two auspicious persons

Dogberry uses the word *auspicious*, meaning promising or favourable. However, we can assume that he intended to communicate that the persons were, in fact, suspicious. Similarly, we can assume that he intended to communicate that these persons had been apprehended (arrested), rather than comprehended (understood). Our assumptions about what he intended to communicate override our knowledge of the semantics of the words that he uses.

As a final example to illustrate the importance of intentions, consider the interpretation of double negatives in English. While modern standard varieties of English use a single negative, double negatives may be found in social or regional varieties, particularly in emphatic contexts such as (26) and (27).

(26) John didn't do nothing wrong

(27) I ain't got no money

When interpreting utterances such as (26) and (27), we once again look for what the speaker intended to communicate. Did she really mean that it was not the case that John did nothing wrong and that therefore he did something wrong, or, more likely, is she emphatically asserting that John did nothing wrong whatsoever? While both are possible, which one we settle on as an interpretation will be driven by what we think the speaker was most likely to have been intending to communicate on that occasion of speaking and in that context. It is not uncommon, of course, for hearers to pretend to have misunderstood the intentions behind such utterances to make a prescriptive, grammatical point. Genuine misunderstandings are, however, much less common, and we will return to consider why these might occur in later chapters.

As examples (23) to (27) illustrate, the key to understanding how the interpretation of an utterance can differ from the encoded meaning of the sentence lies with understanding the speaker's intentions. To work out what someone intends to communicate we must put ourselves in their mental shoes and imagine why they might have chosen to produce that utterance. The ability to do this is known as **mindreading** and requires a cognitive ability known as **theory of mind**. We turn our attention to this ability in the next section.

1.6 Mindreading and Metarepresentation

Imagine that you look out of your window and notice that there is a man with a clipboard knocking on the doors of the houses opposite. What do you think he is doing and why? How have you interpreted his behaviour? You might assume that he is knocking on doors because he wants to speak to the people in the houses about some issue or other. Perhaps he is canvassing in the upcoming local election, perhaps he is collecting for charity, or perhaps he is hoping to sign up customers for his new car-washing business. While you might not know what precisely he is hoping to achieve, you are likely to assume that his behaviour is driven by some goal or other. You do not, for a moment, entertain the possibility that he randomly picked up a clipboard and started knocking on doors for no reason.

As this example illustrates, we view other humans as goal-oriented beings, and we interpret their behaviour accordingly. We think about what might be motivating them or what their goals might be. We think about

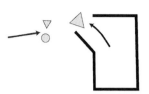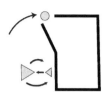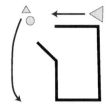

Figure 1.1 The Heider–Simmel animation. An animated movie involving two triangles and a circle. Reproduced from Yanai and Lercher (2020) under Creative Commons Attribution 4.0 International License: https://creativecommons.org/licenses/by/4.0/

what they are wanting to achieve or hoping to achieve. Wanting and hoping are mental states, and so when we do this, we are thinking about what is going on in the mind of the other person. We try to understand the behaviours of other people by attributing mental states to them, and we understand their behaviour in terms of these mental states.

Our urge to view behaviour in terms of motives and intentions is so strong and automatic that we tend to attribute intentions and mental states even in cases where there are none. In 1944 Heider and Simmel carried out a study in which participants were asked to watch a short, animated video. The video showed various geometric shapes moving around a screen. Reproductions of screen shots from the video are shown in Figure 1.1. The participants were then asked to write down what happened in the video. The majority of participants described the shapes as though they were living, sentient beings with emotions, goals, and intentions. They described the two triangles as fighting each other and they reported that one of the shapes was chasing the other. In short, the participants were treating the shapes as though they had minds, and they were constructing theories as to what was going on in those minds to explain the movements that they saw on the screen.

To understand another human's behaviour in terms of goals and mental states we must be able to form a hypothesis about what they are thinking. To do this we have to have thoughts about thoughts. Consider the example in (28).

(28) There is cheese in the fridge

The utterance in (28) describes a state of affairs. Recall from Section 1.3, that utterances are used to express propositions, and that a proposition can be thought of as a representation of a state of affairs. Thus, the utterance in (28) can be used to communicate the proposition that there is cheese in the fridge. The state of affairs that is represented is the state of affairs of there being cheese in the fridge. Now consider example (29).

(29) Fred thinks that there is cheese in the fridge

The utterance in (29) describes the thought that Fred has about the state of affairs described in (28). It expresses a proposition, but that proposition is about another proposition. Propositions are representations, and so we can say that this is a representation about a representation. Representations of representations are known as **metarepresentations.**

The utterance in (30) then expresses a proposition about the proposition in (29).

(30) Isabella believes that Fred thinks that there is cheese in the fridge

Isabella has a belief about Fred's thought about there being cheese in the fridge. It is a representation of a representation of a representation. To be able to put ourselves in other people's mental shoes, we must be able to metarepresent. We must be able to have thoughts about other thoughts. This ability to metarepresent allows us to construct theories about what is going on in other people's minds. For this reason, the ability is often referred to as mindreading or as having a theory of mind.

There is often a tendency to think that it is language, which makes human communication possible, and that inferential interpretation is secondary to the code. This is perhaps not surprising in societies which prize literacy and sophisticated language skills highly. However, Dan Sperber (1994) argues that the key to understanding human communication lies with inference, rather than with code. He suggests that human communication is a by-product of our ability to have thoughts about other people's thoughts (that is, to metarepresent). Not only can we make inferences about what other people are thinking, but we can predict the inferences that other people will make about what we are thinking. This allows us to deliberately change our behaviour to influence these inferences.

Imagine, for example, that you are sitting at dinner with a group of people. One of your fellow diners begins to pour glasses of water from a jug on the table. You can communicate that you would like some water by pushing your glass towards your companion while he is looking in your direction. This is not a coded message. However, you can predict how your companion is likely to interpret such behaviour. You are likely to predict that he will think that you want some water. You are predicting what he will think about what you are thinking. Because you can predict how your action will be interpreted, you can use it to transfer information. You can use the action to communicate.

This ability to metarepresent is key to human communication, and it is this ability to make inferences about other people's mental states that makes inferential communication possible. Of course, the coded signals of language allow us to communicate messages which are much more subtle and complex than 'I would like some water'. We can talk about things that are distant from us in space and time; we can talk about possible events and impossible events; we can discuss highly complex and theoretical issues. It would be hard to communicate the ideas in this book without being able to encode concepts at the specific and detailed level that language allows. However, without the ability to think about what others are intending to communicate, we would be restricted to just this code. As we have seen in this chapter, what we communicate when we produce an utterance almost always goes beyond the code. Language, Sperber (1994) suggests, is a means by which we can make inferential communication more effective. However, it is inference which is at the heart of human communication.

A common way to test for metarepresentational or mindreading ability is by using what are known as **false belief tasks**. These tasks are designed to test for the ability to believe that something is false, while, at the same time, also understanding that somebody else might believe it to be true, or vice versa. We cannot do this unless we can have beliefs about other people's beliefs. A simple version of a false belief task involves two stages. In the first stage, a participant is shown, for example, the cardboard packaging for a toothpaste tube. They are asked what they think is in the packaging. At this point, most participants hold the belief in (31), and answer accordingly.

(31)   There is a tube of toothpaste in the box

However, it is then revcaled that this is a false belief. The experimenter shows the participant that there is, in fact, a pencil in the box and not a tube of toothpaste. The participant will then update their beliefs in line with this new information. Their new belief will be as in (32).

(32)   There is a pencil in the box

In the second stage of the task, the participant is asked to imagine that someone else has come into the room and that they have been shown the packaging box. The participant is then asked to predict what the newcomer will give as an answer when asked what they think is in the box. Most adults, even though they know that there is a pencil in the box, will say that the newcomer will think that there is a tube of toothpaste in the box. That is, they predict that the newcomer will hold a false belief, just as they previously did. The significance of the test is that to answer correctly, the participant must put themselves in the place of the newcomer. They must see the situation from their perspective and answer according to the information that they imagine the newcomer will have. They must attribute a belief that they know to be false to the newcomer and they must answer the question based on that false belief.

Another, slightly more complicated, version of the false belief task is known as the Sally–Anne Test (Baron-Cohen, Leslie, and Frith, 1985). In this test, the participant is shown two dolls and told that one is called Sally and the other is called Anne. Sally has a ball (or marble), which she puts into her basket. Anne has a box. Sally leaves the room, and while she is out of the room, Anne moves the ball from the basket to the box. The participant is then asked to say where they think Sally will look for the ball when she returns. To pass the test the participant must consider the scenario from Sally's perspective. Sally thinks that the ball is in the basket. She has not seen Anne move it and so she will answer based on the information that she has. To reach the correct answer the participant must be able to represent what Sally thinks to be the case, even though it is different to what they themselves think to be the case. That is, they must be able to attribute a false belief to Sally and they must then use this false belief to predict where she will look.

Recent studies in developmental pragmatics have, however, raised questions about how accurately false-belief tasks assess theory of mind abilities. Most five-year-olds will pass the traditional false-belief tasks, while most three-year-olds will fail. This is often taken as evidence of the trajectory of the development of inferential abilities. However, experimental work by Rubio-Fernández and Guerts (2013, 2016) suggests that children below the age of four can pass false-belief tasks if the tasks are streamlined and non-verbal. The classic verbal versions, as described above, can, they suggest, disrupt the child's ability to track perspectives, causing them to give the wrong answer and fail the test. Therefore, while passing the falsc-belief tasks seems to indicate that the participant has mindreading abilities, a failure does not necessarily mean that these abilities are lacking. Indeed, developmental pragmatics is a complex area, and much research is ongoing. Some studies suggest that children as young as two can take the perspective of another person into account when completing some pragmatic tasks. Other studies suggest that difficulties with some elements of pragmatic processing can persist long after the age when most children pass false-belief tasks. We will not delve deeply into developmental pragmatics in this book. However, it is a growing area for research, and studies are revealing more and more about how and when we reach adult pragmatic competency.

1.7 **Organisation of the Book**

In Chapter 2, we take a closer look at the different components that make up a speaker's intended meaning. The aim of this chapter is to give the reader an overview of the breadth and depth of pragmatic work that is involved in everyday communication. As we have seen in Chapter 1, working out what a speaker intends to communicate on any given occasion involves more than just decoding the words that she has uttered. We introduce the main categories of pragmatic processes that are involved in deriving a speaker's overall intended meaning. We start by considering the processes that are involved in working out what the speaker intends to explicitly communicate, discussing reference assignment, disambiguation, and pragmatic enrichment. We then look at the contribution that speech acts and communication of speaker emotion play. Finally, we consider examples of implicitly communicated meaning. In short, this chapter lays out the gaps between what is said and what is communicated and demonstrates how these gaps must be filled to derive a speaker's intended meaning. Chapters 3–9 examine the issues raised in Chapter 2 in more detail and from specific theoretical perspectives.

Chapter 3 introduces speech act theory. We look more closely at the idea that the same sequence of words can be used to perform different acts and to achieve different ends. We explore the idea that utterances can be used to change the world as well as to describe it. We discuss the different sorts of acts that are performed when we produce an utterance, and we think about how we might classify and analyse different kinds of speech acts.

Chapter 4 presents the hugely influential Gricean approach to pragmatics. Grice's distinction between saying and implicating is introduced. We then look closely at his much-discussed cooperative principle and maxims. We work through examples to illustrate how they can be used to explain conversational implicatures. Grice also made a distinction between different types of implicatures, both conversational and conventional, and these are illustrated and discussed at the end of Chapter 4.

In Chapter 5, we critically analyse the Gricean approach to pragmatics, introducing common objections to the framework, along with discussion of the limitations of adopting a purely Gricean account. This provides the reader with the resources to evaluate the Gricean approach both conceptually as a theory and by comparing the predictions that it makes with data, intuitions, and interpretations. We then introduce a key development in the field of pragmatics with a discussion of the neo-Gricean work of Horn and Levinson. We explore how these post-Gricean approaches have built on the work of Grice to try to address some of the issues arising from the maxim-based account.

Chapter 6 provides an outline of another post-Gricean framework for understanding utterance interpretation: relevance theory. Relevance theory moves away from a maxim-based theory of pragmatics towards a framework in which pragmatic processing is seen as taking place within a general theory of cognition. Furthermore, relevance itself is defined and treated as a property of any input to our cognitive systems, with some inputs being more relevant than others. Inferential processes are driven and guided by an assumption that speakers intend their messages to be optimally relevant for their addressees. In this chapter, we define what makes an input relevant and what it means to be optimally relevant. We look at the consequences of these definitions in terms of how hearers go about processing utterances.

In Chapter 7, we discuss how the ideas from relevance theory can be applied to the pragmatic processes and inferential tasks discussed in Chapters 1 and 2. This is a practical chapter with lots of examples and illustrations, and when the reader has worked through the sections and exercises in this chapter, they should be able to use the principles and ideas outlined in Chapter 6 to analyse utterances, texts, and discourse.

Having outlined some major approaches to pragmatics in Chapters 3–7, the book moves on to look at some key issues in pragmatics in more detail. Chapter 8 focuses on figurative language. Rhetorical devices and tropes that have been traditionally analysed as types of non-literal, figurative language include metaphor, hyperbole, and irony, and they pose a particular problem for any theory of pragmatics. We consider how figurative meaning is accounted for by the various pragmatic frameworks, and we provide discussions of some recent and influential accounts of both metaphor and irony.

In Chapter 9, we consider how speakers and hearers negotiate matters of politeness in interaction. Influential work by Brown and Levinson (1987) is introduced. The notion of face is central to this work, and we explore the idea that communication and interaction are rife with face-threatening acts that must be negotiated. We will discuss politeness strategies that are employed to mitigate these acts. The focus in this chapter is on how these strategies are manifested linguistically and in which situations they are likely to be appropriate. This chapter concludes with discussions of more recent developments in the field of politeness. We look at models of impoliteness and consider cross-cultural and discursive approaches to relational work.

In the concluding chapter, the focus turns to practical matters as we outline the various ways in which pragmatics can be researched. The chapter begins with a discussion of the need for research in pragmatics. Neither theoretical work nor experimental work can stand alone if we are to develop our knowledge and understanding of pragmatic processes and of the contributions that they make to communication. Experimental work must be underpinned by theoretical predictions, and theoretical predictions must be tested against experimental data.

Much work in theoretical pragmatics relies, at least initially, on the intuitions of speakers and on thought experiments. We show how constructed examples and counterexamples can be used to test predictions and to fine-tune our understanding. We then turn our attention to experimental pragmatics and discuss a range of experiments which test predictions of pragmatic theories. We think about transcripts, texts, and corpora as sources of data for pragmatic research. Finally, the focus moves onto the practicalities of conducting research, including consideration of ethics and discussion of the importance of diversity.

1.8 Chapter Summary

Pragmatics is the study of how language is used and of what speakers mean by the words that they say. It is the study of utterance interpretation and the role that context plays in communicative acts. At first, this may seem to be a fairly trivial area of study. After all, as we move around the world, we usually have very little difficulty in understanding what the people around us mean when they speak to us. However, a closer look at a few examples has, I hope, illustrated that this task is, in fact, much more complicated than we might realise.

Successful communication using language requires not only decoding, but also inference. The hearer must work out what the speaker is intending to communicate when she utters particular words in a particular context. To infer what a speaker is intending to communicate we must be able to have thoughts about thoughts. That is, we must be able to metarepresent. The chapter closed with a brief look at the general organisation of the information in the rest of the book. In Chapter 2, we begin by exploring the role of inference in communication in more depth. Then in the chapters that follow, we move on to discuss various theoretical approaches to understanding how communication works in context.

Exercises

1a   Can you think of a sentence that would mean the same every single time it was uttered?

1b The examples in (1) and (2) from the chapter, repeated here, as (i) and (ii) could be used to describe the same situation.

    (i)   We made mistakes
    (ii) Mistakes were made

    Example (i) uses the active voice, while (ii) uses the passive voice. What is the difference? In what discourse contexts might each be used and why? What differences are there in the message that each communicates?

1c Look at the utterances in (i) to (v). They could all be used to describe the same situation. What are the differences? What choices has the speaker made in each case, and why do you think this might be?

    (i)   He looked at her
    (ii) Colin stared at Alicia
    (iii) The man looked at the woman
    (iv) The gentleman gazed at the radiant creature
    (v) The rascal stared at his girlfriend

1d Imagine you are at dinner. You would like some salt, but the salt dispenser is at the other end of the table. Think of all the things that you could say (or do) to get the salt passed to you.

1e Think of some different contexts in which the sentences in (10) and (11) (repeated here as (i) and (ii)) might be uttered. What propositions do they express in the contexts that you have provided? What is the speaker implying in each case?

    (i)   I don't watch rubbish
    (ii) It's too hot

1f When might the fragments in examples (13) to (15) (repeated here as (i) to (iii)) be used? What does the speaker intend to communicate in each case?

    (i)   Over there
    (ii) Finally
    (iii) Of course

1g The sentence in (i) was supposedly seen on a sign in the emergency care ward of a hospital. What do you think the message is intended to convey? What does it literally mean? How do you explain the difference?
    (i)   No head injury is too trivial to ignore

Key Terms Introduced in This Chapter
ambiguity, 10
code, 9
context, 2
false belief tasks, 18
implications, 12
implicatures, 11
imply, 5
infer, 11
inference, 11
metarepresentation, 17
mindreading, 15
pragmatic illusions, 14
pragmatics, 2
proposition, 8
proposition expressed, 8
semantics, 2
sentence, 7
sentence meaning, 7
theory of mind, 15
utterance, 7

Further Reading

Mey (2005) provides a brief outline of how pragmatics has developed as a field and considers various ways in which we might define pragmatics and its remit.

Chapman (2011) includes a clear and concise discussion of the difference between social pragmatics and theoretical pragmatics, and for a more detailed and technical discussion of sentences, utterances, and propositions read Clark (2013). Clark (2022) provides an accessible introduction to the general field of pragmatics, with chapters examining specific topics in more detail.

For more about coding and the semantics of language read Valenzuela (2017). Sperber (1994) provides a very readable discussion of how inferential communication works, and he provides examples to illustrate. It is a short chapter full of interesting ideas and is well worth getting to grips with.

Grigoroglou and Papafragou (2019) examine the development of children's pragmatic abilities and they provide an overview of recent relevant work in this area. You can read more about the experiments conducted by Heider and Simmel in their paper from (1944) and you can find versions of the video that was used in the experiment online.

CHAPTER 2

Speaker's Meaning

In This Chapter ...

In this chapter, we take a closer look at the components that make up a speaker's intended meaning. The aim of this chapter is to give an overview of the breadth and depth of the pragmatic work that is involved in everyday communication. Working out what a speaker intends to communicate on any given occasion involves more than just decoding the words that she has uttered. In this chapter, we introduce the pragmatic processes that are involved in deriving a speaker's overall intended meaning.

We start by considering the processes that are involved in working out what the speaker intends to explicitly communicate. This section will include discussion of reference assignment, disambiguation, and pragmatic enrichment. We then look at the contribution that speech acts and the communication of speaker emotion make to the overall meaning of an utterance. Finally, we consider examples of implicitly communicated meaning. In short, this chapter lays out the gaps between what is said and what is communicated and demonstrates how these need to be filled to derive a speaker's intended meaning.

2.1 **Introducing Speaker's Meaning**

In Chapter 1, we saw that understanding an utterance involves working out what the speaker intends to communicate. Consider Bertha's reply to Archie's question in (1).

(1) Archie: Did Charlie get the job?

Bertha (happily): I saw him buying a new suit

On the surface, this seems to be a straightforward conversational exchange. However, as we explore in this chapter, there is a lot more involved in working out what Bertha means than first meets the eye. We must complete various inferential tasks and we must consider not only what Bertha has said but also how she has said it and what she might have implied. If Archie only derives some but not all of the information that Bertha intends to convey, then he will not have fully understood her utterance. Let us look at this example in more detail to illustrate the various tasks involved in deriving speaker's meaning.

First, consider the statement that Bertha makes. When she produces her utterance in (1), Bertha asserts that she saw Charlie buying a new suit. In doing so, she makes a statement about how things are in the world. This is the **explicit meaning** of her utterance, and it is sometimes referred to as the proposition expressed. In Chapter 1, we introduced the idea that a proposition is a representation of a state of affairs, and that it can be either true or false. Now imagine that the same utterance is spoken by somebody else in a different context.

(2) Dennis: How is Freddie doing financially?

Ellen: I saw him buying a new suit

Ellen has uttered the same sentence as Bertha. However, she has expressed a different proposition. Ellen has expressed the proposition that she (Ellen) saw him (Freddie) buying a new suit. The same words have been uttered in the same order, but they have been used to express a different proposition.

To work out what proposition a speaker is intending to express when she produces an utterance, we must take the context of the utterance into account, and we must perform inferential processes. This observation that we cannot work out what a speaker is explicitly communicating without using inference is summed up in what Robyn Carston (2002) calls the **underdeterminacy thesis**. According to the underdeterminacy thesis, the meaning that is encoded by the linguistic content of an utterance underdetermines the proposition that it expresses. The inferential processes that are involved in working out the proposition expressed include **reference** assignment, disambiguation, and **pragmatic enrichment**. We look at each of these in more detail in the following sections. For now, it is enough to notice that the pronouns in (1) and (2) pick out different individuals in the world, and that this affects the proposition that the speaker expresses when she produces the utterance.

Next consider what is communicated by the replies in (1) and (2), beyond the propositions that they express. Both Bertha's utterance in (1) and Ellen's utterance in (2) are indirect answers to yes/no questions. We saw similar examples in Chapter 1. The propositions that are expressed by these utterances do not by themselves answer the questions that have been asked. To reach an answer to the yes/no questions that Archie and Dennis have asked, we must go beyond the proposition that has been expressed and infer what the speakers intended to imply. That is, we must work out what the implicatures of the utterances are. As outlined in Chapter 1, implicatures are intended implications. Once again, we see that by changing the context, the same sentence can lead to different implicatures. In (1) Bertha implies that, yes, Charlie got a new job. In (2), however, the implicature is different. When uttered in this discourse context, the sentence tells us nothing about Charlie or about his job. Instead, Ellen implies that Freddie is doing well financially. These implicatures are part of the speaker's intended meaning, and we look more closely at this sort of implicated meaning in Section 2.7.

There are two more components of the speaker's intended meaning to take into account. First, we must consider any attitudinal or emotional information that the speaker intends to convey. Bertha utters her reply in (1) happily, and this conveys information that appears to be part of her overall intended meaning. We consider the intentional communication of emotions and attitudes in Section 2.6. Second, to work out what a speaker intends to communicate, we must make an inference about the speech act that the speaker intends to perform. Are they asking a question, issuing an instruction, or making a statement, for example? We consider speech acts and the role they play in speaker's meaning in Section 2.5. First, however, we start with a more detailed look at the inferential tasks that contribute to the speaker's explicitly communicated meaning: reference assignment (Section 2.2), disambiguation (Section 2.3), and pragmatic enrichment (Section 2.4).

2.2 Reference Assignment

When we communicate, we refer to things. We refer to people, objects, and places, and we also refer to concepts, ideas, and abstractions. To refer to things we use **referring expressions**. These include pronouns (*he*, *she*, *it, they, we*), definite descriptions (*the cat, the man on the bike, the girl with the skateboard*), indefinite descriptions (*a horse, an angry customer, a beautiful day*), demonstratives (*this, that, those ideas, these answers*), and names (*John, London, Mr Sumner*).

The interpretation of referring expressions is context-sensitive. As we saw with the interpretation of the pronouns in (1) and (2), the interpretation of referring expressions makes a difference to the proposition expressed. Consider example (3).

(3)   He is wearing a blue coat

It is only when we have made an inference about who the speaker intends to refer to that we can form a hypothesis about the proposition that is expressed. If the speaker of (3) is intending to refer to Raamy, then she is expressing the proposition in (4).

(4)   Raamy is wearing a blue coat

If, however, the speaker utters (3) intending to refer to Lee, then she is expressing the proposition in (5).

(5)   Lee is wearing a blue coat

While the same sentence has been uttered, the difference in the assignment of referents means that a different proposition has been expressed. We must take context and speaker intentions into account when we assign reference, and we then use this to identify the proposition that the speaker is expressing.

Reference assignment is an inferential task. While the pronoun *he* encodes information that we can use to help us assign reference, it does not encode unique information about the intended referent. The pronoun *he* could refer to any male person or thing, living, dead, or fictional. The sentence in (3) could be used to express an indefinitely large number of different propositions, one for each male person or thing. So far, we have focused on pronouns, but the same principle applies to any referring expression. Consider the definite descriptions (*the man, the red tie, the blue house*) in (6).

(6)   The man with the red tie lives in the blue house

There are many men, red ties, and blue houses in the world. To work out the proposition that the speaker of (6) is expressing, we must infer which man, tie, and house she was intending to refer to. The words in the descriptions help us to do this, but the hearer must also take the context into consideration. The hearer will also only ever be making a best guess (or inference) about what the speaker intended.

In sum, reference assignment is an inferential process that contributes to what is explicitly communicated by an utterance. We must assign reference to referring expressions to form a hypothesis about the proposition that the speaker is intending to express. Reference assignment is not the only inferential process that contributes to a speaker's meaning in this way. In the next section we turn our attention to disambiguation, which, again, we will see plays a crucial role in the derivation of the proposition expressed.

2.3 **Disambiguation**

As we have seen, a sentence in English is usually, if not always, compatible with more than one proposition expressed. We do not find a one-to-one correspondence between form and meaning in English, or indeed in any other language we might choose to examine. In a straightforward coded system, such as traffic lights, a given signal corresponds with a given meaning or message. In language, however, we have ambiguity. That is, we have words and sentences that are compatible with more than one meaning. In English, we find a great deal of **lexical ambiguity**. Consider examples (7) and (8).

(7) The coach was waiting for the football team after the match

(8) Matthew keeps his bat in the shed

In these examples, we have instances of lexical ambiguity. The sentences contain words that correspond to more than one meaning or concept. The words *coach*, *bat*, and *match* have more than one encoded meaning. While a coach is a type of vehicle often used to transport groups of people, the same word can also mean a person who trains another person or group of people in some sort of skill. There is nothing in the word itself that tells us which is the intended meaning on any particular occasion of use. The hearer must decide which they think the speaker intended. This process of deciding is an inferential process.

To work out a speaker's intended meaning, the hearer must select one of the possible different meanings. If the use of *coach* in (7) is taken to refer to a vehicle, then the utterance will be taken to have expressed a different proposition than if it is taken to refer to a person who runs training sessions. In (7), either interpretation is plausible. Football players often have training coaches, and they often travel to and from matches in a vehicle called a coach. Therefore, a hearer will need to look to the broader context to work out which proposition the speaker intended to express.

Notice that the English word *match* also has more than one meaning. It can be used to describe an event in which opponents compete at some sort of game or sport, and it can also be used to describe a small, thin object used to start a fire. In (7), the other information associated with each of these meanings makes one far more plausible than the others. A football match is an event, and so happens at a certain time. It is therefore possible for something else (in this case the act of the coach waiting for someone or something) to happen after it. The other meaning relates to an object, rather than an event. As such, it is hard to see how something could happen after it, in the way described in the sentence. However, notice that, even though this act of disambiguation seems trivial and obvious, it is driven by the context and not by what is encoded by the word itself.

In (8), we have the lexically ambiguous word *bat*. This could be used to mean a type of flying mammal, or it could be used to mean a hitting instrument commonly used in sport. As with *coach* in (7), without further information, both are plausible interpretations for (8). Matthew might keep his pet bat in his shed, or he might keep his sports bat in his shed. Again, a hearer would need to know more about the discourse context to form a hypothesis about the intended meaning. If we move away from written utterances and focus only on spoken examples, then we have further ambiguities. There are many words in English that may be spelled differently, but which sound the same when pronounced: *weak*, *week*; *eye*, *I*; *here*, *hear*; *loan*, *lone*. When spoken, the spelling information is not available to the hearer, and so he must work out which of the different meanings the speaker intended.

Along with lexical ambiguity we also have structural or **syntactic ambiguity**. Consider example (9).

(9)   Helen saw the man with the binoculars

The sentence in (9) is compatible with at least two different interpretations. However, this time, the ambiguity does not come from the encoded meaning of the words. Rather, the sequence of words is compatible with more than one syntactic structure. When we change the syntactic structure, we change the way in which words or phrases relate to one another. This changes the meaning. On one interpretation of (9), the prepositional phrase *with the binoculars* is part of the noun phrase that describes the man. On this interpretation, the man is described as having the binoculars. Helen is the person who saw him, but she has no direct connection with the binoculars herself. On another interpretation, the prepositional phrase *with the binoculars* attaches to the verb phrase and so describes the act of seeing. In this case, Helen uses the binoculars to see the man, and the man has no connection with the binoculars. These two interpretations map onto different syntactic structures, and thus we have a structural ambiguity. To infer the proposition that the speaker is intending to express, we must resolve this ambiguity and decide which of the two possibilities is intended.

While language is rife with ambiguity, we very rarely notice it in everyday conversation. We become most aware of it when misunderstandings occur or when speakers deliberately use ambiguous terms or phrases. This is perhaps most obvious in cases of word play or puns, as illustrated in (10).

(10)   Two goldfish in a tank. One says to the other, 'How do you drive this thing?'

The humour arises from the lexical ambiguity in the word *tank*. We assume that goldfish will most naturally be in a fish tank, but then this assumption is turned upside down in the second half of the joke when we realise that they are, in fact, in a military vehicle.

Choosing between the possible meanings of lexical items and resolving syntactic ambiguities are inferential acts. The intended meaning of ambiguous words and expressions is not accessible through decoding alone. The hearer must use information from the context to form a hypothesis about the speaker's intended meaning. Disambiguation is a pragmatic task.

2.4 **Pragmatic Enrichment**

Even once we have decoded the linguistic content, assigned reference to all referring expressions, and disambiguated any ambiguous expressions or structures, we may still find that we cannot completely determine the proposition that the speaker is intending to express. As we saw in Chapter 1, some words encode incomplete concepts that must be enriched during the interpretation process. This pragmatic enrichment process contributes to the proposition that is expressed by the utterance. Some examples are given in (11) to (14).

(11)   He lived close to the airport
(12)   She sat close to the fire
(13)   Did you buy enough food for the week?
(14)   Have you eaten enough for lunch?

In each of these examples, we need to go beyond the encoded content to infer the proposition that is expressed. Decoding alone will not provide us with the meaning that the speaker of these utterances intends. Even after we have assigned reference to the pronouns in these utterances, we must do more inferential work. The utterances in (11) and (12) both include the word *close*. While the word is the same, the contribution that it makes seems to be different in each case, and, crucially, this contribution depends on the interpretation of the word in context. We might describe someone who lives a kilometre away from the airport as living close to the airport. However, it would seem ridiculous to describe someone as sitting close to the fire if the fire were a kilometre away.

In (13) and (14) we have two questions. Both questions contain the word *enough* and both relate to food. It seems clear, however, that the amount of food that constitutes enough is likely to be different in each case. The amount of food you might need for a week is going to be considerably more than the amount you would need for one lunch. We find a similar effect with gradable adjectives. A small elephant will still be a lot bigger than a large mouse. Words such as *close*, *enough*, *small*, and *large* are not, however, ambiguous. There is some shared meaning between each of the uses. To form a hypothesis about the intended proposition expressed, the shared meaning must be enriched in the context, and this must happen on each occasion of use.

In (11) to (14), a hearer must pragmatically enrich the encoded content to reach a proposition expressed. Now consider example (15) and think about what Clare means when she utters it to her son Jacob after he has fallen over and hurt his knee.

(15) Stop crying! You're not going to die

If we assign reference to the pronoun *you* and disambiguate the verb *to die* from its homophone (although not homograph) *to dye*, we are left with the proposition in (16).

(16) You [Jacob] are not going to die [pass away]

However, we do not, generally, take Clare to be promising her son immortality when she utters (15). Rather, she seems to be reassuring him that he will not die from this injury at this time. That is, what Clare intends to communicate might be close to that given in (17).

(17) You [Jacob] are not going to die [pass away] [from this injury in the near future]

There is nothing in the encoded content of Clare's utterance that gives us this extra information. Rather, we infer it based on general assumptions about the world and about what Clare is intending to communicate. Furthermore, it would seem unreasonable if, many years later, on his deathbed, Jacob accused his mother of lying to him when he was a small boy because he is now going to die.

As another illustration, consider example (18).

(18)   The sun is shining

If we do not allow for pragmatic enrichment when interpreting an utterance, (18) will be trivially true whenever it is uttered. It is, after all, almost certain to be the case that the sun is shining somewhere in the world (or, indeed, the galaxy) at any given time. Without pragmatically enriching the meaning in this case, every utterance of (18) would communicate the same thing. This is clearly not the case. If Jamie utters (18) in Cape Town on Monday at 3pm, then it means that the sun is shining in Cape Town on Monday at 3pm. If Jamie utters (18) in Helsinki at 11am on Wednesday, then it means that the sun is shining in Helsinki at 11am on Wednesday. The pragmatically enriched proposition expressed by (18) is, therefore, something like that given in (19).

(19)   The sun is shining [at the time of the utterance] [in the place of the utterance]

Thus, to identify the proposition that a speaker is intending to express, we not only have to disambiguate and assign reference. We also must pragmatically enrich the content in other ways. If we fail to do so, we will not have fully understood the speaker's intended meaning.

2.5 Speech Acts

Even when a hearer has formed a hypothesis about the proposition that the speaker is intending to express, his inferential work is not done. A speaker can express the same proposition but use that proposition to do different things. That is, the same sentence can be used to perform different speech acts. Consider the sentence in (20).

(20)   Winter is coming

If we only view this sequence of words in terms of its syntax and semantics, then we will conclude that it is a statement about winter coming. It expresses the proposition that winter is coming. However, if we stop at this point, we miss the fact that this sequence of words can be used to do different things. The speaker may be using the sentence in (20) to tell the hearer something. This speech act can be represented as in (21). However, it is also possible that by uttering (20), the speaker is warning the addressee that winter is coming, as in (22).

(21)   [I tell you that] winter is coming
(22)   [I warn you that] winter is coming

We might also be able to think of contexts in which (20) could be uttered as a threat or as a bet. Furthermore, if we add a question mark to the written form of (20) or use rising intonation when we speak it, we can turn the same sequence of words into a question. By asking a question rather than making a statement we are very clearly using the words to do something different.

The speech act that the speaker intends to perform is part of her speaker's meaning. If we think someone is telling us something when they are, in fact, asking us a question, we have misunderstood them. If we think they are promising us something when they are, in fact, intending to issue a warning, then we have misunderstood them. In Chapter 3 we look much more closely at different kinds of speech acts. We consider how they act in different ways and how we might account for them in terms of pragmatic meaning.

2.6 Attitudes and Emotions

Consider examples (23) and (24) and think about what Jane has intentionally communicated on each occasion.

(23) Jane (happily): I couldn't believe it! Geoff came to the party!
(24) Jane (angrily): I couldn't believe it! Geoff came to the party!

While Jane has uttered the same words in the same order in (23) and (24), it seems clear enough that she has not communicated exactly the same meaning. The way in which she has uttered the words and perhaps the facial expressions, gestures, or body language that accompany her words tell us something about her emotions and attitude. In (23), not only is Jane communicating that Geoff came to the party, but she is also communicating that she is happy about this. In (24), on the other hand, she is communicating that Geoff coming to the party is something that makes her feel angry. We will have misunderstood if we do not attribute to her the same attitude that she intended to communicate.

When information about our attitudes or emotions is intentionally and openly communicated it becomes part of the speaker's meaning. In (23) and (24), this does not affect the proposition that is expressed. It does not seem that we could reasonably accuse Jane of lying if we later found out that she was not happy/angry that Geoff came to the party. We might, however, feel that she had misled us or been disingenuous.

Information about the speaker's emotions and attitudes may be encoded by the lexical choices that the speaker makes. Jane may, for example, have chosen to utter (25).

(25) Jane: I'm so angry! I can't believe Geoff came to the party!

In this case, Jane has explicitly expressed the proposition that she is angry. However, as (23) and (24) illustrate, emotions and attitudes may also be conveyed non-linguistically. We may communicate how we are feeling by our facial expressions, gestures, and body language, or by our tone of voice. While this is a complicated and broad field of study, the interpretation of these parts of the message will almost always depend on contextual factors, and interpretation will be driven by pragmatic processes.

2.7 Implicit Meaning

Speaker's meaning not only includes the statements that we make. When working out what a speaker intends to communicate by producing an utterance, we must also consider what she may have been intending to imply by her utterance. That is, we must form a hypothesis about her intended **implicit meaning**. We have already seen that speakers often answer questions indirectly. Another example is given in (26).

(26) Mel: Shall I get you a coffee?

Nuria: Coffee will keep me awake

Mel has asked a yes/no question, but Nuria's reply does not provide a yes or no answer. Rather, she makes the statement that coffee will keep her awake. If Mel does not go beyond the proposition expressed to try to work out what Nuria is implying, she will not have an answer to her question and she will have failed to completely understand Nuria's message.

If Mel does not have access to any further relevant information, it is likely that she will infer that Nuria is turning down her offer of a coffee. It is normal and courteous to offer an explanation when refusing an offer. Acceptances, however, do not usually require explanations. It is possible, however, that the same utterance can lead to a different implicature if it is uttered in a different context. Imagine, for example, that both interlocutors know that Nuria has an important deadline at 11pm that day. She needs to focus and work non-stop to meet it. In this context, Mel is likely to take Nuria to be implying that, yes, she would like Mel to get her a coffee. In both cases the implied meaning is part of what Nuria intends to communicate. It is part of the speaker's meaning of her utterance. She intends to not only communicate whether or not she would like a coffee. She also intends to communicate her reasons for this. This part of her meaning cannot, however, be inferred without knowledge of the context in which the utterance has been produced.

Now consider what Harriet is intending to communicate in her answer to Juliette's question in (27).

(27) Juliette: Have you read the latest novel by Ermintrude Brooks?
      Harriet: I don't read trash

Harriet explicitly makes the statement that she does not read trash (novels), and most people would agree that she is implying that she has not read the latest novel by Ermintrude Brooks. However, this implicature does not exhaust Harriet's implied meaning. She is also using her answer to imply that Ermintrude Brooks novels are, in her opinion, trash. This is also part of the intended meaning of her utterance, and if we do not access this part of her meaning, we have not fully understood what Harriet has communicated.

Of course, implicatures are not restricted to indirect answers to yes/no questions. Whenever a speaker communicates something indirectly, but still intentionally, we have implicated meaning. To derive implicatures, hearers must make inferences based on evidence, and these will usually depend on information from the context. Some further examples are given in (28) to (30).

(28) It's cold in here
(29) How long until it finishes?
(30) The Prime Minister looked tired today

The speaker of (28) may be implying that she wants the heating to be turned up. The speaker of (29) might be implying that the movie she is watching is boring. The speaker of (30) might be implying that the Prime Minister is not coping well with the pressures of power and office. In each case, what is implied depends on the context of the utterance. Consider how the implicated meaning of (31) will change from context to context.

(31) I hope you get what you deserve

The speaker of (31) explicitly states that she hopes that the addressee gets whatever it is that he deserves. If the speaker thinks that the addressee deserves good things to happen to him, then by uttering (31) she is implying that she hopes good things will happen to him. If, however, she thinks that the addressee deserves a punishment or hardship of some sort, then she is implying that she hopes that these bad things will befall the addressee.

Implicatures also arise when language is used figuratively. This is a major topic in pragmatics. We briefly discuss these implicatures in more detail in the next section and return to the topic again in Chapter 8.

2.8 **Figurative Meaning**

In Section 2.3, we saw that in cases of lexical ambiguity, the same word encodes more than one meaning. In Section 2.4, we saw that the encoded meaning of words must often be pragmatically enriched if we are to reach the speaker's intended meaning. In this section, we briefly introduce the idea that words and utterances may be used non-literally to generate implicatures. Consider the examples in (32) to (34).

(32) His bedroom was a pigsty!

(33) I'm starving!

(34) Michelle (after falling over her own feet): I'm so graceful!

The bedroom in (32) is not, we assume, literally a pigsty. Rather the speaker is using a **metaphor** to communicate that the bedroom was untidy, messy, and, perhaps, dirty. In (33), the speaker uses **hyperbole** to communicate that she is very hungry, and in (34), Michelle ironically describes herself as graceful. In each case, what is literally encoded by the utterance is not what the speaker intends to communicate. If the hearer relies only on decoding, there will be a misunderstanding in these cases.

2.8.1 Metaphor

Metaphors are often thought of as poetic or literary devices. We might, for example, be asked to find the metaphors in a particular piece of poetry or analyse an author's use of a metaphor in a novel or short story. In (35), Romeo in Shakespeare's *Romeo and Juliet* (Act 2, Scene 2, Line 4) uses a metaphor to capture his experience of seeing Juliet on the balcony. In (36), the narrator in Toni Morrison's novel *Song of Solomon* describes how the character Milkman thinks of his long-term partner Hagar in terms of a beer that he might drink. She no longer excites him or gives him pleasure. He simply consumes her because she is there.

(35) Juliet is the sun

(36) She was the third beer (Morrison, 1977/1989, p. 91)

Notice that, in both cases, it is impossible to precisely paraphrase what is communicated by these metaphors and, indeed, we often resort to further metaphors when we attempt to do so. We might think of Juliet as being as beautiful as the sun, but the metaphor communicates more than that. She is radiant. She lights up Romeo's life. She is the centre of his universe. We could go on attempting to paraphrase aspects of what is communicated by the metaphor in (35), but none would entirely capture everything that is conveyed. Indeed, some of what Romeo conveys here is beyond words and is perhaps more about his feelings and emotions. Likewise, in (36), the parallel between Milkman's attitude towards Hagar and his attitude towards a third beer is hard to sum up in a paraphrase or two. Again, notice that, while explaining the context, I found myself resorting to a related metaphor ('He simply consumes her').

While it is certainly the case that metaphors are an established and common feature of poetry and literature, they are not the sole preserve of high culture. We find them both in popular culture and in everyday conversation. Examples (37) and (38) are taken from the lyrics of popular music tracks.

(37) Baby, you're a firework (Perry, Eriksen, Hermansen, Wilhelm, and Dean, 2010)

(38) I'm a hot air balloon that could go to space (Williams, 2013)

In (37), by describing the addressee of the song as a firework, the singer Katy Perry communicates a general feeling of positivity, potential, and vibrancy. Once again, however, the precise meaning is difficult to paraphrase. In (38), Pharrell Williams uses the metaphor of a hot air balloon rising impossibly high to capture feelings of happiness and of being carefree. Now consider the rather more everyday examples in (39) and (40).

(39) My office is a sauna

(40) Jeremy is a devil

We can quite easily imagine (39) being used to convey the stifling heat in a non-air-conditioned office on a hot day, and (40) could be used to communicate some sort of quality about a person called Jeremy. Perhaps he has done something unspeakably bad, or perhaps Jeremy is a small boy who is often cheeky and naughty. In each case, the speaker uses a metaphor to convey her meaning in what are typical, everyday contexts.

Metaphors, by definition, involve describing something as something that it literally is not. Given this, what proposition is the speaker expressing when she uses a metaphor? Consider example (39) again. Intuitively, the speaker of (39) has said something true if her office is so hot that it feels like a sauna. It would seem unreasonable to accuse her of lying on the basis that her office is not an actual, literal sauna. Similarly, consider the grounds on which we might reasonably object to the metaphorical utterance in (40). In (41) the speaker is objecting based on the literal interpretation, while in (42), she is objecting based on a metaphorical interpretation.

(41) That's not true. Jeremy is a human

(42) That's not true. Jeremy is a nice person!

The objection in (42) is intuitively more appropriate. Meanwhile, a speaker uttering (41) as an objection to (40) would appear to have misunderstood the intended meaning. In sum, when we examine our intuitions about what speakers are intending to communicate when they use metaphors, it appears that the literal meaning is not part of the speaker's meaning.

2.8.2 Hyperbole

Hyperbole or exaggeration is closely related to metaphor. Some examples are given in (43) to (45).

(43)   There were a million people at the party

(44)   I was starving when I got to the restaurant

(45)   The room was boiling hot

As with the metaphorical examples, the speakers of (43) to (45) are, we assume, saying something that is not literally true. They are exaggerating to describe an extreme situation. There were very many people at the party in (43), the speaker of (44) was very hungry when she got to the restaurant, and the room in (45) was very hot.

As with metaphor, we find examples of hyperbole, not only in everyday life, but also in literary works, as in (46), and popular culture, as in the Lady Gaga song lyrics in (47).

(46)   I had to wait in the station for ten days – an eternity (Conrad, 1902/1994, p. 26)

(47)   You're giving me a million reasons to let you go (Germanotta, Lindsey, and Ronson, 2016)

Ten days is not literally an eternity, but the character in Joseph Conrad's *Heart of Darkness* describes it as such in (46). Similarly, it is unlikely that the addressee of the lyrics in (47) has literally given the singer Lady Gaga a million reasons to end the relationship. In both cases hyperbole is used to communicate something about how the narrator is feeling.

2.8.3 Irony

In cases of verbal **irony**, a speaker says something that she does not believe, and by doing so usually communicates her attitude towards a person, object, situation, or event. It is worth taking a few lines at this point to make some terminological clarifications. The field of pragmatics is chiefly concerned with verbal irony. In cases of verbal irony, a speaker says something that she does not mean. This is often, although not always, the opposite of what she intends to communicate. Some illustrations are given in (48) and (49).

(48) [when it has been raining for weeks on end]: It's another beautiful, sunny day!

(49) [when your computer crashes just before a deadline]: Perfect! That's just what I need right now!

We often hear these sorts of comments described as being examples of sarcasm. Indeed, it is not always clear where the difference between the two terms lies. Different speakers appear to use them differently. For some, they are interchangeable, and for others, sarcasm is a particularly cruel or mocking type of irony, usually with a victim. For the purposes of the discussions in this book, I will mainly use the term irony, as it is the term which has the broader meaning.

Verbal irony is distinct from both situational and dramatic irony. Situational irony arises when something happens which is completely incongruous with what we might expect, and is, indeed, perhaps the very last thing we might have expected. Examples would include a fire station burning down, a pilot being afraid of heights, or a book about the dangers of censorship being banned. In cases of dramatic irony, the audience of a drama knows something that the characters in the drama do not. For example, at the end of *Romeo and Juliet*, Romeo kills himself because he thinks that Juliet is dead. The audience, however, knows that Juliet has only taken a drug to make her appear dead, and is actually alive. Similarly, in the *Superman* movies and comics, Lois Lane confides in her co-worker Clark Kent about her love for Superman, not knowing that Clark Kent is Superman. The audience is aware of his double identity throughout, and so we have dramatic irony.

For the purposes of working out what a speaker intends to communicate, pragmatics is only really concerned with verbal irony, and that will be the focus in this book. We examine verbal irony in more detail, along with metaphor and hyperbole in Chapter 8.

2.9 Chapter Summary

In this chapter, we have looked at the various components that make up speaker's meaning. We started by looking at the various inferential processes that are involved in working out what a speaker is explicitly communicating. We considered reference assignment, disambiguation, and pragmatic enrichment. We saw that each of these processes contributes to the proposition that is expressed. We then moved on to think about the speech acts that a speaker might be performing when she produces an utterance and how this forms part of speaker's meaning. In Section 2.6 we briefly considered how a speaker may intentionally communicate information about her emotions or attitudes when she produces an utterance. The final sections of the chapter considered implicitly communicated meaning. We discussed examples and saw how these form part of the speaker's intended meaning. Finally, we briefly considered figurative language, focusing on three key rhetorical devices: metaphor, hyperbole, and irony. Each of these topics will be considered in more detail in the chapters that follow, and we will see how different pragmatic theories and frameworks have sought to characterise and explain the role that these processes play in the intentional communication of meaning.

Exercises

2a   Look at the sentences in (i) to (v). What inferential work do you need to do to form a hypothesis about the speaker's intended explicit meaning?

(i)   John wrote a letter
(ii) The students told the teachers they had to leave
(iii) Everyone came to the party
(iv) Aisha lives near the station
(v)   We will be there tomorrow

2b   Identify the ambiguity (or ambiguities) in examples (i) to (vi). In each case, is the ambiguity lexical or syntactic? What are the possible interpretations?

(i)   James checked his room for bugs
(ii) Visiting students can be interesting
(iii) Celia decided to go to Paris on Tuesday
(iv) Kevin sat on a bench by the bank
(v)   The chicken is ready to eat
(vi) Olivia bought new glasses for the party

2c   What are the possible interpretations of the sentence in (i)? Notice which of these interpretations occurred to you first? Which do you think is most compatible with your encyclopaedic knowledge of the world? Does this surprise you?

(i)   That sheepdog is too hairy to eat

2d   It has been said that there are ambiguous sentences, but no ambiguous utterances. What might this mean? How does this link to the idea of speaker intentions that we explored in Chapter 1?

2e   Choose a paragraph from a book, newspaper, or website. Look at each lexical item in turn. Ignoring the context in which they are used, consider whether each has more than one encoded meaning? How much ambiguity do you find?

2f   The following examples (i) to (v) were submitted to the BBC Radio 4 comedy news show *The News Quiz* (BBC, n.d.). Where is the ambiguity in each case? Why are they funny?

  (i)   News story: A 12-week-old kitten was rescued from inside a living room sofa after fire officers chopped it up with hacksaws and hydraulic cutters

  (ii)   Personal advertisement: Hello. I'm looking for a free or cheap double mattress. I'm heavily pregnant so I would be extremely grateful if you are also able to deliver

  (iii) Advertisement in local newspaper: Six-foot boa constrictor. Free to a good home. Very friendly, good eater, likes children.

  (iv)   A warning to competitors at a marathon: Please do not bring plastic bin bags to wear. We've had runners tripping over them, and they just end up in landfill

  (v)   News story: A group of primary school children toured the Houses of Parliament this week thanks to their guide, Watford MP Richard Harrington. The children had an opportunity to grill Mr Hamilton before lunch

2f   How might a communicator intentionally convey information about their attitudes and emotions? Think of as many examples as possible. How do these affect the meaning that is conveyed?

2g   Choose a favourite poem, novel, or song and identify any uses of metaphor, hyperbole, or irony. What do they contribute to the piece?

Key Terms Introduced in this Chapter

Further Reading

Most of the topics covered in Chapter 2 will be explored in more depth in later chapters. Valenzuela (2017) includes more detailed discussion of the semantically encoded meanings of lexical items and provides a useful introduction to figurative meaning, with a focus on metaphor.

Carston (2002) introduces and discusses the underdeterminacy thesis in detail. This text is recommended for any reader who would like to focus on the various ways in which what we say underdetermines what we mean. Tim Wharton (2009) provides a detailed and comprehension examination of non-verbal pragmatics, and his work is crucial reading for those interested in how we might intentionally communicate our emotions and attitudes.

CHAPTER 3

Speech Act Theory

In This Chapter ...

In this chapter, we think about the different things that we *do* when we produce utterances. Communication is not only about the exchange of information. We also perform acts and, in some cases, change the world when we speak, sign, or write. To fully understand what a speaker is communicating, we must infer which act (or acts) she is intending to perform. Is she simply describing the world as she sees it, or is she using her utterance to make a request, ask a question, or issue a warning? Speech act theory emerged as a means of understanding and analysing the things we do when we use language. In this chapter, we track the development of speech act theory, focusing on the work of two influential thinkers in the field: J. L. Austin and John R. Searle.

We begin by looking at what Austin called performatives. These are utterances which effect a change in the world when they are produced. They include acts such as resigning, placing a bet, and making a promise, and to be successful they must satisfy what Austin called felicity conditions. We then move on to explore Austin's observation that when we produce an utterance, we perform three different types of speech act: locutionary acts, illocutionary acts, and perlocutionary acts. These are defined and compared in Section 3.2.2.

John R. Searle's work responds to and develops the work of Austin. He identifies four categories of felicity condition and uses these to propose a classification system for illocutionary acts. We consider Searle's discussion of indirect speech acts as a key contribution to speech act theory and pragmatics more widely. The chapter ends with a brief overview of how speech act theory has been applied and developed since the work of Austin and Searle.

3.1 **Doing Things with Words**

A speaker can use an utterance to perform a range of acts. When we speak, write, or sign, we are not limited to describing the world around us or to stating facts. We can use utterances to assert or promise something. We can use them to beg or to threaten someone. Language can also be used to make bets, to name ships, and even to marry one person to another.

In Chapter 2, we briefly looked at the example repeated here as (1). While this utterance describes a state of affairs in the world, there are some occasions on which it might be used, not only to describe, but to do something else as well.

(1) Winter is coming

Imagine, for example, that John and Claire have been discussing their household maintenance. There is a hole in the roof and a radiator has stopped working. John thinks that these are not urgent matters, and he suggests that they concentrate on redesigning the garden rather than fixing the roof or heating. In response to this suggestion, Claire utters (1). While her utterance describes a state of affairs, it could also be understood as a warning. She is warning John that if they do not focus on the roof and radiators, they will be cold when the weather worsens in the winter.

Identification of the speech act that is being performed by a speaker is a key task in the interpretation of an utterance. The same sentence can be used to perform different **speech acts**. As with the other pragmatic aspects of communication discussed in this book, speech acts are inferred by the hearer, and this act of inference involves forming a hypothesis about the intentions of the speaker. If Claire intends her utterance in (1) to be understood as a warning, but John interprets it merely as a description, then a misunderstanding has taken place.

Speech act theory is a field within pragmatics which is concerned with the speech acts that speakers perform. Much of the work of speech act theory stems from the key observation that we can use utterances to do various things. It focuses on analyses of the acts that are performed when we utter a sentence, and it aims to capture the range of functions that language can perform. Here we focus on the work of J. L. Austin and John R. Searle.

Austin's influential work begins from his observation that we do more with language than simply making statements and describing states of affairs. Austin's thinking around speech acts is laid out in his book *How to Do Things with Words* (1962), and when approaching his ideas, it is helpful to be aware that he reveals his position gradually over the course of this book. Austin presents distinctions early in the text which he later distances himself from, and he takes the reader with him as he builds an argument to support his conclusions. We will broadly follow his line of argument here, and much of the terminology that we use to talk about speech acts stems from Austin's original ideas and discussions. As we will see, John R. Searle then took these ideas, criticised some aspects of Austin's approach and developed others to produce his own analysis. We begin our discussion of Austin's work by looking at a set of utterances which most obviously *do* something. These are utterances which change the way things are in the world. Austin called these **performatives**.

3.2 Austin's Speech Act Theory

3.2.1 Austin and Performatives

Consider examples (2) to (4), and think about how the world is different after they have been spoken, compared to before.

(2) I pronounce you husband and wife

(3) I bet you £50 that Roger Federer will win Wimbledon this year

(4) I apologise for what I said last night

In each of these cases, the speaker is using a declarative sentence to *do* something specific. She is using her words to change the world. By uttering (2) the speaker changes the official relationship between the addressees. Before (2) is uttered, they are not married, and after it is produced, they are. By uttering (3), the speaker makes a bet. When she produces the utterance, she sets out the terms of the wager and at the same time commits herself to the deal. Finally, in (4), the act of uttering the words *I apologise* constitutes the apology itself. In each of these cases the world is changed by the act of uttering particular words.

Austin called these utterances performatives. He contrasted them with utterances which declare something to be the case, which he called **constatives**. Constatives can be true or false. However, it does not make sense to ask whether a performative utterance is true. Instead, we tend to think of performatives in terms of whether they have been successful or not. By producing a performative utterance, a speaker carries out an action.

Felicity conditions are the conditions that must be in place for that action to be considered successful. For example, I cannot successfully marry two people simply by uttering the words in (2). Certain other conditions must be in place. Amongst other things, the two people must be of a certain minimum age, they must both be currently unmarried, and I must have been granted some sort of authorisation to carry out marriage ceremonies. If these conditions are not satisfied, uttering the words will not cause a change in the way things are in the world. The two addressees will not be married.

Austin identifies two ways in which a performative can fail, and he links these to the felicity conditions associated with that performative. First, a performative utterance can **misfire**. A misfire occurs when the procedure associated with the performative has not been followed. As we have just seen, my attempt to marry two people will fail if I do not have the appropriate authorisation. It will also misfire if certain declarations are not made by the appropriate people in the appropriate circumstances. For example, in United Kingdom law, both parties must declare that they know of no legal reason why they cannot marry, and both parties must utter a promise or contract stating their intention to enter into the marriage. If the ceremony does not include both of these elements, then the couple are not legally married and the act of pronouncing them so will misfire.

The misfiring of a performative is often associated with formal and ritualised acts. We have already seen this in the example of a marriage ceremony. However, we find felicity conditions and associated misfirings applying in many other contexts. For example, in the United Kingdom legal system, a person is not arrested until the police officer has told them that they are being arrested. Similarly, a court session is adjourned only when a judge states that it is adjourned. The status of a player in a baseball game changes when an umpire calls him or her out (or makes an equivalent gesture). Notice that if a spectator who is watching from the sidelines shouts the word *out*, this makes no difference to the status of the player in the game. The spectator does not have the requisite authority, and the act misfires. In each of these cases, the success of the act is contingent on the satisfaction of certain conditions to do with the people, circumstances, and procedures involved and/or with the specific wording used.

The other means by which a performative can fail are related to the intentions and sincerity of the participants, and Austin refers to cases that fail in this way as **abuses**. All conventional procedures may have been followed and all participants may have uttered the right words and phrases. However, if the intentions of the participants are not sincere, then, according to Austin, some acts will not be felicitous. For example, in UK law, a forced marriage can be declared null on the grounds of a lack of consent. The participants may have uttered the appropriate words, but if it is later revealed that they were forced or coerced into doing so against their will, the marriage is considered never to have taken place. Alternatively, consider an apology that is uttered insincerely. A conventional apology may have been uttered, but if the speaker did not mean it, then it feels as though an apology has not, indeed, been made. The act is hollow and insincere. We do not need a particular position of authority or role to make an apology or a promise, but the sincerity of the speaker is important.

The main verbs in performative utterances in English tend to be first person singular, present tense, and in the active voice. We can see this in (2) to (4). However, as Austin observed, there is no clear association between the grammatical form of an utterance in this sense and whether that utterance is performative or not. The same grammatical construction can be performative on one occasion of use and constative on another. To illustrate, consider the exchanges in (5) and (6).

(5) Nick: You've broken my favourite mug
     Theresa: I apologise
(6) Nick: What do you do if you forget someone's birthday?
     Theresa: I apologise

In both cases, Theresa has produced the same grammatical sequence of words. In (5), she is performing the act of apologising, and her utterance is therefore performative. In (6), however, she is describing what she does, and thus her utterance is constative. A first-person present tense active utterance is, therefore, not a clear and unambiguous sign that we are dealing with a performative.

Furthermore, as Austin notes, performatives can be in the second or third person, as in (7) and (8), and they can also be in the passive voice, as the following examples (taken from Austin, 1962, p. 57) illustrate.

(7) You are hereby authorised to pay …
(8) Passengers are warned to cross the track by the bridge only
(9) Notice is hereby given that trespassers will be prosecuted

How then, might we identify performative utterances if there is no definitive connection between the grammatical form of an utterance and its status as a performative or constative? Performatives, Austin notices, often include the word *hereby*, as in (7) and (9). *Hereby* is an explicit indication that the speaker is doing something by saying something, and Austin suggests that we can identify performatives by testing to see whether *hereby* can be inserted. This works for the performatives in (10) to (12).

(10) I hereby pronounce you husband and wife

(11) I hereby promise to pay my debt

(12) I hereby name this ship *La Farruca*

Notice, however, how it fails with the constative utterances in (13) and (14).

(13) ?John is hereby borrowing your pen

(14) ?I hereby work in a bar every Friday night

Constatives are, however, by their very nature, assertions or statements about states of affairs, and we can use *hereby* with the verbs *state* and *assert* to produce acceptable utterances. Consider the examples in (15) and (16).

(15) I hereby state that today is Tuesday

(16) I hereby assert that the sun is shining

Suddenly acts (stating and asserting) that are associated with constative utterances are behaving like performatives. The boundary between the two has become blurred, and it certainly does not seem possible to distinguish between them based on their surface form alone.

Austin's solution to this problem is to introduce a different distinction. Rather than categorising utterances as constative or performative, he suggests that a distinction be drawn between what he calls **explicit performatives** and **primary performatives**. An explicit performative contains an explicit performative verb which describes the action being performed. This might be *name*, *promise*, *apologise*, *bet*, *warn*, *state*, or *assert*, for example. A primary performative, on the other hand, is an utterance that is used to perform an act, but which does not contain an explicit performative verb. We have seen various examples already, but some more are given in (17) to (19).

(17) The floor is wet (uttered as a warning)

(18) I will come on Tuesday (uttered as a promise)

(19) Out! (uttered by a baseball umpire)

We should, Austin suggests, be able to rephrase primary performatives as explicit performatives, as in (20) to (22).

(20) I warn you that the floor is wet

(21) I promise you that I will come on Tuesday

(22) I call you out!

Once again, however, Austin points out a problem. There are cases where someone is clearly performing an action when they produce an utterance but for which there is no explicit performative verb. The act of verbally insulting someone is one example. We may use an utterance to perform the act of insulting someone, but we cannot insult someone simply by using the verb *insult*. Think about the utterance in (23).

(23) I insult you

Uttering (23) describes the act of insulting, but it does not, in and of itself, perform that act. Compare this with Theresa's apology in (5).

Furthermore, there are some utterances which can be both performative and constative at the same time. Consider the example in (24).

(24) I blame you for the team losing

Here the speaker appears to be both performing the act of blaming and describing the way that she feels. Similarly, if we perform the act of apologising by uttering (25), we are both apologising and describing how we feel.

(25) I am sorry

Finally, we seem to be able to make any constative utterance into a performative simply by adding an explicit verb such as *state* or *assert*. We saw this in (15) and (16). It seems that all utterances perform some sort of action, even if it is an action that we might associate with constatives, such as stating or asserting.

Ultimately, Austin concluded that it was not possible to draw a clear line between performatives and constatives, and that a different approach was needed. As he explains (Austin, 1962, p. 91), 'It is time to make a fresh start on the problem. We want to reconsider more generally the sense in which to say something may be to do something'. This brings us onto the next key distinction in speech act theory and to another way of thinking about the acts that we perform when we produce an utterance. We turn our attention to this in the next section.

3.2.2 Types of Speech Act

Austin's attempt to classify utterances into performatives and constatives breaks down, and the boundary between the two categories becomes blurred. However, this leads him to adopt a new approach which has been influential in the development and application of speech act theory. Austin develops his account by looking more closely at the different things that we do when we produce utterances. He notices that each individual utterance can be understood as performing three different sorts of act at the same time. To fully understand what a speaker is doing when she produces an utterance, we must consider each of these acts separately. The difference between the three types can be rather hard to grasp, and so it is easiest to start with an example. Imagine that Sara utters (26) to Dan as he enters their kitchen.

(26)   The floor is wet

When Sara utters the words in (26), she performs an act of locution. She speaks a series of words, and she produces a sentence of English. Austin called this the **locutionary act.** It is the act of using language. If we were to describe the locutionary act that Sara has performed in this case, we could simply quote her words or perhaps report what she said. A locutionary act is the act of creating an utterance.

Usually we do not, however, produce utterances just for the sake of producing utterances. We produce utterances to perform what Austin calls **illocutionary acts.** The sentence in (26), for example, could be intended as a simple statement of fact (an assertion), or it could be intended as a complaint, a warning, or even as a threat. Each of these is a different illocutionary act. For (26), let us assume that Sara is intending to warn Dan that the floor is wet. She is performing the illocutionary act of warning. The same sentence uttered in a different context, with a different intention would perform a different illocutionary act.

Finally, distinct from the locutionary and illocutionary acts, we have what are known as **perlocutionary acts.** By producing her utterance in (26), Sara may have intended to achieve some effect. In this discourse context, when uttered as a warning, it is likely that she hoped her utterance would cause Dan to walk more carefully across the floor so as not to slip. This is an example of a perlocutionary act. As Austin (1962, p. 101) explains:

> Saying something will often, or even normally, produce certain consequential effects upon the feelings, thoughts, or actions of the audience, or of the speaker, or of other persons: and it may be done with the design, intention, or purpose of producing them.

The distinction between the illocutionary act and the perlocutionary act can be difficult to grasp, and Austin himself admitted that it was blurry. However, it can help to think about the different ways in which we might answer the question 'What did Sara do?' If we are thinking about the illocutionary act, then we will answer this question by saying that she warned Dan. However, if we are answering the question in terms of the perlocutionary act, we will say that she stopped Dan walking on the wet floor (assuming that the act is successful).

The illocutionary act is about the nature of the speech act that is performed, and it is determined by the conventions of the grammar and the intentions of the speakers. The perlocutionary act is about the consequences or effects of the utterance, and it depends on the context in which the utterance is produced. The perlocutionary act that is performed may be part of what the speaker intended, but an utterance may also lead to unintended consequences. Sara's warning to Dan in (26), for example, may irritate or annoy him as he realises that he is not able to get to the cupboard without stepping on the wet floor. It was not Sara's intention to provoke these feelings, but it is an effect of her utterance, and so it is part of the perlocutionary act that has been performed.

We can also distinguish between the three different types of act by thinking about how the speaker might fail in performing each of them. Sara's locutionary act in (26) would fail if, for some reason, she did not manage to get her words out. Perhaps she has just swallowed some water and it causes her to cough when she tries to speak. We might also struggle to perform a locutionary act in a language in which we do not have fluency. We may not be able to clearly articulate the words, or we may lack the vocabulary to produce the full utterance.

Sara's illocutionary act, on the other hand, would fail if, for example, Dan interprets her utterance as a complaint, rather than as a warning. In that case, he does not correctly infer what she was trying to do with her utterance. She was not complaining but giving a warning. Perlocutionary acts are the consequences or effects that follow from the utterance. A speaker might intend for her utterance to perform one perlocutionary act, but it might perform quite a different act as well or instead. We have already considered how Dan might react to Sara's well-intentioned warning in (26) in a way that she did not intend. As another example, imagine that you tell a friend a joke, but rather than being amused, they are offended by the subject matter. In this case, the perlocutionary act that you intended to perform has failed.

The distinction between locutionary, illocutionary, and perlocutionary acts allowed Austin to revisit his distinction between constatives and performatives. Those utterances that were previously considered to be constatives could now be viewed in terms of the illocutionary acts that they perform. Constatives are utterances which perform the illocutionary acts of describing, asserting, or informing. Looked at this way, constatives do not form a meaningful class that is different from performatives. Rather, Austin (1962, p. 150) identifies what he calls 'more general *families* of related and overlapping speech-acts'. He tentatively proposes a set of five such classes, identified via associated verbs and the illocutionary acts that they are used to perform. The five classes are verdictives, exercitives, commissives, behabitives and expositives, and Austin (1962, p. 163) provides the following summary of their functions:

the verdictive is an exercise of judgement, the exercitive is an assertion of influence or exercising of power, the commissive is an assuming of an obligation or declaring of an intention, the behabitive is the adopting of an attitude, and the expositive is the clarifying of reasons, arguments, and communications.

Austin himself seemed somewhat dissatisfied with these groupings and perhaps saw them as ripe for further development and refinement. Indeed, this is precisely what John R. Searle did in his work on speech acts which we turn to next.

3.3 Searle's Speech Act Theory

3.3.1 Searle's Felicity Conditions

Searle (1979, p. 8) considers Austin's five categories to be 'an excellent basis for discussion'. However, he argues that the taxonomy should be revised to be more systematic and consistent. His main criticism of Austin's system is its focus on classifying verbs. As an alternative, Searle proposes that it is the properties of the illocutionary acts that should be 'the basis for constructing a classification' (1979, p. 12). To this end, he identifies four categories of felicity conditions and uses these as a framework to analyse and classify illocutionary acts.

Searle's four categories of felicity conditions are **propositional content conditions, preparatory conditions, sincerity conditions,** and **essential conditions.** Each illocutionary act can then be assessed against these four categories to produce a 'list of conditions for the performance of a certain illocutionary act' (Searle, 1969, p. 56). This classification system then allows us to compare illocutionary acts, describe how they differ, and group them together.

To illustrate each category of felicity condition and to show how they can be used to analyse illocutionary acts, consider the utterances in (27) and (28). In (27) the speaker makes a promise and in (28) she makes a request.

(27) I promise to clean my room

(28) Please clean your room

Each illocutionary act will have propositional content conditions. Different propositions place different conditions on the illocutionary act. For example, the proposition in (27) is a promise, and a promise must relate to something that the speaker themselves will do. You cannot successfully make a promise on behalf of someone else. Similarly, a promise must be about an action that will take place in the future. You cannot, according to Searle, make a promise about a past action. These conditions follow by virtue of the propositional meaning of the verb *to promise*. Compare this with the act of requesting. Like a promise, a request must necessarily be about future actions, but in this case, it must relate to the future actions of the hearer, rather than the speaker.

Preparatory conditions are the states of affairs that need to be in place for the successful performance of the speech act. For example, for a promise to be felicitous, the speaker must believe that the hearer wants the speaker to do the promised action (or at least that she prefers that the speaker does it, rather than does not do it). For the utterance in (27) to be felicitous as a promise, the speaker must believe that the hearer wants the speaker to clean her (the speaker's) room. For a request such as (28) to be successful, the hearer must be able to perform the action. We cannot felicitously request that someone does something impossible or unreasonable.

The sincerity condition for an illocutionary act is determined by requirements on the psychological state of the speaker towards the propositional content of the utterance. The nature of this psychological state varies depending on the act that is being performed. In the case of the promise in (27), for example, the speaker must intend to clean her room. In the case of the request in (28), the speaker must want the hearer to do the action.

Finally, illocutionary acts have what Searle calls an essential condition. To satisfy the essential condition the speaker must intend that the utterance be acted upon in an appropriate way. That is, the utterance must count as an attempt to perform the speech act. For example, for an act of promising to be felicitous, the speaker must intend that by uttering the promise, she places herself under an obligation to do the action or deed. For a request to be felicitous, the utterance must count as an attempt to get the hearer to do the act.

Searle's felicity conditions for promising and requesting are summarised in Table 3.1 (adapted from Searle, 1979, p. 44).

Analysing illocutionary acts in this way allows us to compare them. It reveals the ways in which they are similar as well as what makes them different from one another.

3.3.2 A Taxonomy of Illocutionary Acts

Having established the four felicity conditions as a means by which to analyse and compare illocutionary acts, Searle proposes an alternative classification to that of Austin. He describes his aims as:

Table 3.1 *Searle's felicity conditions for promising and requesting*

	Promise	Request
Propositional Content Condition	The speaker predicates a future action of the speaker.	The speaker predicates a future action of the hearer.
Preparatory Condition	The hearer wants the speaker to perform the action. The speaker is able to perform the action.	The hearer is able to perform the action.
Sincerity Condition	The speaker intends to do the action.	The speaker wants the hearer to do the action.
Essential Condition	The utterance counts as the undertaking by the speaker of an obligation to do the action.	The utterance counts as an attempt by the speaker to get the hearer to do the action.

> to explicate the notion of an illocutionary act by stating a set of necessary and sufficient conditions for the performance of a particular kind of illocutionary act (Searle, 1965, p. 2).

He goes on to suggest that:

> If I am successful in stating the conditions and the corresponding rules for even one kind of illocutionary act, that will provide us with a pattern for analysing other kinds of acts (Searle, 1965, p. 2).

There are, he proposes, five basic categories of illocutionary act. The first category is **assertives**, which Searle also refers to as **representatives**. Speech acts in this category commit the speaker to something being the case. For example, if I utter the sentence in (29), I am committing to it being the case that it is Thursday.

(29) Today is Thursday

My words and the truth of them is determined by the state of affairs in the world, and it is a property of assertives that they can be assessed as true or false.

Searle's second category is **directives**. These are attempts to get the hearer to do something, including invitations to do something, suggestions to do something, or insistences that the hearer do something. For Searle, questions are a subset of directives as they are an attempt to get the hearer to provide information. All directives share common propositional content conditions and sincerity conditions. The propositional content is always that the hearer does some action in the future, and the sincerity condition is that the speaker wants the action to be undertaken.

Commissives are illocutionary acts which commit the speaker to some future action. For a commissive act to be felicitous, the speaker must intend to do the action described in the propositional content. For example, in (30), the propositional content is that the speaker will be on time tomorrow.

(30)   I promise to be on time tomorrow

For the promise in (30) to be felicitous, the speaker must intend to be on time tomorrow.

Preparatory conditions can help us to distinguish between different commissives. For example, both promises and threats are commissives, and, as such, both commit the speaker to some future action. However, in the case of promises, the future action is desirable for the hearer, but, in the case of threats, it is not.

As Searle observes (1965, p. 11), there are seemingly problematic cases, such as (31), where the verb *promise* may be used with an action that is not desirable for the hearer.

(31)   I promise you I will have my revenge on you

However, Searle's classification is based, not on verbs, but on the nature of the illocutionary act. Regardless of the verb that is used, (31) performs the illocutionary act of threatening, rather than promising.

The utterances in (32) to (34) are examples of illocutionary acts that fall into Searle's category of **expressives**.

(32)   Congratulations on your promotion
(33)   Thank you for the present
(34)   I apologise for forgetting your birthday

Expressives communicate the psychological state of the speaker or her emotional reaction towards a proposition. For illocutionary acts in this category, the sincerity condition relates to the emotional or psychological state that the speaker is feeling. For a case of thanking to be sincere, for example, the speaker must feel grateful or appreciative, and in the case of congratulating, the speaker must feel pleased about the hearer's achievements.

The final category of illocutionary acts proposed by Searle is **declarations**. Declarations are utterances which change the world by the very fact that they have been produced. We saw this type of utterance classified as performative in Section 3.2. When a baseball umpire calls a player out by producing the utterance in (35), the status of that player changes. Similarly, if a judge passes a guilty verdict, it is the uttering of that verdict, as in (36), which changes the status of the accused from innocent (until proven guilty) to guilty in the eyes of the law.

(35) You're out!

(36) I find you guilty

Declarations require the speaker and hearer to occupy special places within what Searle calls 'an extra-linguistic institution' (1979, p. 18). Only the umpire can call someone out (successfully) in baseball, and only a judge can declare someone guilty in certain court systems.

According to Searle, declarations do not have sincerity conditions. The act of saying them makes them so, regardless of the sincerity of the speaker's intentions. Imagine, for example, that the baseball umpire does not think that a player from Team A is out because she does not believe that the player from Team B successfully tagged him. (Tagging is one way in which a player can be put out in baseball.) However, before the game, she accepted a bribe to help Team B win, and so she calls the player out. That player is now out, regardless of the umpire's beliefs or honesty. The very act of (felicitously) uttering a declaration effects a change and brings the world into line with the propositional content of the utterance.

According to Searle, these five categories capture the different and varied things that we do when we use language. Each illocutionary act has associated felicity conditions, and these can be used to distinguish between different acts and to group them together. Searle (1979, p. 29) sums up his key approach and conclusion, as follows:

> If we adopt illocutionary point as the basic notion on which to classify uses of language, then there are a rather limited number of basic things we do with language: we tell people how things are, we try to get them to do things, we commit ourselves to doing things, we express our feelings and attitudes and we bring about changes through our utterances. Often, we do more than one of these at once in the same utterance.

This final observation that a speaker may perform more than one illocutionary act via the same utterance underpins one of Searle's key contributions to speech act theory: his work on indirect speech acts. We turn our attention to this in the next section.

3.3.3 Indirect Speech Acts

As we saw in Chapters 1 and 2, there is often a gap between what a speaker literally and explicitly says and the full extent of what she means to communicate. Searle was particularly interested in a subset of cases where a speaker says one thing but means something more. Consider examples (37) and (38).

(37) I would like you to leave

(38) Can you leave?

On the surface, the utterance in (37) is a statement, and it can be assessed as true or false. It will be true if and only if the speaker would like the addressee(s) to leave, and it will be false if she would not. On the surface, the utterance in (38), is a question about the addressee's ability to leave. However, most hearers would interpret both (37) and (38) as also being requests. They are **indirect speech acts**. The speech act of requesting is performed indirectly via another type of act.

According to Searle (1979, p. 30), such utterances perform two illocutionary acts. Both (37) and (38) are primarily requests. However, in each case, the speaker performs this primary illocutionary act indirectly via a secondary illocutionary act of a different sort. In (37), the speaker does this by making a statement, and in (38), she does this by asking a question. These secondary illocutionary acts are, according to Searle, literal, while the primary, indirect acts are non-literal.

Searle goes on to ask how it is possible for a hearer to understand an indirect, non-literal illocutionary act from the performance of a literal, but secondary act. This issue, of course, goes to the heart of pragmatics as it is an example of a speaker meaning more than she says. As we have seen, explaining how this gap between saying and meaning is bridged is a key aim of pragmatic theories and analyses.

Searle proposes that one of the key means by which a speaker can perform a speech act indirectly is by using the secondary act to refer, in some way, to the felicity conditions for the primary act. Recall the preparatory and sincerity conditions for the act of requesting (see Table 3.1). The hearer must be able to do the action (preparatory condition), and the speaker must want the hearer to do the action (sincerity condition). If we look again at the indirect requests in (37) and (38), we can see that each of the secondary, literal illocutionary acts relates to the felicity conditions for the primary, indirect act. The statement in (37) ('I would like you to leave') is an assertion that the sincerity condition is satisfied. The speaker wants the hearer to do the action of leaving. The utterance in (38) ('Can you leave?') is a question about the hearer's ability to perform the action of leaving. It is therefore a question about whether the preparatory condition for the request is satisfied.

These examples demonstrate that a speaker can perform an indirect speech act of requesting by stating that the sincerity condition has been fulfilled or by asking whether the preparatory condition has been fulfilled. She can also do so by asserting that the preparatory condition has been fulfilled. The utterance in (39), while literally a statement about the hearer's ability to leave now, could be used as a request for the hearer to do just that.

(39) You can leave now

Finally, a speaker might make an indirect request by stating that the propositional content condition obtains, as in (40), or by asking whether it does, as in (41)

(40) You will leave now

(41) Are you leaving now?

Thus, we can see that the indirect means of performing an illocutionary act are not random or arbitrary. They are directly linked to the felicity conditions for the primary illocutionary act. The hearer must infer that the speaker is referring to these conditions as an indirect means of performing an associated primary illocutionary act.

As Searle (1979) notes, indirect means of performing illocutionary acts may become conventionalised. Expressions such as *can you*, *would you*, and *are you able to* have become conventionalised ways of making a request, for example. Finally, indirectness is often motivated by politeness, and we return to think about how indirect utterances might be used to maintain and enhance speaker–hearer relationships in Chapter 9.

3.4 Further Developments, Applications, and Responses

The core of this chapter has provided an overview of the work of two of the most influential thinkers in speech act theory. It is necessary to understand the origins of this area of pragmatics if one is to use the insights and classifications that it offers. However, speech act theory does not end with the work of Austin and Searle. Current thinkers in pragmatics continue to investigate speech acts as a key aspect of pragmatic meaning, and ideas from speech act theory continue to be applied to new areas and data, some of which we return to in later chapters of this book. In Chapter 9, we return to the topic of indirectness as we consider politeness and impoliteness. Speech acts play a key role in understanding how speakers do politeness and relational work. A speaker may choose to make a request indirectly, rather than directly, for reasons of politeness, and some speech acts may be associated with a lack of politeness or even with impoliteness.

Indirect speech acts necessarily involve implicitly communicated meaning. As we explore approaches to pragmatics over the next four chapters, we will discuss several examples of indirect speech acts. In Chapter 7, we will see how speech act information is accounted for on the relevance-theoretic framework for utterance interpretation.

Speech act theory has not, of course, been without its critics. Levinson (1983, p. 240), for example, suggests that Searle's taxonomy is not as 'definitive or exhaustive' as claimed, and raises questions about how systematically felicity conditions are applied in the analysis. Levinson goes on to suggest that the construction of classification systems for speech acts is not as worthwhile as it might at first seem. Rather, for many, the focus in pragmatics has shifted towards viewing illocutionary acts in terms of communicative intentions. Such approaches are aligned with the work of Grice, and we turn our attention to that in the next chapter.

Despite these criticisms, insights from speech act theory are often used to analyse discourse, and they undoubtably provide a useful model for doing so. Speech act theory has been used in the analysis of communicative strategies in institutional contexts such as education, healthcare, and politics. It has also proved useful in the study of children's pragmatic development. Speech act theory provides a framework for analysing and tracking the development of children's language and communication abilities. We can ask, for example, whether children are performing speech acts (and if so, which ones), before they have reached full grammatical competence. Clark (2004, p. 570) discusses evidence that pre-linguistic gestures are 'proto-versions of the speech acts of asserting (points) and requesting (reaches)'. Classifications of speech acts can then be used to track the repertoires of children as they develop.

More recently, speech act theory has been applied fruitfully in the study of digital communication. The emergence of new media has led to the development of new forms of communication, and speech act theory has been used to analyse memes, GIFs, emoji, and status updates, amongst other online phenomena (Scott, 2022).

Other recent work using speech act theory has attempted to develop accounts that align with other areas and approaches within pragmatics. For example, work by Ruytenbeek (2017, 2019, 2021) focuses on indirect requests. He analyses the results of experimental studies into the comprehension of indirect requests and discusses their relation to politeness and the social context. Kissine (2013, p. 2) argues that current models of 'cognitively oriented pragmatics' do not sufficiently cover the issue of how illocutionary force is assigned to an utterance. He seeks to redress the balance by offering new analyses of constatives, directives, and commissives, and by arguing for further 'study of speech acts within cognitive pragmatics' (p. 166). As these studies show, speech act theory is far from dead, and the work of Austin and Searle continues to prove useful to those approaching language and discourse from a pragmatic perspective.

3.5 **Chapter Summary**

In this chapter, we took a closer look at the different things that we can do when we use language. We thought about the contributions that speech acts make to speaker's meaning, and we discussed two influential approaches to their study. We began with Austin's observation that some utterances (performatives) produce a change in the world simply by virtue of having been uttered. Following Austin's line of argument, we explored the different acts that a speaker performs when she produces an utterance, thinking about locutionary acts, illocutionary acts, and perlocutionary acts. We saw how Austin's proposal for a classification of illocutionary acts prompted a response from Searle. Searle's own classification system focuses on the properties of each illocutionary act and the conditions under which they can be felicitously performed. Searle's work on indirect speech acts provides us with insight into how we can say one thing, but mean another, and how this might be linked with considerations of politeness. Finally, we briefly considered the influence that speech act theory continues to have on the study of language, communication, and pragmatics.

Exercises

3a Which of the following (i) to (vii) are performatives according to Austin's analysis? Could any of them also be used as constatives? If so, specify the context in which this would be the case.

(i)   I resign
(ii) He broke his promise to me
(iii) I dedicate this book to my mother
(iv) I told him I was sorry
(v)   She won the bet
(vi) I declare this festival open!
(vii) I promise I will call you at 8pm this evening

3b What are the felicity conditions are for the following acts? Can you identify when an attempt to perform them might misfire or be an abuse (in Austin's terms)?

(i)   Placing someone under arrest
(ii) Making a bet
(iii) Passing sentence in a court of law

3c   Imagine that you are on the set of a television drama series while it is being filmed. You witness a scene in which two of the characters go through a wedding ceremony. Are the two actors married after they have performed this scene? If not, why not? Explain your answer in terms of Austin's theory of performatives?

3d   In Section 3.2, we saw the sentence (17) ('The floor is wet') used as a warning. Think of some other contexts in which the same sentence might be used to perform a different illocutionary act. What would the likely perlocutionary act(s) be in each case?

3e   According to Searle, there are five basic categories of things that we can do with language, summarised in (i)–(v).

(i)   tell people how things are
(ii)   commit ourselves to doing things
(iii) bring about changes
(iv)   get people to do things
(v)   express our feelings and attitudes

Match up his descriptions with the categories that he proposes, given in (a)–(e), and give an example of each.

(a)   Declarations
(b)   Assertives
(c)   Commissives
(d)   Expressives
(e)   Directives

3f   How might you make a promise via an indirect speech act? What is the secondary (literal) illocutionary act that you have performed? Can you link your indirect promise to the felicity conditions for making a promise (as given in Table 3.1)?

Key Terms Introduced in this Chapter

Further Reading

Speech act theory is indebted to the work of Austin and Searle, and anyone interested in applying speech act analyses should, if possible, read their original works. Austin lays out his arguments over the course of his 1962 book *How To Do Things With Words* and the key distinctions from this chapter are discussed in detail. Searle then discusses and develops these ideas in a series of publications including: *What Is a Speech Act?* (1965), *Speech Acts* (1969), and *Expression and Meaning* (1979).

There are accessible introductions to speech act theory in many books on pragmatics including Clark (2022), Chapman (2011), and Mey (2005). Levinson (1983) talks through the development of speech act theory and in particular the relation between Austin's ideas and Searle's work. He provides an accessible critical evaluation of their ideas.

Those readers interested in how speech act theory has developed after Austin and Searle should look at the work of Bach and Harnish (1979). Bach's (2006) chapter on *Speech Acts and Pragmatics* provides a shorter overview of both speech act theory and the work of Bach and Harnish. Both works mentioned in Section 3.4 (Kissine 2013 and Ruytenbeek 2021) offer comprehensive overviews of speech act theory along with discussion of their own arguments and developments. Fogal, Harris, and Moss (2018) includes papers on a range of speech act-related issues and applications. The introductory chapter provides an overview of the 'contemporary theoretical landscape' (p. 1) which more advanced students will find useful.

CHAPTER **4**

Gricean Pragmatics

In This Chapter ...

In this chapter, we introduce the influential work of H. Paul Grice, focusing on his claims about indirectly communicated meaning. Grice is generally acknowledged as the first person to propose an account of how hearers derive implied meaning. He coined the now widely accepted term *implicature* to describe any proposition that is communicated without being directly stated, and he offered an account of how hearers derive implicatures by working out what a speaker meant to communicate beyond what has been directly and explicitly stated in an utterance.

We begin this chapter by exploring Grice's distinction between 'what is said' and what is implicated. We then move on to what is, perhaps, Grice's most famous and widely discussed contribution to the field of pragmatics: the cooperative principle (CP) and its associated maxims. Speakers, it is claimed, abide by certain norms when they take part in a conversation. We outline Grice's formulation of these norms, and the role they play in inferential processes and implicature derivation. The chapter closes with a discussion of the different categories of implicature that Grice identified. We look at examples to illustrate the role that context plays in inferential processes for each category of implicature.

4.1 Grice and Pragmatics

As we have seen in the previous three chapters, we very often mean more than we say. Questions relating to implicated meaning have been discussed since (at least) the time of Aristotle (Horn, 2004; Chapman, 2005). However, no comprehensive account of how we bridge the gap between what speakers say and what they mean had been offered prior to the work of H. Paul Grice. Grice (1989) proposed a framework for understanding how we make inferences about what speakers are indirectly communicating. He suggested that the interpretation of utterances is driven by general assumptions about how people behave. His ideas on inference and implicature in conversation have arguably inspired all subsequent work in linguistic pragmatics, and his influence cannot be overstated.

In this chapter, we focus on Grice's work on implicature, and in particular, on his groundbreaking work that was published in *Logic and Conversation* and the associated *Retrospective Epilogue* (Grice, 1989). He did, of course, work on many other areas in philosophy and linguistics, and some of these will be of interest to students of language and communication. His work on meaning, for example, has been hugely significant in certain areas of semantics, and continues to influence ideas and theories to this day.

We will explore the details of Grice's proposal about communication and implicature in more detail in the following sections. However, the overarching idea that drives Grice's account is that communication is a cooperative activity. When we interpret utterances, we assume that the speaker is trying to be cooperative. We then use this assumption of cooperation when we are calculating (or inferring) what the speaker was intending to communicate. This allows us to explain why hearers draw the inferences they do, and it allows us to show how these inferences are calculated.

Many of Grice's most influential ideas were delivered as part of the William James lectures given at Harvard University in 1967. These were then published as part of a collection of Grice's work, which includes a *Retrospective Epilogue* written around ten years later and about a year before Grice's death. While the essays have been influential, they are fairly complicated, and the style of writing is, perhaps, not always immediately accessible to the modern student. Anyone interested in studying and using Grice's ideas is, however, strongly encouraged to read the original texts. In this chapter, you will find the original terminology alongside explanations of technical terms and notions. We begin, in the next section, by introducing a key distinction that is central to Grice's work: the distinction between what a speaker says, and what she implicates.

4.2 Saying and Implicating

Grice made an important distinction between two layers of communicated meaning: '**what is said**' and **what is implicated**. 'What is said' is used to describe the basic proposition that has been asserted by the speaker. This is the statement that the speaker has made, and it is this that she can be held to in terms of truthfulness. '[W]hat someone has said' is, according to Grice, 'closely related to the conventional meaning of the words (the sentence) he has uttered' (Grice, 1989, p. 25). We can understand the conventional meaning of a word to be simply the accepted meaning that is encoded by that word.

Grice made specific claims about how a hearer works out what is being said. First, the hearer must decode the words that have been used. Decoding was discussed in Section 1.4 and depends on the hearer being sufficiently familiar with the language in which the utterance is produced to access the coded meaning of the words. As we saw in Chapter 2, many words have more than one encoded meaning, and so a second task for the hearer is to disambiguate any ambiguous words. Finally, the hearer must determine who or what is being referred to by any referring expressions that have been used. To see how this might work in practice, consider the example in (1).

(1) He ate his lunch by the bank

To determine what the speaker has said in the Gricean sense, we need to access the meaning of the individual words, and then perform the two other tasks: disambiguation and reference assignment (p. 25). We must disambiguate the word *bank*. That is, we must decide whether it should be taken to mean financial institution/building or the land alongside a river. We must then decide who the pronoun *he* refers to, and whether the possessive pronoun *his* is referring to the same person, or to someone different. When a speaker utters (1), she could, for example, be intending to communicate the proposition given in (2), or she could be intending to communicate the proposition in (3), or any one of a range of other possibilities.

(2) Jeremy ate Jeremy's lunch by the building that houses the financial institution

(3) Nigel ate Arthur's lunch by the riverbank

Any meaning that is communicated beyond 'what is said' is considered to be part of what is implicated by the utterance. What is implicated is everything that is suggested, implied, or hinted at without being explicitly stated. Consider again the example in (4), first discussed in Chapter 1.

(4) Gemma: Did Luisa get the job?
Pauline: She looked happy

What Pauline has said, in Gricean terms, is that Luisa looked happy. We work this out by decoding the meaning of the words and assigning Luisa as the referent of the pronoun *she*. Pauline does not directly *say* anything about whether Luisa got the job or not. However, what she says clearly does not exhaust what she has communicated, and it can be assumed that Pauline has implicated that Luisa did indeed get the job. Notice that as Pauline has not said this directly, it would be unreasonable to accuse her of having said something false if we later discovered that Luisa did not, in fact, get the job. However, we have not fully understood what Pauline intended to communicate if we do not move beyond what she has said to also consider what she has implicated.

This idea of implicated meaning should be familiar by this point, and the notion of implicature was introduced in Chapter 1. While *implicature* has now become a standard term in linguistics and pragmatics, it was Grice who first proposed it as a term for those propositions that a speaker implicates, rather than directly states or *says*. The term *implicature* is also distinct in important ways from the term *implication*. Implicatures are intended implications. The notion of intention is key to understanding a speaker's overall meaning. Consider the conversation in (5), focusing on what Arnie might infer from Bertha's utterance.

(5) Arnie: Did you go out last night?
Bertha: It was the final of Love Island!

Given general knowledge about the popular television reality show *Love Island*, and a general assumption that people are often at home when they watch television shows, Arnie is likely to infer that Bertha did not go out last night. This is what she intends to implicate, and so this is an implicature of her utterance. Now assume that Arnie has a low opinion of people who watch reality television shows. He thinks that they are superficial. Bertha's utterance may well cause him to lower his opinion of her and to infer that she is superficial. This is unlikely to be part of what Bertha intended to communicate, and so while it is an implication of her utterance, it is not an implicature.

Much of Grice's focus in *Logic and Conversation* is on what he calls non-conventional or **conversational implicatures**. These are implicatures that arise because of assumptions about how interlocutors interact and behave. In the next section, we examine these assumptions in more detail. In doing so, we introduce some key components of the Gricean approach: the **cooperative principle** and **maxims**.

4.3 The Cooperative Principle and Maxims

4.3.1 The Cooperative Principle

Perhaps the most famous and discussed aspect of Grice's work is the claim that when we engage in conversation, we expect our conversational partners to be cooperative. The idea is that participants in a conversation should, ideally, be working towards a common goal. Grice (1989, p. 28) likens the act of engaging in conversation to the act of working with someone to fix a car or bake a cake. Just as two (or more) people must work together and cooperate if they want to achieve a practical goal, so the participants in a conversation must work together and each contribute in an appropriate, timely, and cooperative manner if they wish to achieve the goal of successful communication. Grice proposes that conversation is governed by a general principle of cooperation. The cooperative principle, or CP, is as follows:

> Make your conversational contribution such as is required, at the stage at which it occurs, by the accepted purpose or direction of the talk exchange in which you are engaged (Grice, 1989, p. 26).

When introducing the CP, Grice describes it as a 'rough general principle' (p. 26). It is intended to capture a general notion of cooperation that participants in a conversation are expected to observe. Cooperative speakers should contribute to the conversation in a way that is appropriate, based on the requirements of the conversation. That contribution should be at an appropriate time, and it should move the exchange towards the overall communicative purpose or goal of the conversation. Utterance interpretation is then driven by the assumption that speakers are following this general cooperative principle. If we assume that our conversational partners are aiming to be cooperative, then we will infer whatever additional meaning is necessary to maintain this assumption. We will see in Section 4.4 how the cooperative principle underpins conversational implicatures.

Having established this general, overarching principle, Grice then outlines a set of rules or maxims which, if followed, will lead to communicative behaviour that satisfies the requirements of the CP. The maxims are divided into four themed groups or categories: **Quantity**, **Quality**, **Relation**, and **Manner**. Each category contains one or more maxims, and we consider each of these in turn in the next sections.

4.3.2 Quantity (or Informativeness)

The maxims of quantity relate to how much information is provided by the utterance and whether this satisfies the requirements of the conversation. The maxims in this category are also sometimes referred to as the maxims of informativeness. They are as follows:

1. Make your contribution as informative as is required (for the current purposes of the exchange)
2. Do not make your contribution more informative than is required

The speaker is expected to provide neither too much nor too little information. Consider the exchanges in (6) and (7) which take place between Arnie and Bertha in London, UK. In each case, Bertha's reply feels uncooperative. We can understand this in terms of how much information she supplies and how this relates to the current purpose of the talk exchange.

(6) Arnie: Do you know what the time is?
    Bertha: Yes, I do
(7) Arnie: Do you know what the time is?
    Bertha: Yes, it's 4:30 pm in Hong Kong, 3:30 am in Bogota, and 9:30 am in London

In (6) it is reasonable to assume that Arnie is not only asking whether Bertha knows what the time is, but also that, if she does know, she should tell him. It is also reasonable to expect Bertha to realise this. Therefore, her answer in (6) is not informative enough and is uncooperative in this respect. Although her response may provide a literal answer to Arnie's question, it does not provide enough information for the purposes of the talk exchange and might perhaps lead us to think that she is being deliberately difficult or obstructive.

It is also reasonable to assume that when Arnie asks the question, he is interested in knowing the time for their current location. While Bertha provides this in her answer in (7), she also provides additional information that is not required. This makes her utterance uncooperative with respect to the second quantity maxim. It provides more information than is necessary. We will see below that providing more or less information than is required can lead to quantity maxim implicatures. These are discussed in Section 4.4.

In (8) Bertha gives a cooperative answer that provides neither too much nor too little information, but just the right amount.

(8) Arnie: Do you know what the time is?
     Bertha: Yes, it's just coming up to 9:30

4.3.3 Quality (or Truthfulness)

Maxims within the quality category are related to the truth of what has been communicated. They are also sometimes referred to as the maxims of truthfulness. Within this category, Grice identifies a supermaxim:

- Try to make your contribution one that is true

This is then broken down into two more specific submaxims:

1. Do not say what you believe to be false
2. Do not say that for which you lack adequate evidence

There are some important points to notice about the supermaxim and submaxims in this category. First, the supermaxim deals with the speaker's contribution as a whole. The submaxims, on the other hand, focus on what the speaker is saying. Remember that, for Grice, what a speaker says is only part of what she communicates. 'What is said' does not exhaust the communicative contribution.

Second, the two submaxims focus on different aspects of the quality of 'what is said'. According to the first submaxim, a cooperative speaker should not say something if she does not believe that what she is saying is true. The second submaxim makes stronger demands on the quality of 'what is said'. Not only should the speaker avoid saying something she knows is false, but she should also avoid saying something if she does not have sufficient evidence that it is true. Consider (9) and (10) as alternative answers to Arnie's question about the time, thinking about how Bertha's reply might be uncooperative in terms of the submaxims of quality.

(9) Bertha (looks at her watch and sees that it is 9:30am): It's just after 8am

(10) Bertha (realising she does not have a watch and guessing): It's 8am

In (9), Bertha is deliberately deceptive. She knows that it is not 8am, and so by uttering (9) she is saying something that she believes to be false. The situation in (10) is slightly different. She does not know what the time is, and so she hazards a guess. However, without adequate evidence to support this guess, this too is considered uncooperative in terms of quality.

Grice presents the first maxim of truthfulness as the most important of all the maxims. He briefly considers whether it should even be included with the others, rather than given some special status. The other maxims, he says, 'come into operation only on the assumption that this maxim of Quality is satisfied' (p. 27). Making your contribution truthful is, therefore, a key quality of a cooperative speaker in the Gricean sense.

Finally, when first encountering the work of Grice, it is easy to assume that the maxim of quality is just designed to rule out lying and deception. There are, however, various other occasions on which a speaker might say something that is not strictly and literally true. These include when using metaphor or irony, or when telling stories or jokes. We return to consider how these fit into the Gricean account in Section 4.4.

4.3.4 Relation

The category of relation contains only one maxim:

1. Be relevant

Grice acknowledges that this maxim is potentially problematic. He raises various questions about what it means for something to be relevant and about how the different ways in which it is possible for something to be relevant might fit into the picture. He is also aware that speakers change the subject as a normal part of a conversation, and he acknowledges that there is a need to address this in future work. However, setting aside these issues, at a basic and intuitive level, we can understand how a speaker might be viewed as being uncooperative if, as in example (11), she provides information that is not relevant to the conversation.

(11) Arnie: Do you know what the time is?
      Bertha: Madrid is the capital of Spain

Bertha's reply in (11) in no way answers Arnie's questions, and so, on the surface at least, appears to be uncooperative. Not only is Bertha's cooperative response in (8) informative and (we assume) truthful, but it is also relevant.

4.3.5 Manner

The final category of maxims is slightly different to the others in that it relates to the way in which something is said, rather than what has been said. As with the quality maxim, Grice provides us with a supermaxim of manner, along with several more specific submaxims:

- Be perspicuous
  1. Avoid obscurity of expression
  2. Avoid ambiguity
  3. Be brief (avoid unnecessary prolixity)
  4. Be orderly

According to the supermaxim 'Be perspicuous,' a speaker should aim to be clear. The submaxims then break down the subtasks involved in achieving this clarity. The speaker should avoid obscure expressions and ambiguity. She should be brief and succinct, and she should present information in an orderly fashion. In sum, a cooperative speaker should construct her utterances in such a way as to make the information as easily accessible and understandable as possible. We might, for example, expect a series of events to be described in chronological order, as in (12).

(12)   Stelios got up, got dressed, and ate breakfast

While (12) would strictly speaking be true if Stelios ate breakfast in bed, then got up, and finally got dressed, we expect a cooperative speaker to present such events in the order in which they happened.

Students often find the language used in these maxims challenging. However, it can be helpful to think that Grice was himself demonstrating, and perhaps ridiculing, uncooperative behaviour in his wording here. It would, ironically, be clearer if the supermaxim was 'Be clear', rather than 'Be perspicuous'. Similarly, removing the unnecessary prolixity in the added phrase 'avoid unnecessary prolixity' would make the third submaxim briefer. It seems unlikely that Grice was unaware of these points, and so we can assume this wording was deliberate and knowing.

4.4 Conversational Implicatures

4.4.1 Deriving Implicatures

Having outlined the CP and maxims, we are now able to discuss the role that they play in deriving conversational implicatures. Recall that for Grice, verbal communication is a rational and cooperative activity. In some cases, however, if we only consider what the speaker actually says, it may appear that she is not behaving cooperatively or in line with the maxims. Perhaps, for example, she has not given as much information as the hearer might like, or she has said something that is, on the face of it, not directly relevant to the current conversation. While the speaker's utterance may not comply with all the maxims at the level of 'what is said', the hearer will maintain the assumption that the speaker is being cooperative overall. The hearer uses this assumption to work out what the speaker is intending to communicate, including what she is communicating indirectly, via inference.

Conversational implicatures arise when a hearer must add something to what has been said to maintain the assumption of cooperation. Grice identifies three categories of conversational implicature that arise in this way. The three categories capture the different ways in which what the speaker says relates to the maxims. In each case, an overall assumption of cooperation is maintained, and this drives the derivation of implicatures.

First, let us look at cases where implicatures follow simply from the assumption that the CP and maxims are being maintained.

Consider example (13), used by Grice (1989) himself in *Logic and Conversation* to illustrate how implicatures in this category may arise.

(13) Arnie: I am out of petrol

   Bertha: There is a garage around the corner

In terms of 'what is said', Bertha does no more than assert the existence of a garage around the corner. However, for this information to be relevant and informative in the context of Arnie being out of petrol, we must infer that (Bertha thinks that) the garage is likely to be open and that it is the type of garage that sells petrol. If Bertha does not think these things, then her utterance would not be cooperative. We must attribute these assumptions to Bertha if we wish to maintain the assumption that she is being cooperative and observing the maxims. These assumptions are part of what she communicates, implicitly, to Arnie. Arnie is likely to derive the implicatures in (14) to (16) from Bertha's reply.

(14) The garage around the corner is open now

(15) The garage around the corner is the typc of garage that sells petrol

(16) I [Arnie] can buy petrol from the garage around the corner

These implicatures arise because the hearer assumes that the speaker is obeying the maxims. Implicatures of this sort are by far the most common type, and when deriving them, most hearers barely notice that their interpretation goes beyond what the speaker has strictly stated.

4.4.2 When Maxims Clash

The second category of conversational implicatures identified by Grice arises when two maxims clash. Consider example (17). This is also adapted from one of Grice's original examples. Arnie and Bertha are discussing the possibility of visiting Colin as part of an upcoming vacation.

(17)   Arnie: Where does Colin live?

Bertha: Somewhere in the South of France

Given the context, a more informative answer to Arnie's question would be appropriate. The purpose of the conversation is to establish whether it is possible to take a trip to wherever Colin lives, and so we would expect precise details. However, we only get a vague, under-informative answer. Bertha appears to be violating the maxim of informativeness. Her contribution is not as informative as is required.

However, we assume that Bertha is still being cooperative overall. The apparent violation results from a clash of maxims. If Bertha does not have any more precise information, then she is forced to choose between quantity (informativeness) and quality (truthfulness). She could provide Arnie with more precise information, but this would mean having to hazard a guess. In doing so she would be saying something for which she lacked adequate evidence and thus violating one of the maxims of truthfulness. In this case, it is not possible for Bertha to be both fully informative and truthful.

As we have seen in Section 4.3.3, Grice considers the first maxim of quality (truthfulness) to be the most important of the maxims. Bertha must prioritise being truthful. The clash therefore leads her to produce an under-informative utterance. However, the assumption that Bertha is being cooperative leads us to infer that she has done so because she does not have more precise information. Thus, Arnie will derive the implicature in (18) as part of Bertha's meaning.

(18)   Bertha does not know exactly where Colin lives

This implicature arises because of the clash of maxims and the assumption that the speaker is being cooperative.

4.4.3 Flouting

The final category of implicatures arises when a maxim is openly violated, or flouted, at the level of 'what is said'. Again, to reconcile this behaviour with the assumption that the speaker is being cooperative overall, the hearer must try to work out why the speaker might have done this. He will draw inferences to understand the speaker's behaviour, and these inferences will form part of what is communicated by the utterance. Again, it is useful to use an adapted version of Grice's original example to illustrate this.

Imagine that you work for a high-profile international company and have been asked to recruit a new member of staff. You receive what looks like a promising application and so you request a reference from the applicant's university tutor. When the reference arrives, it contains only the sentence in (19).

(19) Stuart always arrived on time for class and was smartly dressed

According to Grice (1989, p. 33), this response constitutes a **flouting** of the first maxim of quantity. The university tutor surely knows that more information is required. You would expect her to provide information about the applicant's skills, abilities, attributes, and suitability for the role. You would also reasonably expect that the tutor would be able to provide this information. The fact that she has not done so implies that she wishes 'to impart information that [she] is reluctant to write down' (p. 33). By responding with the utterance in (19), the tutor is indirectly communicating that there was nothing more positive to say about her former student. She was able to produce a more informative utterance but chose not to do so. We can infer that this was because she did not want to be openly critical. She flouted the first maxim of quantity to implicate that the applicant is not a suitable candidate for the position.

A speaker may also flout one or more of the maxims from the manner category if she makes her utterance less brief or clear to implicate additional meaning. Imagine that a friend is telling you about what happened at a recent party that she attended. Compare the utterances in (20) and (21) as possible ways to describe what happened.

(20) The music started playing and Chris started to dance
(21) The music started playing and Chris started to move his limbs around in time to the beat

The act of dancing would, we might assume, usually involve moving limbs around in time to the beat of some music. Using the verb *dance* would be the briefest and clearest way in which to convey this meaning. Therefore, if the speaker has chosen to utter (21) instead, we must infer that she has done so for a reason. The speaker is implying that Chris's attempts to dance were so bad that they could not reasonably be described as dancing.

As we saw in Chapter 2, figurative uses of language including irony and metaphor are key issues in any theory of pragmatics. Grice's approach to figurative, non-literal uses of language is to treat them as cases of flouting. However, as these are central issues, they will be considered separately in the next section.

4.4.4 Figurative Language

According to Grice, uses of figurative language, including metaphor, hyperbole, meiosis, and irony, can be explained as floutings of the maxims of truthfulness. The act of flouting triggers a related implicature. Consider examples (22) to (25).

(22) (Uttered after dropping and breaking a vase): That's just what I needed!

(23) (Uttered on a hot day): My office is a greenhouse

(24) (Uttered by someone who skipped lunch that day): I'm starving!

(25) (Uttered after a serious argument has taken place): It's a little tense in here

Let us start by considering the case of irony in example (22). It would be ridiculous to think that dropping and breaking a vase was just what the speaker needed. The speaker of (22) has clearly said something that, on the face of it, is untrue. The first maxim of quality states that a speaker should not say something that she believes to be false. However, this is clearly what the speaker is doing here, and, furthermore, she must know that the hearer will realise that what she is saying is false. The speaker is therefore flouting the maxim of truthfulness. The hearer will, however, assume that this flouting was intended to be cooperative in some way, and that the speaker was trying to communicate something true by saying something obviously false. Grice claims that the most obvious related proposition that the speaker could be intending to communicate is the opposite of what she has said.

The Gricean account of metaphor follows a similar story. The speaker of (23) cannot reasonably be communicating that her office is actually and literally a greenhouse, and, again, we can understand this as a flouting of the maxim of quality. However, in this case, the opposite of what was literally said would be that the speaker's office is not a greenhouse. This would be stating the obvious, and so, the hearer must seek a different interpretation. Grice suggests that in these metaphorical cases the most likely interpretation is that the speaker is attributing some features of being a greenhouse to her office. We end up with the proposition that the office is like a greenhouse in some way. The cases of exaggeration and understatement that we find in (24) and (25) respectively work in a similar way. A blatant flouting of the maxim of truthfulness triggers the derivation of a related implicature.

4.4.5 Maxim Violations

Finally, let us consider some cases where speakers violate the maxims without necessarily intending the hearer to derive implicatures. While Grice suggests that cooperative speakers should try to abide by the maxims, he acknowledges that there are various other circumstances in which the maxims are violated. For example, while the maxim of quality states that speakers should not say things that they know to be false, we know that people can and often do lie. Lying is a covert violation of the maxim of quality (truthfulness). It is covert because, while the speaker has violated the maxim, she does not want her hearer to know that she has done so. This contrasts with the cases of overt violation (or flouting) discussed in the previous sections.

Speakers may also 'opt out' of a maxim by, for example, communicating that they are not going to give the required information. Finally, the maxims may be suspended in certain contexts, for example, when telling jokes or in fiction. Consider the contexts in which we might hear examples such as (26) and (27).

(26) A man walked into a bar …

(27) Once upon a time there was a magical land far away …

While we might not accept what is being described as true, we suspend our usual expectation of truthfulness when interpreting jokes or stories. We do not consider the speaker to be lying or being deceptive, but rather we suspend or opt out of the expectation that 'what is said' will be strictly and literally true.

4.5.6 Some Common Misunderstandings

Grice's cooperative principle and maxims are one of the most widely known notions in pragmatics, and, perhaps because of this, they have a life beyond that originally intended by Grice. Their use and interpretation are also often subject to misunderstandings and misapplications, and in this section, we discuss a few of the more common of these.

Students of pragmatics often fall into the trap of thinking that the Gricean approach must be wrong because speakers often violate maxims. It is very common for those encountering Grice's work for the first time to find a case of maxim violation in everyday conversation and conclude that speakers are not cooperative. It is, however, crucial to remember that Grice did not claim that speakers never violate maxims. Indeed, he systematically discusses different types of maxim violation in *Logic and Conversation*. What he does claim is that overall speakers are aiming to be cooperative.

Maxims may be violated because they clash (Section 4.4.2) giving a speaker no choice but to choose between them, and maxims may be overtly violated, or flouted, at the level of 'what is said' to trigger implicatures and thereby maintain the overall assumption of cooperation. Maxim violation is a key component of Grice's theory of conversational implicatures. Therefore, when we come across an apparent case of maxim violation, rather than rejecting the Gricean approach outright, we should ask ourselves why the speaker has violated the maxim and what we need to infer to maintain the overall assumption of cooperation.

A related misunderstanding is that if a speaker violates a maxim, they are being uncooperative. Imagine, for example, an exchange such as (28) where a speaker violates the maxim of relation (and possibly also quantity) by changing the subject dramatically.

(28) Adam: What do you think of Tina? Isn't she awful?

Meg: Ghastly weather we've been having recently, isn't it?

Adam has asked a specific question about Meg's opinion of Tina. By replying with an utterance about the weather, Meg is violating the maxim of relation. From this it might be easy to assume that she is an unco-operative conversational partner. However, by changing the subject in this way, Meg implicates that she does not wish to answer the question and perhaps that she feels Adam's question is inappropriate. While these implicatures may not answer the question directly, they only arise because of the assumption that Meg is being cooperative overall. If there were no expectation that speakers are relevant and informative, then Meg's reply in (28) would not be unusual or unexpected. If it were not unexpected or unusual, then the hearer would not be forced to infer anything further to maintain the assumption of cooperation. It is, according to Grice, only because we assume that speakers are cooperative and only because they follow the maxims where possible, that conversational implicatures of this sort arise.

Finally, the maxims are often discussed as rules that we should follow if we want to speak or write well. The maxims have an intuitive appeal that makes them popular in guides for how to write and communicate effectively. Indeed, it makes sense that if you want to communicate clearly, whether in writing or speech, you should provide enough, but not too much information, make your language use orderly and clear, and as relevant as possible. However, Grice did not intend for the maxims to be treated as a guide to good communication. Rather, the CP and maxims govern all communication, regardless of style, register, or medium. For Grice, com-municating in a cooperative manner is thought to be the rational strategy to adopt to successfully achieve your communicative aims.

4.5 Categories of Implicatures

4.5.1 Particularised Conversational Implicatures

Most of the implicatures that we have seen so far are what Grice called **par-ticularised conversational implicatures** (PCIs). They arise because a particu-lar speaker has produced the utterance at a particular time, in a particular place, and with particular contextual conditions in place. Consider the utterance in (29).

(29) He doesn't like long books

To work out 'what is said' in this example, a hearer need only assign reference to the pronoun *he*. Let us imagine that (29) is uttered about someone called Dan. According to Grice, what the speaker says in uttering (29) is that Dan doesn't like long books. It is a statement about a particular person's opinion of a particular subcategory of books. Without any further contextual information, it is impossible to know if the speaker intended to communicate anything further. However, if we provide more context, then implicatures emerge. Consider the utterance as part of the exchange in (30).

(30) Helen: Has Dan read *War and Peace*?
      Sara: He doesn't like long books

In this context, Sara's utterance not only communicates that Dan doesn't like long books, but it also implicates that (a) *War and Peace* is a long book and (b) Dan hasn't read *War and Peace*. Now consider the alternative exchange in (31).

(31) Helen: Has Dan read *Moby-Dick*?
      Sara: He doesn't like long books

While what is being said remains the same, what Sara is implicating has now changed. Her reply now implicates that (a) *Moby-Dick* is a long book and (b) Dan hasn't read *Moby-Dick*. These are different implicatures from those generated by her reply in (30). Finally, consider another possible conversational exchange involving the same sentence.

(32) Helen: Do you think you'll go on a second date with Dan?
      Sara: He doesn't like long books

Once again, changing the context leads to different implicatures. Now the most obvious interpretation is that Sara does not think she will go on a second date and that this has something to do with the fact that Dan doesn't like long books. In this context, Helen is also likely to derive some implicatures about Sara's attitude towards people who read and perhaps about what she is looking for in a romantic partner. The three different contexts lead to three different sets of implicatures. These implicatures are particular to the context in which the utterance has been produced.

   Now consider the utterance in (33).

(33) Jeremy is a pig

This could be used literally, to communicate the name of the pig, or it could be used metaphorically, to comment on some aspect of Jeremy's behaviour or personality. To determine which use is intended, the hearer needs to know particular details of the context. Furthermore, once the hearer has determined that the speaker is using *pig* as a metaphor, he must draw on contextual information to infer the ways in which Jeremy is like a pig. Jeremy could be rude, lazy, greedy, or untidy. Which meaning is intended by the speaker will depend on the context in which she produces the metaphor. Similarly, a sentence that is uttered ironically in one context might be meant literally and sincerely in another.

(34) What beautiful weather we are having!

The speaker of (34) might sincerely think the weather is beautiful or might be ironically implicating that the weather is awful. It is impossible to know without knowing details of the context. Particularised conversational implicatures arise because of the context in which the utterance has been produced, and the hearer must use information from the context to derive them.

Grice observed, however, that there are some conversational implicatures that arise without the need for particular or specific reference to the context. He called these **generalised conversational implicatures**, and we consider these next.

4.5.2 Generalised Conversational Implicatures

Generalised conversational implicatures (GCIs) are conversational implicatures which arise without the need for a particular or specific context. Let us look at some examples to illustrate.

(35) I broke a finger last year

(36) Siobhan went for a drink with a man yesterday

Even without any further contextual information, hearers tend to agree on what is communicated by these utterances. It is generally assumed, when interpreting (35), that the finger that the speaker broke was her own finger. Notice, however, that this is not specified in the encoded meaning of the sentence. Similarly, when hearers interpret (36), they are likely to infer that Siobhan went for a drink with a man who was not her brother, father, son, or husband, but rather a man that she has recently met, with a likely romantic connection of some sort. In both cases, the hearers infer additional meaning beyond 'what is said'. That is, they infer meaning beyond what is encoded by the words themselves and beyond what is yielded from the processes of reference assignment and disambiguation. It is also very common for hearers to not be consciously aware that they are deriving these implicatures. When asked, hearers very often struggle to identify them as implicatures until it is pointed out that the additional information is not encoded by the sentence itself.

A specific, and much discussed, subcategory of generalised conversational implicature arises when scalar terms are used in a sentence. Scalar terms represent different points on scales of meaning. For example, the scale in (37) is made up of adjectives that describe temperature, ranging from coolest to hottest.

(37) <lukewarm; warm; hot>

The quantifiers *some* and *all* also sit on a scale. Part of this scale is given in (38) and shows their relative positions.

(38) <some; all>

To understand the scalar nature of these terms and the role that this plays in the derivation of implicatures, consider the example in (39).

(39) The children ate some of the cakes

Logically, if one has eaten all the cakes, then one has also eaten some of the cakes. The reverse is not, however, true. It is possible to have eaten some of the cakes without having eaten all of them. Therefore, *all* is a more specific, more informative term than *some*. When hearing (39), and without needing any further contextual information, (adult) hearers tend to infer that the children ate some *but not all* the cakes. From a Gricean perspective, if we assume that the speaker of (39) is being cooperative, then we expect her to use the more informative option if it applies. The fact that she did not choose to do so, therefore implicates that it does not apply in this case. The inference that the children ate some, but not all, of the cakes follows. This is considered a generalised conversational implicature because we do not need access to any further contextual information to derive the inference. These **scalar implicatures** will be discussed in more detail in Chapter 5 as they feature significantly in several post-Gricean approaches to pragmatics.

4.5.3 Conventional Implicatures

Alongside the conversational implicatures discussed in the last two sections, Grice identified a category of implicatures which he called **conventional implicatures**. In these cases, an instruction to derive the implicature is encoded into a linguistic expression. Knowing the meaning of the word is to know which implicature a speaker is intending the hearer to derive when she uses that word. Consider the example in (40), paying particular attention to the role played by the word *but*.

(40)   It's raining but it's not cold

The claim is that words like *but* do not change what the speaker has said in the Gricean sense. In (40), the speaker has said or asserted that it is raining, and she has also asserted that it is cold. Whether she is telling the truth or not depends on whether those two things are true. If it is raining and it is not cold, then the speaker of (40) has said something true.

Imagine now that we replace *but* in (40) with *and* to give us the utterance in (41).

(41)   It's raining and it's not cold

Even though we have changed a word in the sentence, the truth of what has been asserted depends on the same conditions. As with (40), the utterance in (41) will be true if it is both raining and not cold. What then do words like *but* add to what is communicated?

According to Grice, discourse connectives like *but* encode what he calls conventional implicatures. These are implicatures that follow because a particular word has been used. In (40), for example, the use of *but* conventionally indicates that the hearer should infer a contrast between the two statements. When a speaker utters (40), she is, according to Grice, performing speech acts at two different levels. First, she is asserting two 'ground-floor' statements. These are that it's raining and that it's not cold. However, by using *but*, she is also performing the 'higher-order speech-act' of contrasting the two lower-level statements. To fully understand what the speaker is communicating, the hearer should infer that there is a contrast between the two asserted statements. According to Grice, it is the conventional meaning of the word *but* which determines this inference. Unlike conversational implicatures, conventional implicatures do not draw on the CP and maxims. In the next section, we briefly consider a further feature of conversation implicatures which, according to Grice, sets them apart from their conventional counterparts: cancellability.

4.5.4 Implicatures and Cancellability

According to Grice, a key feature of conversational implicatures is that they are cancellable. That is, they can be cancelled by information which is not compatible with the implicature. This information can come either from a further utterance or from the context. Consider the conversation in (42).

(42)   Helen: Has Dan read Moby-Dick?

Sara: He doesn't like long books, but he made an exception because he is obsessed with whales

The first part of Sara's reply seems to implicate that Dan has not read Moby-Dick. However, the second part of her utterance provides information which contradicts this. Implicatures are explicitly cancellable in this way if the speaker can add a statement that contradicts the implicature without creating a nonsensical utterance. The example in (42) is a particularised conversational implicature (PCI). However, generalised conversational implicatures (GCIs) are also cancellable, as demonstrated by (43) to (45).

(43) I broke a finger last year … It was my brother's finger. I accidently hit him on the hand while we were fixing the fence. He was very angry with me

(44) Siobhan went for a drink with a man yesterday, but don't get excited … It was only her brother

(45) The children ate some of the cakes … In fact, they ate all of them!

In each case, the second half of the utterance leads the hearer to cancel the implicature but does so without making the first half untrue or nonsensical.

A conversational implicature will be contextually cancellable if it is possible to find contexts of use in which the implicature does not arise. Consider the example in (46), uttered after a soccer match.

(46) Harry scored three goals

We might expect the hearer of (46) to derive the scalar implicature that Harry scored exactly three goals and no more. Notice that this is an implicature because what the speaker of (46) asserts is logically compatible with Harry scoring four, five, or more goals. Imagine, however, that Harry needed to score at least three more goals to become his team's highest scoring player. When used in this context, (46) is unlikely to lead to the implicature that Harry scored three and only three goals. Rather, the hearer will take the speaker to be communicating that Harry scored at least three goals.

As we saw in Section 4.5.3, conventional implicatures arise because of the meaning of a particular lexical item. Unlike conversational implicatures, they are not cancellable. Once the lexical item has been used, the inference has been triggered, and attempts to cancel the implicature feel distinctly odd or insincere. Imagine, for example, that a speaker utters (47).

(47) John is old but he likes rap music … I don't mean to imply that it is surprising or unusual for an old person to like rap music

The use of *but* triggers the implicature that there is some sort of contrast between John being old and him liking rap music or that his liking of rap music is unexpected in some way because he is old. The speaker's subsequent denial that she was implicating this sense of contrast or unexpectedness seems rather unconvincing. By using the word *but*, the speaker has committed herself to the associated implicature, and she cannot cancel it by stating a contradictory position.

According to Grice, cancellability is one of the ways in which conversational implicatures differ from conventional implicatures, and he suggests that all conversational implicatures are cancellable. Cancellability is often discussed as a potential test for conversational implicatures. However, Grice (1989, p. 44) stops short of making this claim, acknowledging that such a test would sometimes fail.

4.6 Chapter Summary

In this chapter, we introduced the key notions in the Gricean account of implicature. We saw that Grice makes an important distinction between 'what is said' and what is implicated. 'What is said' is determined by a combination of decoded meaning, disambiguation, and reference assignment. Any other meaning that is communicated beyond this is implicated. We then explored Grice's account of implicated meaning, focusing on conversational implicatures. According to Grice, conversational implicatures arise from the assumption that speakers are following the cooperative principle (CP), and that, as such, they are contributing to the conversation in a cooperative fashion. Conversational implicatures arise when a hearer must infer some additional information to maintain the assumption that the speaker is being cooperative. Grice identifies four categories of maxims which, if followed, should lead to a cooperative utterance. These categories relate to the quality, quantity, relevance, and manner of the utterance. Implicatures may arise from the assumption that the speaker is obeying the maxims, or they may be generated to maintain an overall assumption of cooperation when the maxims clash or are flouted.

In the last section of the chapter, we discussed the different categories of implicature as recognised by Grice. We saw that conversational implicatures can be divided into those that depend on specific contextual conditions (particularised conversational implicatures) and those that arise generally (generalised conversational implicatures). Alongside conversational implicatures, Grice discusses conventional implicatures. These arise because of the use of a particular word or expression, and, unlike conversational implicatures, cannot be cancelled by subsequent utterances or contextual circumstances.

Exercises

4a For each of the replies in the exchanges in (i) to (iii) work out what the speaker (Bella) is saying ('what is said') and what she is implicating.

    (i)   Arthur: Are you going to London on holiday?
           Bella: I don't like the rain
    (ii) Arthur: Do you want me to close the window?
           Bella: It's rather cold in here
    (iii) Arthur: Would you like a cup of coffee?
           Bella: Coffee keeps me awake

4b Look again at the uncooperative examples in Section 4.3. In each case, propose a cooperative alternative. There may be more than one possibility!

    (i)   Arnie: Do you have the time?
           Bertha (has the time):
    (ii) Arnie: Do you have the time?
           Bertha (does not have the time):

4c Look at the replies in the exchanges in (i) to (v). What is the speaker (Brenda) implicating in each case? How can we explain the implicature using the CP and maxims? Be as specific as possible. Which maxim is involved? Why does the implicature arise?

    (i)   Albie: We need more milk
           Brenda: There's a shop just around the corner
    (ii) Albie: What time does the next train for Edinburgh leave?
           Brenda: Some time after 3pm
    (iii) Albie: Is Delia a good dancer?
           Brenda: She's enthusiastic
    (iv) Albie: Shall we stop for lunch?
           Brenda: I'm starving!
    (v)   Albie: Are you angry with me?
           Brenda: Of course not. It's fantastic that you spilled coffee on my new white carpet.

4d Identify the generalised conversational implicatures (GCIs) in the following utterances. On what basis might the implicature be cancelled in each case?

(i) Manchester United scored three goals in their last match!
(ii) Edward's exam results were satisfactory
(iii) Usain Bolt can run 100 m in 9.58 seconds
(iv) I've got £100 to last me until the end of the month
(v) The plumber made a reasonable job of fitting the new boiler

---

4e Look at the highlighted words in (i) to (iv). What do those words add to the meaning? Keeping Grice's notion of conventional implicature in mind, propose an analysis of them in terms of what they indicate to the hearer. Explain why it would be strange to cancel them.

(i) *Even* Patrick passed the test
(ii) Luisa was late *too*
(iii) Steve is happy, *so* he's coming to the party
(iv) Steve is happy. *After all*, he's coming to the party

Key Terms Introduced in this Chapter

conventional implicatures, 81
conversational implicatures, 68
cooperative principle, 68
flouting, 75
generalised conversational implicatures, 80
manner, 69
maxims, 68
particularised conversational implicatures, 78
quality, 69
quantity, 69
relation, 69
scalar implicatures, 81
what is said, 66
what is implicated, 66

Further Reading

Grice's writing on implicature in *Logic and Conversation* and the associated *Retrospective* Epilogue (Grice, 1989), while by no means an easy read, is more accessible than some of his other papers, and anyone using Grice in an analysis should attempt to read the original.

For those who are interested in Grice's work more broadly, or who want to read about his work in a broader context, Siobhan Chapman's (2005) book *Paul Grice: Philosopher and Linguist* provides a comprehensive account of his life and work. Chapman's (2011) book on pragmatics, also includes a useful and accessible section on Grice and implicature.

Most textbooks on pragmatics include an introduction to Grice's ideas about pragmatics. Those which discuss the topic in more detail include Levinson (1983) and Clark (2013). Levinson provides an in-depth discussion of how we might test for implicatures, and discusses issues relating to cancellability, as briefly touched on at the end of this chapter

For readers who are interested in Grice's work on meaning mentioned at the beginning of this chapter, the work of Tim Wharton (2003, 2009) is recommended. He provides a clear overview of Grice's work on meaning and considers how the ideas might be developed and applied more broadly.

CHAPTER 5

Pragmatics Beyond Grice

In This Chapter ...

In this chapter, we look at how the field of pragmatics has developed following Grice's hugely influential work. Many of the ideas and analyses that have developed out of Grice's work have been motivated by the aim of addressing apparent problems or limitations with his approach. Therefore, we begin this chapter with a discussion of some common questions, problems, and objections that arise in relation to Grice's work on pragmatics. While Grice is without a doubt one of the most influential figures in pragmatics, his work has been criticised on several grounds, and we explore some of these here. We look at general issues relating to the origins and universality of the Gricean framework, as well as asking more specific questions about the operation of individual maxims.

A key criticism of Grice has been that his work is rooted in one social and cultural context. We discuss a key study by Elinor Ochs Keenan in which she considers how conversations and interactions play out in a community with cultural assumptions, which differ significantly from the world in which Grice developed his ideas. We then move on to consider two influential accounts that have developed out of Grice's work, but which broadly maintain his overall approach. Such approaches are known as neo-Gricean. We outline work by Laurence R. Horn and Stephen Levinson, and we see how their proposed principles explain various types of inference and implicature.

5.1 Grice and Beyond

It is impossible to study pragmatics without studying the work of Grice. His cooperative principle and maxims may often be the only introduction to pragmatics that many linguistics and language students receive, and his work has influence beyond those working specifically in pragmatics itself. Grice's framework was the first real attempt to understand and explain how conversational implicatures arise. His revolutionary contributions to the field include the central idea that communication is a rational activity and that, as communicators, we have assumptions and expectations about how our interlocutors will behave. We see these key notions persisting in both the post-Gricean approaches outlined in this chapter and in relevance theory, which is introduced in Chapter 6.

Despite his undeniable influence on pragmatics as a discipline, Grice's work has, of course, drawn a range of criticisms. Indeed, he revisits some of his own ideas in his retrospective epilogue and identifies areas that he considers in need of further consideration and development. While in this chapter we spend some time considering problems, questions, and short-comings associated with the Gricean framework, the intention is not to dismiss or even downplay Grice's contribution. Rather, the aim is to sit-uate his work as the inspiration and starting point for much, if not all, of the work that has followed. Theories and frameworks develop when they are applied to new data and new examples and when they are questioned, tested and, subsequently, adapted. In this chapter, we consider some of the issues that have been raised in relation to Grice's work, and we will see that it is out of these issues, that new and exciting approaches have developed.

5.2 Are We Always Cooperative When We Communicate?

Cooperation is at the heart of the Gricean approach to pragmatics. Grice (1989, p. 26) describes conversations as being 'cooperative efforts' with 'a common purpose or set of purposes, or at least a mutually accepted direction'. Furthermore, the derivation of implicatures is driven by the assumption that interlocutors are obeying the cooperative principle.

Is it, however, reasonable to claim that speakers are always cooperative? Are there, for example, instances of successful communication where the participants cannot reasonably be described as cooperating? There are certainly conversations that are hostile in nature, and which do not feel very cooperative, and there are others in which the participants might have very different aims or objectives from one another. In cases of cross-examination, for example, the person being questioned may well be decidedly uncooperative. A police suspect who repeatedly answers 'no comment' to every question that she is asked is fully aware of the accepted purpose of the discourse in which she is engaged. However, she is choosing not to cooperate with it. Of course, we might ask if a one-sided interrogation of this sort can really be classified as a conversation. Perhaps not. However, the participants are communicating with one another nonetheless, and so some explanation as to how this is achieved is needed.

While speakers often compose their messages in a cooperative manner, a question remains over whether they can always be said to be behaving cooperatively. That is, should cooperation be taken as the supreme principle that governs communication? How do we allow for the fact that there seem to be cases where communication takes place in the absence of cooperation? There are two strategies available to us at this point.

One option is to reject the assumption that cooperation is the underlying principle that drives communication, and to seek some alternative approach. As we will see in Chapter 6, this is the route that has been taken by one post-Gricean approach: relevance theory.

A second option is to maintain the assumption that cooperation is the central driving factor in communication, and to look for a way to accommodate apparent examples of non-cooperative communication. In his retrospective epilogue, Grice does just this. He discusses hostile cases such as cross-examination and argues that these apparent counterexamples can be said to be simulating rationality and cooperation. That is, he maintains that even in these apparently non-cooperative scenarios, the cooperative principle is still in operation.

When laying out his general approach, Grice uses the analogy of working with someone to bake a cake or fix a car to capture the joint, goal-driven nature of conversation as he sees it. These activities have clear end goals. If they are successfully completed, the participants will end up with a baked cake and a fixed car, respectively. It is less clear, however, that conversations necessarily always have agreed outcomes or goals. The cooperative principle refers to 'the accepted purpose or direction of the talk exchange in which you are engaged', and this raises several questions. Who decides on the 'accepted purpose' of a talk exchange, and on what basis does it become 'accepted'? How do we deal with conversations that appear to have no clear or agreed purpose or direction?

Grice (1989, p. 370) himself considers the case of what he calls 'over-the-garden-wall chatter'. We might also refer to this kind of conversation as small talk or **phatic communication**. Such discourse appears to be motivated by social aims, rather than by the aim of communicating information. Furthermore, it achieves these social goals by the very fact that it has little purpose or direction. Grice's suggestion is that in such conversations the common aim is 'that each party should, for the time being, identify himself with the transitory conversational interests of the other' (p. 29). We consider phatic communication from a different perspective in Chapter 7.

5.3 Questions about the Maxims

5.3.1 Questions around Terminology

At first glance, Grice's maxims appear to give us clear guidelines for how we should go about making a cooperative contribution to a conversation. We should tell the truth, we should give an appropriate amount of information (not too much, not too little), we should keep our contributions relevant, and we should say things in a cooperative manner. The maxims give us a good general idea about what is expected of us when we communicate.

However, when we interrogate them a little further, questions arise about what precisely is meant by each maxim and how we should interpret the terminology used. For example, how brief is brief? How should we judge brevity? Should we judge it by counting the number of words, the number of syllables, or perhaps the number of syntactic units? How is a contribution judged to be obscure? Who decides what is an orderly way to present information? And perhaps most significantly, how are we to judge something as relevant? Indeed, the maxim of relation is particularly vague, commanding us, as it does, to simply, 'Be relevant.' What makes something relevant? How relevant is relevant enough? How do we allow for the fact that what is relevant to one person may not be relevant to another? These are questions and issues that Grice explicitly acknowledges when he first introduces the maxim of relation. As he says:

> Though the maxim [of relevance] itself is terse, its formulation conceals a number of problems that exercise me a good deal: questions about what different kinds and focuses of relevance there may be, how these

shift in the course of a talk exchange, how to allow for the fact that subjects of conversation are legitimately changed, and so on. I find the treatment of such questions exceedingly difficult, and I hope to revert to them in later work (1989, p. 27).

As Clark (2013, p. 58) notes, Grice never did return to these questions specifically, and he never provided a more precise definition of what it means to be relevant. However, a general sense of what it means to be relevant is often good enough when we are discussing and analysing utterances from a Gricean perspective. To be relevant, a contribution should relate to the topic of conversation. For example, as we saw in Chapter 4, when we ask somebody what the time is, we expect an answer that in some way relates to the time, and anything else is likely to be judged as irrelevant.

Attempts to provide more specific and precise definitions of the terminology that Grice used have played a key role in the development of post-Gricean theories and frameworks. We see in Section 5.6 how two of these accounts have translated the maxims into their own principles, and in Chapter 6, we see that a more precise definition of what it means to be relevant is a key part of Sperber and Wilson's relevance-theoretic pragmatics.

5.3.2 Where, Why, and How?

Grice's maxims have undeniably had a huge influence on the discipline of pragmatics and beyond. However, various questions concerning both their nature and origin remain. We often see the maxims treated as prescriptive in nature. That is, we find them presented as rules or guidelines for how cooperative speakers should behave. The maxims are often cited as rules for effective communication, and we find them quoted in various guides for how to speak or write well. This was not, however, how Grice originally intended them to be used. As Bach explains (2006, p. 24), the maxims are not 'sociological generalizations about speech, nor [are they] moral prescriptions or proscriptions on what to say or communicate'. Rather they should be seen as a description of how cooperative speakers do, in fact, behave. As Bach goes on to explain (2006, p. 24), they are better thought of as 'presumptions about utterances, presumptions that we as listeners rely on and as speakers exploit'.

This still, however, leaves various questions unanswered. Where do the maxims come from? Are they something we are born with or are they learned? Are they universal or do we see some variation cross-culturally? Could there be other maxims? Could we do without any of the maxims? Again, we find that Grice considered these questions himself, and his thoughts on the matter give us further insight into how he conceived of the maxims. According to Grice (1989, p. 29):

it is just a well-recognized empirical fact that people do behave in these ways; they learned to do so in childhood and have not lost the habit of doing so; ... I would like to be able to think of the standard type of conversational practice not merely as something that all or most do in fact follow but as something that it is reasonable for us to follow, and that we should not abandon.

Thus, for Grice, observing the cooperative principle and maxims is simply the rational way to behave.

A further question arises about the maxims themselves and their relation to one another. They are generally presented as a set of four independent maxims of equal importance and significance. However, as Grice himself acknowledges in Strand Six of his retrospective epilogue (Grice, 1989, pp. 368–72), this presentation may be misleading. First, the maxims are not completely independent of one another. We saw in Chapter 4 that some implicatures arise from a clash of maxims. On other occasions, we seem to have an overlap between the maxims. For example, to observe the maxim of quantity, we must judge how much information is required. However, to do this, we must take the topic of the conversation into consideration and decide what is relevant to that topic. Thus, there is likely to be some overlap between the work done by the maxim of quantity (informativeness) and the work done by the maxim of relation (relevance). If a speaker has included more information than is required, then that information will also be irrelevant, and so again, we have some overlap.

Grice also notes that the maxims do not all contribute to communication in the same way. Unlike the quality, quantity, and relation maxims, the maxims of manner are to do with clarity of presentation, and they are much less likely to lead to implicatures than the other maxims. They are about how we say things, rather than what we say.

Finally, the maxim of quality (truthfulness) has a significance that sets it apart from the other maxims. As Grice (1989, p. 27) notes, 'other maxims come into operation only on the assumption that this maxim of Quality is satisfied'. He reiterates this point in his retrospective epilogue when he explains that '[f]alse information is not an inferior kind of information; it just is not information' (p. 371). Thus, in practice, the different maxims play slightly different roles to one another, they contribute to meaning in different ways, and they have slightly different statuses.

5.3.3 Questions about the Maxims of Quality

Grice considers the supermaxim of quality (truthfulness) to be the most important of the maxims. This supermaxim states that as a speaker you should '[t]ry to make your contribution one that is true'. Of course, speakers do not always tell the truth. We lie, we tell stories, and make jokes that are not true. We also use language non-literally in metaphors and ironies. Grice was aware of these non-truthful uses of language and accounted for them as various types of maxim violation.

Lies are covert violations of the maxim of truthfulness. When a speaker tells a lie, even though she is saying something that she knows to be untrue, she does not intend the hearer to recognise this. Indeed, when telling a lie, the speaker hopes that the hearer will assume that what has been said is true. That is, the speaker hopes that the hearer will accept that she is obeying the maxim of truthfulness. In the case of jokes and fiction, the maxim of truthfulness is suspended. The speaker overtly opts out of it, and the hearer does not assume that what is being said is the literal truth. Finally, as discussed in Chapter 4, figurative uses of language, including metaphor and irony, are overt violations, or floutings, of the maxim of truthfulness. By appearing to say something that is obviously and undeniably untrue, the speaker triggers the search for a related, true implicature.

However, as Wilson (1995) and Wilson and Sperber (2002) discuss, there are various instances which do not fit into any of these categories, but which still appear to be examples of speakers uttering something that is not literally true. Consider the examples (1) to (3).

(1) The wedding cost £20,000

(2) The room fell silent

(3) Jeremy had a square face

Suppose that you ask your friend how much her son's wedding cost, and she replies with the utterance in (1). You then later find out that the wedding actually cost £20,104. Would you feel that your friend had lied to you? She has not strictly speaking said something that is true. However, we are unlikely to feel as though we have been lied to or deceived in this case. The approximation in (1) feels true enough. Similarly, the room that is described in (2) was unlikely to have been completely silent. Perhaps there were sounds of people breathing or the hum of an electrical fixture. Perhaps the wind could be heard whistling in the distance through an open window. Any of these would mean that the room was not completely silent and yet, once again, we would be unlikely to think that (2) was a deceitful description so long as nobody was speaking and the room was more or less silent.

Finally, it is not possible for a human to have a square face if we take the word *square* literally. Therefore, the speaker of (3) appears to have said something untrue. It is, however, possible to imagine situations in which

(3) might be uttered and in which it might feel as though the speaker were saying something true. In none of these cases do we feel that the speaker has lied, and, perhaps just as significantly, neither do we feel that they have flouted the maxim of truthfulness. It is not clear how such examples are to be accounted for on the Gricean framework.

Finally, consider cases of non-declarative and negative metaphors, such as (4) and (5).

(4)   Be an angel!

(5)   Jacqui is no angel!

These trigger metaphorical interpretations even though they cannot be said to be untrue and so do not flout the maxim of truthfulness. We will return to these examples in Chapter 8 when we come to consider figurative uses of language. However, for now, it is enough to start thinking about whether truthfulness is as central to communication as Grice's supermaxim might suggest.

5.3.4 Questions about the Maxims of Manner

Grice's manner maxims certainly seem, at least from a style perspective, to make good sense. It seems reasonable that speakers should aim to be clear, brief, orderly, and to avoid ambiguity and obscurity. However, again, if we take a closer look at the ways in which speakers actually use language, all is not quite so simple.

Language is full of ambiguity, both lexical and syntactic. It would be virtually impossible for a speaker to avoid using ambiguous words or structures for any length of time. There also appears to be little need to avoid ambiguity. As we saw in Chapter 2, disambiguation is a very common pragmatic task. Hearers usually infer the intended meaning without much difficulty, and indeed, they are often not even consciously aware that there has been an ambiguity. It may only be when misunderstandings occur or when an ambiguity is used for comic effect that we even notice that a word or phrase is compatible with more than one meaning. Furthermore, it is likely that Grice's use of the word *ambiguity* was not limited strictly to lexical or structure ambiguity, but rather was intended to capture any cases where two or more interpretations are possible. As we have seen throughout our discussions, utterances are often compatible with more than one interpretation.

Grice lists various maxims within the category of manner. However, on some occasions it will necessarily be difficult to obey all of them at once. Legal texts, for example, are deliberately written to be as unambiguous as possible. Ideally, there should be no room for inference or individual interpretation when it comes to the law. As a result, these texts are unlikely to be brief. Spelling everything out explicitly necessarily makes an utterance longer than it would be if some information had been left unsaid.

Finally, there are other contexts in which a speaker might legitimately make her utterance less brief than it might otherwise have been. Consider the utterances in (6) and (7), as discussed by Wilson and Sperber (1981, p. 173).

(6) (a) Peter is married to Madeleine

(b) It is Peter who is married to Madeleine

(7) (a) Mary ate a peanut

(b) Mary put a peanut into her mouth, chewed, and swallowed it

In each case, the same basic information is conveyed by both versions. However, the (b) versions are longer than the (a) versions, and so a speaker obeying the maxims of manner should always prefer the (a) versions. It is not difficult, however, to imagine contexts in which a speaker might utter (6b) or (7b) appropriately and without any sense that she is being unnecessarily verbose. Perhaps the speaker of (6b) is correcting a misconception that Madeleine is married to John, and perhaps (7b) is being used to communicate, not only that Mary ate a peanut, but that she did so in a considered and contemplative manner. Being as brief as possible does not seem to be necessarily always the best strategy for a speaker to adopt.

5.4 Keenan and Cross-Cultural Pragmatics

Linguistic anthropologist Elinor Ochs Keenan (1976) raises an altogether different objection to the Gricean approach to pragmatics. Following ethnographic fieldwork with Malagasy speakers in Madagascar, she questions how far the cooperative principle and maxims can be applied cross-culturally. Philosophers, she claims, tend to focus their work on the behaviour, interaction, and communicative norms that they observe in their own cultures and societies. While this is understandable as a starting point when developing a theory or hypothesis about communication, we should not assume that patterns observed in one culture or society will necessarily be found in another.

While Grice does not explicitly claim that the cooperative principle and maxims are universal, they do seem to be presented as general claims about how humans behave. Indeed, Grice presents them as a rational and reasonable way to behave. A natural extension of this assumption would be that any cultures, groups, or individuals who do not behave in this way are somehow irrational or unreasonable. This is a problematic position to take, and Keenan's data from Madagascar raise questions about how the maxims might most usefully be applied.

Keenan focuses on the quantity maxims, and in particular, on the first maxim of quantity which instructs the speaker to make her contribution as informative as is required. According to this maxim, a speaker is expected to 'meet the informational needs of their interactional partner' (Keenan, 1976, p. 69) as far as she is able. If a speaker does not give as much information as is required, then the hearer is likely to infer that the speaker did not have that information. That is, the only reason that a cooperative speaker would not provide the required information is if she is unable to do so. However, the Malagasy people, Keenan (1976, p. 70) claims, 'regularly provide less information than is required by their conversational partner, even though they have access to the necessary information'. Consider the exchange in (8) taken from Keenan's data.

(8) Speaker A: Where is your mother?

     Speaker B: She is either in the house or at the market

According to Grice's cooperative principle and the first maxim of quantity, Speaker B should only provide an answer like this if she knows that her mother is either in the house or at the market but does not know for sure which is the case. Thus, B's answer would implicate that B was not able to give more specific information.

However, according to Keenan, in Malagasy society this implicature does not follow. There is no expectation that speakers will satisfy the hearer's informational needs. Keenan suggests two reasons for this. First, Malagasy is a close-knit society in which very little remains private. New information is a prized commodity, and it is not given away easily. Knowing something that other people do not know provides one with a form of prestige, and anyone requesting information will expect to have to put some effort into persuading the speaker to share it. Information is more likely to be withheld if it is significant and if the interlocutor could not easily find it out for themselves.

Second, Keenan claims that in this society there is a general fear of explicitly committing to a claim. If communicating the information were to lead to negative consequences, then the speaker would feel responsible for those consequences. Similarly, if a speaker were to make a commitment to a future event that did not come to pass, the speaker would suffer a loss of face. This leads to utterances that might appear underinformative or uncooperative. Keenan (1976, p. 71) provides the following example:

Thus, when I once asked an elderly woman when I might find her brother at home, she gave me this answer, 'If you don't come after five, you won't find him.' She was not willing to guarantee that if I did come after five, I would find him.

The elderly woman uses a double negative, and in doing so communicates that her hearer should come after five to look for the brother, but she does so without committing herself to him being there. If Keenan arrives after five, but the brother is not there, the elderly woman will not have lost face.

In Chapter 4, we saw examples of Grice's generalised conversational implicatures (GCIs) in which an indefinite referring expression such as *a man* leads a hearer to infer that the man is not previously known or familiar to the speaker. The fear of explicitly committing to a claim means that this implicature also does not follow in Malagasy discourse. According to Keenan (p. 73), '[w]hen someone in a Malagasy village says, "I see a person," those listening do not infer that the speaker is not closely associated with the referent'.

Keenan concludes that whether and to what degree speakers conform to the maxims of quantity depends at least in part on cultural and social factors. Furthermore, this cultural variation is not restricted to the close-knit Malagasy community and their fear of losing face. As Keenan points out, professional roles such as priest, doctor, or lawyer might require that a speaker withhold information at certain times, and, indeed, there are likely to be situations in every society in which an individual will withhold information if it is in their best interests to do so.

For Keenan, the value of Grice's work is that it provides a framework that can be used to compare conversational practices in different social and cultural communities. She interprets Grice's claim that 'it is just a well-recognized empirical fact that people do behave in these ways' (1989, p. 29) to be presenting the maxims as 'social facts' (p. 79). She objects to this, and rather considers their value to lie in offering a starting point for analysing and understanding real language in use.

5.5 What Is NOT Wrong with Grice

When students first encounter Grice, a common initial reaction is to object to the maxims as simple descriptions of how speakers always behave. People do not always tell the truth. Indeed, they often lie. On some occasions, a speaker will give us more information than we might have required, and on other occasions, they may give us less. It is easy to fall into a trap of assuming that because people do not always obey the maxims, Grice must be wrong.

However, this is to misunderstand the nature and purpose of the maxims. Grice never claimed that everything we say always conforms to the maxims. His claim, however, was that communication is a rational and cooperative activity, and that we always assume that speakers are being rational and cooperative overall, even if they appear to be violating individual maxims. It is this assumption that speakers will be cooperative that drives the generation of implicatures. That is, when we interpret an utterance, we infer those things that are necessary to maintain our assumption that the speaker is being cooperative overall. Horn (2004, p. 8) sums this up as follows:

> conversational implicature operates through the mechanism of exploitation. … pragmatic principles and convention do as much work when they are apparently violated – when speaker S counts on hearer H to recognise the apparent violation and to perform the appropriate contextual adjustment – as when they are observed or ostentatiously violated.

If implicature depends on exploitation and violation of principles, then we need to have principles that can be exploited and violated. Grice's framework provides us with these.

Finally, it is worth reminding ourselves at this point that an objection to the specifics of a maxim does not singlehandedly discredit the entire approach or analysis. We do not throw out an entire framework or theory and all its associated insights simply because there are counterexamples or question marks in relation to specific parts of it. Rather, we use the questions and counterexamples to drive the development of our understanding.

Our knowledge about how communication and language work is continually developing. New approaches build on what has gone before. To completely disregard Grice because of some objections to the details of his approach is to disregard significant developments in our knowledge and understanding of pragmatics and of utterance interpretation. As Wilson and Sperber (1981, p. 155) explain:

> The value of Grice's work derives not so much from the detail of his analyses as from the general claim that underlies them … The broad outline of this position is extremely convincing … However, it seems to us that its detail needs considerable modification if any further progress is to be made.

In the rest of this chapter, and in the chapters that follow, we move on to look at some of the approaches to pragmatics that have grown out of Grice's insights. We explore the modifications that have been suggested and we think about how these seek to address the issues raised in the first half of this chapter. We begin by turning our attention to two key accounts that retain many of Grice's key ideas while developing others in specific ways. As they are still closely aligned with the original Gricean framework, these accounts are commonly referred to as **neo-Gricean**.

5.6 Neo-Gricean Pragmatics

In this section, we consider two influential pragmatic accounts that developed directly out of Grice's work on conversational implicature. Both Laurence Horn (1984; 2004) and Stephen Levinson (1987, 2000) developed accounts which, while broadly Gricean in nature, seek to address some of the problems or limitations of the original programme. As such, they represent the two main branches of neo-Gricean pragmatics.

Both Horn and Levinson take a reductionist approach and they seek to develop and improve on Grice's original programme by proposing a smaller and less complex set of principles. Horn reduces the maxims down to two principles, while Levinson's proposal comprises three principles. Both Horn and Levinson view the work done by Grice's maxim of quality as fundamental, and, as such, they treat a requirement for truthfulness as sitting outside of their proposed principles. According to Horn (1984, p. 12), if the speaker is not obeying the maxim of quality, 'the entire conversational … apparatus collapses'.

5.6.1 Horn

Laurence Horn (1984) argues that Grice's conversational maxims can be boiled down to two principles, and that these principles and the interaction between them can be used to explain the inferences that hearers make. The two principles are related to two factors which drive and constrain communication.

To communicate you need to produce some sort of communicative act. This might be an utterance, a gesture, or something else. You will be unable to convey your message and achieve your desired outcome if you do not do something. This motivation to achieve your aims drives you to communicate. However, at the same time, we do not want to expend any more energy than is necessary. This drives a speaker to use the minimum mental and physical effort possible. Therefore, we have two factors working in opposition to one another: the drive to communicate and the desire to conserve effort. According to Horn, it is these forces and the interaction between them that generates implicatures. He formalised these two factors in his two principles: the **Q Principle** and the **R Principle**.

Horn argues that all of Grice's maxims except for the maxim of quality (truthfulness) are captured in these two principles, and he defines them as follows:

(9) The Q Principle (hearer-based):
     Make your contribution sufficient
     Say as much as you can (given R)

(10) The R Principle (speaker-based):
     Make your contribution necessary
     Say no more than you must (given Q)

The Q Principle sets the lower limit on what a speaker should say. She should make her contribution sufficient, and she should say as much as she can, given the constraints of the R Principle. The R Principle, on the other hand, sets the upper limit on what a speaker should say. The speaker should make her contribution necessary, and she should say no more than necessary, allowing for the constraints of the Q Principle. Notice that the interaction between the principles is written into Horn's definition. A speaker must follow each principle as far as allowed given the other principle. This means that there is a tension between the two. As we will see, it is this tension that drives much implicature derivation.

Notice that the Q Principle is presented as 'hearer-based'. It is about providing the hearer with sufficient information, and it sets the lower limit on what the speaker must do to achieve this. The R Principle, on the other hand, is presented as 'speaker-based'. It is about the speaker saying what is necessary for communicating the message, but no more. As such, it sets the upper limit on what the speaker should say.

According to Horn, between them, these two principles do the work of Grice's maxims of quantity, relation, and manner. The Q principle covers the same ground as Grice's first quantity maxim ('Make your contribution as informative as is required.'), and the R Principle subsumes the work done by the second quantity maxim ('Do not make your contribution more informative than is required.'). The R Principle also covers the work done by the maxims of relation and manner.

As we have seen, the Q Principle requires that a speaker says as much as she can. The assumption that a speaker is obeying this principle drives the derivation of Q-based implicatures. These are implicatures that arise via the assumption that if a speaker has not said more, this is because she was not able to say more. The most discussed category of Q-based implicatures are scalar implicatures. Examples of scalar implicatures were introduced in Section 4.5.2.

Consider the examples in (11) and (12), paying particular attention to the contribution made by the terms in italics: *possible* and *certain*.

(11) It is *possible* that Diane will get the job

(12) It is *certain* that Diane will get the job

Notice that for something to be certain, it must also be possible. Therefore, the meaning of the word *certain* entails the meaning of the word *possible*. If it is certain that Diane will get the job, then it is also possible that she will get the job.

The reverse is, however, not the case. It is not the case that if something is possible, it is also necessarily certain. Therefore, *certain* is more informative than *possible*. If a speaker is following the Q Principle and saying as much as she can, then we would expect her to describe things that she knows to be certain as *certain*, and not merely *possible*. Therefore, if she chooses to describe something as *possible*, it is reasonable to infer that the speaker did not feel that it was appropriate to describe it as certain. By using the word *possible* in (11), the speaker implicates that she is not certain that Diane got the job.

As discussed in Chapter 4, scalar implicatures occur wherever we have words which form the same sort of one-way implicational scale as we find with *possible* and *certain*: <possible; certain>. Other examples include <some; all>, <warm; hot>, <sometimes; often; always>, <like; love>, and <good; excellent>. Numbers also form a scale. The utterance in (13), for example, would usually be taken to implicate that no more than three goals were scored, even though a team that scores four goals has also scored three goals.

(13) Chelsea scored three goals at the weekend

As Chapman (2011) explains, Q-implicatures are negative implicatures, in that they implicate that something is not the case. They are based on 'what could have been said but wasn't' (Horn, 2004, p. 13).

The R Principle states that a speaker should say no more than is necessary. Horn describes R-based implicatures as involving 'social rather than purely linguistic motivation' (Horn, 2004, p. 13). That is, if, given the discourse context, a hearer can reasonably be expected to infer a particular detail or aspect of the intended meaning, then there is no need for the speaker to explicitly spell this out in her utterance. This drives a hearer to assume stereotypical or **unmarked** interpretations unless specifically directed otherwise. He can be expected to fill in details that he might reasonably be able to infer.

Something is unmarked if it is the usual and expected way to express a concept or idea. If the speaker chooses to use a less usual and more unexpected expression to communicate a concept or idea, we say that that expression is marked. Now consider the utterance in (14).

(14) Max took out his keys and opened the door

The order of the two events described in (14) has not been specified, and it would strictly speaking be true if Max opened the door and then took out his keys, or vice versa. However, a hearer assuming the R Principle will look for the most unmarked, stereotypical interpretation and so is likely to infer that the keys were taken out and then the door was opened. Indeed, the hearer is also likely to infer that the keys were used to open the door, even though this has not been explicitly stated either.

According to the R Principle, the speaker should say no more than is necessary, and so if the hearer can be expected to infer a detail, then there is no need for the speaker to make that detail explicit. Consider (15), which was discussed in Chapter 4, and which is usually taken to communicate that the speaker broke one of her own fingers.

(15) I broke a finger last year

According to the R Principle, the speaker should not say more than she has to say. The speaker of (15) does not need to specify that it was her own finger that she broke, as this is the most usual, stereotypical interpretation. The speaker can therefore trust the hearer to fill in these details himself.

Horn (2007) suggests that R-based effects play a role in lexical processes such as blending, clipping, and abbreviation. Some words or expressions, such as those in (16) to (18), may be so frequently used that a speaker can reduce or abbreviate them, trusting that this will not interfere with the communication of meaning.

(16) Motor hotel > motel

(17) Examination > exam

(18) Telephone > phone

The reduced versions may then become the standard and unmarked ways of referring to these items.

R-based implicatures are also associated with the interpretation of indirect speech acts and with politeness effects. As Horn (1984) discusses, enquiries as to whether one can pass the salt will usually be interpreted as requests for the salt to be passed, rather than as genuine enquiries as to the hearer's ability. The speaker can avoid a direct order or request whilst being confident that the hearer will be able to infer the intended meaning.

Imagine that a speaker follows either the Q Principle or the R Principle without regard for the other. A speaker following only the Q Principle would spell out every little detail and specific point of her message. A speaker following only the R Principle, on the other hand, may not say anything at all. It is only by balancing these principles and by determining what she can say as relative to what she must say and vice versa, that a speaker produces cooperative utterances. However, it is the inevitable tension between the two principles that allows us to explain other instances of implicated meaning.

Consider again the example in (15). The possessive pronoun *my* is more specific and more informative than the indefinite article *a*. Therefore, we might expect a speaker who is obeying the Q Principle to produce the utterance in (19) if she is able to do so. That is, if the finger she is referring to is her own finger.

(19) I broke my finger last year

We might also then expect that a speaker who utters (15) instead of (19) would be taken to be implicating that it was not her own finger that was broken. However, as we have seen, this is not, in fact, the most common interpretation. The speaker of the utterance in (15) is usually taken to be referring to her own finger. Recall that Horn's principles each include reference to the other. A speaker should say as much as she can, given R, and a speaker should say no more than she must, given Q. When interpreting (15), we have very strong expectations about the most usual and normal scenarios in which people break fingers, and so, in this case, the R Principle overrides the Q Principle.

We also see the interaction of the Q and R Principles in the differing interpretations of utterances that include semantically similar expressions. Consider the pairs in examples (20) to (22), taken from Horn (2004).

(20) (a) Her blouse was pale red
      (b) Her blouse was pink
(21) (a) He got the machine to stop
      (b) He stopped the machine
(22) (a) It's not impossible that you will solve the problem
      (b) It's possible that you will solve the problem

While for each of these pairs the two utterances are more or less semantically equivalent, one version is what we would consider unmarked. Application of the R Principle leads to an association between unmarked expressions and unmarked interpretations. If the speaker has described a thing or an event in an unremarkable way, then, the hearer will assume an unremarkable, normal, or stereotypical interpretation. In each of the pairs in (20) to (22), the (b) version uses the unmarked expression. There is no reason to think that there is anything strange or unusual about the pinkness of the blouse in (20b) or that the machine in (21b) was stopped in anything other than a normal, unremarkable way.

Compare these, however, with the (a) versions. In each case, the speaker uses a marked expression. Rather than *pink*, the blouse is described as *pale red*, and rather than having *stopped the machine*, the participant is described as having *got the machine to stop*. The speaker has used a longer, more unusual, and more complicated phrase in each case. Remember, that the R Principle states that a speaker should say no more than she must. Therefore, the hearer will infer that there must have been some reason for the speaker to choose the marked version. The Q Principle then also plays its part. The hearer will assume that the reason that the speaker used the marked version is because the unmarked version was not sufficient in some way or other. The blouse in (20a), for example, was not appropriately described as pink, and the act of stopping the machine in (21a) departed, in some way, from the normal, expected way of doing so. Notice, however, that the hearer must still infer the way in which the things described are marked. This will depend on the context in which the utterances are spoken and will vary accordingly.

5.6.2 Levinson

Like Horn, Stephen Levinson (1987, 2000) takes a broadly Gricean approach to pragmatics, and like Horn he suggests that the original maxims can be reduced to several principles. He suggests that we think of Grice's maxims not as rules, but as 'inferential heuristics' (2000, p. 35). That is, they should be thought of as rule-of-thumb strategies for making inferences. Behavioural norms then emerge from these strategies.

Levinson proposes that there are three principles which line up with three different types of inference: the Q, I, and M Principles. Each of these heuristics provides a general principle or strategy, and Levinson's proposal spells out what this means from the perspective of the speaker and the hearer. For each principle, he provides a description of what the speaker is instructed to do: the speaker's maxim. He also gives us a description of what the hearer can assume to be the case, based on what the speaker has said and on how she has said it: the recipient's corollary. The three principles interact and are defined relative to one another, and so it is necessary to present them in full first, before discussing each in greater depth. The summary in Table 5.1 draws on Levinson's (1987, 2000) discussions, with some simplifications.

Each of these principles, and the associated maxim and corollary, leads to inferences. Levinson's Q Principle does the work of Grice's first maxim of quantity ('Make your contribution as informative as is required'), and it broadly parallels Horn's Q Principle in that it specifies that the speaker

Table 5.1 *Levinson's Q, I, and M principles*

Principle	General Heuristic	Speaker's Maxim	Recipient's Corollary
Q	What isn't said, isn't.	Do not provide a statement that is informationally weaker than your knowledge of the world allows, unless providing an informationally stronger statement would contravene the I-Principle.	Take it that the speaker made the strongest statement consistent with what he knows.
I	What is expressed simply is stereotypically exemplified.	Say as little as possible to achieve your communicative ends.	Enrich the informational content of the speaker's utterance, assuming that the speaker has not said things that can be taken for granted.
M	What's said in an abnormal way, isn't normal.	Indicate an abnormal, non-stereotypical situation by using marked expressions that contrast with those you would use to describe the corresponding normal, stereotypical situation.	What is said in an abnormal way indicates an abnormal situation, or marked messages indicate marked situations.

should say enough. The corollary spells out that, based on this principle, if a speaker does not say something, then the hearer can assume that it is not the case.

As with Horn's Q Principle, Levinson's Q Principle is associated with scalar implicatures. That is, it can be used to explain why, in some situations, use of a particular term implicates that a related, but informationally richer term can be taken not to apply. In Section 5.6.1, we saw (11) and (12) using *possible* and *certain*, and a very similar explanation emerges when we apply Levinson's Q Principle. If a speaker describes an event as *possible*, then we can infer that the event is not, as far as the speaker knows, *certain*. If it were certain, then we would expect the speaker to say so, and as she has not said so, we can assume that it is not the case.

Consider the exchange between Hannah and Jasmine in (23).

(23) Hannah: Did you read the article?

Jasmine: I read the introduction

From Jasmine's answer, Hannah can infer that Jasmine has only read the introduction and not the rest of the article. Notice that to read an article, it is necessary to read the introduction of that article. So, Jasmine's answer is not logically incompatible with her having read the whole article. However, according to Levinson's Q Principle, what isn't said, isn't the case. Jasmine has not said that she has read the whole article, and therefore, we can assume that she has not done so.

Whereas both Horn's Q Principle and Levinson's Q Principle are about saying enough, Horn's R Principle and Levinson's **I Principle** are about not saying too much. They do the work of the second part of Grice's quantity maxim ('Do not make your contribution more informative than is required'). The I Principle sets the upper limit on what the speaker should say. In practical terms, a speaker need not explicitly state those things that would otherwise be assumed to be the case. She should only say what is required. The hearer can assume that, unless otherwise stated, things are to be interpreted in a stereotypical, unexceptional way. Therefore, when interpreting the utterances in (24) to (26), the hearer is entitled to assume that each of the activities happened in a normal, unmarked manner.

(24) He opened the door

(25) She ate the sandwich

(26) The runners crossed the finishing line

In (24), the door was opened in the normal way, perhaps by turning a handle and pushing. In (25), the sandwich was eaten in the way that sandwiches might stereotypically be eaten, for example, by picking it up by hand and taking several bites. Finally, the runners in (26) can be assumed to have crossed the finishing line in a stereotypical manner, perhaps raising their arms in the air in triumph. We would be entitled to presume that they were not running backwards or in slow motion.

Levinson (2000) discusses a range of different inferences that follow from the I Principle, including **bridging inferences**. Bridging inferences are inferences that arise to connect two ideas. Consider example (27).

(27) Lydia walked into the kitchen. The window was open

We are likely to infer that the window referred to in the second part of the utterance is the window of the already mentioned kitchen. When we make this inference, we connect the two parts of the utterance. The speaker of (27) does not need to explicitly state that the window is the kitchen window, because she knows that the hearer is likely to assume this anyway.

A key difference between Horn's approach and Levinson's approach is that Levinson proposes a third principle, his **M Principle**. This principle is concerned, not with what is said, but with how it is said, and the M Principle replaces the various submaxims that fall under the Gricean category of manner. As we have just seen, according to the I Principle, if something is said in a normal way, then the hearer can assume that a stereotypical interpretation is intended. The M Principle guides interpretation in cases where a marked or abnormal expression is used. In short, if the speaker says something in an abnormal way, then the hearer can infer that something unusual or marked was intended. Consider the example in (28), taken from Levinson (2000, p. 39).

(28)   Bill caused the car to stop

The unmarked way to describe Bill stopping a car would be the utterance in (29).

(29)   Bill stopped the car

Had the speaker uttered (29), the hearer would have inferred, via the I Principle, that Bill stopped the car in the usual way by pressing his foot down on the brake pedal. However, by uttering (28), the speaker has chosen a marked expression. According to the M Principle, the hearer should therefore infer that there was something marked or unusual about the way that Bill stopped the car. Perhaps he was not driving the car but stopped it by stepping out in front of it. Perhaps the main brakes had failed, and Bill had to use the handbrake to stop the car. Whatever the specifics of the situation, we can infer, via the M Principle, that there is something unusual about the way that Bill stopped the car in (28).

The M Principle also explains the interpretation of some double negatives. Consider the examples in (30) and (31).

(30)   Fan is happy
(31)   Fan is not unhappy

As these examples illustrate, in language, two negatives do not necessarily equal a positive. Logically, we might expect that by adding two negative elements to the positive statement in (30) we would achieve another positive. However, in practice, the two utterances do not communicate the same meaning. The M Principle offers an explanation as to why this might be.

The unmarked way to describe someone as happy is to simply say that they are happy. The use of *not unhappy* in (31) is therefore marked. According to the M Principle, marked messages indicate marked situations. We must therefore assume that the speaker of (31) means something other than that Fan is happy. With gradable adjectives such as *happy*, we are, of course, not restricted to a binary choice between happy and unhappy. Not being able to describe Fan as unhappy does not therefore mean that she must be happy. Rather, the utterance in (31) states that she is not unhappy, while simultaneously implying that she cannot appropriately be described as happy either.

5.7 Chapter Summary

In this chapter, we have considered how the field of pragmatics has developed following Grice's revolutionary ideas and proposals. We started by considering some issues, problems, and questions that have been raised in relation to the cooperative principle and the maxims. Some of these are related to general assumptions that Grice makes about the nature and universality of his approach. Other issues relate to specific maxims and to the terminology used. We briefly discussed work by Keenan which considers the extent to which the maxims may be applied cross-culturally. In the final section of the chapter, the focus turned to neo-Gricean approaches to pragmatics, and proposals by Horn and Levinson were outlined and briefly discussed along with examples of the different inferences that they seek to explain.

Exercises

5a   Can you think of examples where communication cannot reasonably be described as cooperative? Return to Grice's cooperative principle to check your ideas against the wording in his definition.

5b   Think of a time when you have taken part in phatic communication or 'small talk'. What would you say the goal or aim of the conversation was? How might this fit into Grice's picture of communication?

5c   Consider Keenan's claims about the value of information in the Malagasy society and its implications for the maxim of quantity. Can you think of any situations in which a speaker might not immediately reveal information that they have? Hint: Think about childhood games, educational contexts, and gossip to get you started.

5d How might the Gricean maxims be applied to poetic language? Take a poem of your choice and discuss it in terms of the manner maxims. Does the poet use ambiguity? Is everything described briefly, clearly, and in an orderly manner? Rewrite the poem so that it strictly conforms to the manner maxims and reflect on how this changes the text.

5e Describe the implicatures that arise from the examples in (i) to (viii) and explain them using (a) Horn's principles and (b) Levinson's principles.

(i) Some of the apples were rotten
(ii) Abi is my father's wife
(iii) I often get up late on Sundays
(iv) Tim sat next to a woman on the train home
(v) Aybige broke a tooth yesterday
(vi) It was not impossible to find a shirt that he liked
(vii) You can have tea or coffee with your breakfast
(viii) We went to a French restaurant. The waiter was Italian

Key Terms Introduced in this Chapter
bridging inferences, 107
I Principle, 107
M Principle, 108
neo-Gricean, 100
phatic communication, 91
Q Principle, 100
R Principle, 100
unmarked, 102

Further Reading
Clark (2013) includes a detailed discussion of Grice's theory and goes into more detail concerning many of the objections and questions covered in this chapter. The continuing influence of Grice's work is evident in Petrus (2010) which includes a wide range of essays related to his work and ideas. Chapman (2011) includes an accessible introduction to neo-Gricean pragmatics and discusses both Horn and Levinson's proposals in some detail. Horn's (1984, 2004) work on scalar implicatures and 'Horn Scales' has been particularly influential, as has Levinson's (2000) account of *Presumptive Meanings*. Horn (2007) provides a more detailed introduction to the ideas that inspired his model and principles, and he discusses how they might be applied to issues in language development and change. Birner and Ward (2006) bring together a collection of more recent work inspired by Horn's neo-Gricean approach.

CHAPTER 6

Relevance-Theoretic Pragmatics

In This Chapter ...

In this chapter, we introduce the main ideas behind an influential theory of pragmatics: relevance theory. We begin by considering how it developed out of the Gricean approach to pragmatics, and we look at how it differs from that approach. Relevance theory is a cognitive pragmatic theory of how we process utterances, and, indeed, how we process information, in context. The chapter begins with a discussion of relevance and cognition, and we outline the relevance-theoretic characterisation of context. This then leads us to a definition of what it means for something to be relevant, and from this we move on to introduce the two principles which drive the relevance-theoretic approach to utterance interpretation. When information is intentionally communicated (both in utterances and in other forms of communication), we say it is ostensive. Ostensive communication is, according to relevance theory, special. It raises expectations of how relevant it will be for the addressee, and this has important consequences for how we process information and how we understand utterance interpretation. We will see that this leads us to the relevance-theoretic comprehension procedure which describes how we go about processing intentionally communicated information.

6.1 A Cognitive Theory of Communication

6.1.1 From Grice to Relevance Theory

In Chapter 4, we saw that Gricean pragmatics is driven by the idea that speakers are fundamentally cooperative. While a speaker may violate a maxim, it is assumed that she is ultimately trying to make her utterance cooperative. In Chapter 5, we saw that this can make it difficult to explain some of the ways in which speakers behave. Interlocutors are not always cooperative, and on some occasions, they may not have a clear purpose driving their conversational exchanges beyond conforming to social niceties. Furthermore, it is not entirely clear where the maxims come from or why speakers should obey them. Some of the definitions are vague, and, as Grice acknowledged, require more thought and development. In Chapter 5 we also saw how neo-Gricean approaches to pragmatics have responded to these issues and developed Grice's ideas.

In the 1980s Dan Sperber and Deirdre Wilson developed an alternative, post-Gricean framework for understanding how we interpret utterances: **relevance theory**. Sperber and Wilson were inspired by many of the underlying ideas of Grice, and, like Grice, they based their approach on the assumption that the recognition of intentions is central to successful communication. If an addressee recognises the speaker's intended meaning, then successful communication has taken place. To illustrate, consider the following example. Imagine that I intend to ask you if you know where the nearest car park is. However, when I utter the question, I suffer a slip of the tongue and produce the phrase 'par cark' instead. You are not left confused and unable to answer my question, even though the words *par* and *cark* do not have standard meanings relevant to this context in English. Rather, you will focus on working out what I intended to say, and you will answer my question based on what you think my intention was. I intended to say, 'car park', even though that is not what I produced. Recognition of intentions is key to both the Gricean and relevance theory approaches to pragmatics. Recall, however, that for Grice, the key to working out what a speaker intends to communicate is the assumption that they are being cooperative. Sperber and Wilson move away from this assumption, and instead argue that what drives interpretation is an assumption of **relevance**.

One of the criticisms levelled at the Gricean approach is that much of the terminology used is vague. It is not necessarily clear, for example, what is meant by the maxim 'Be relevant,' and it is not clear how a hearer or speaker is supposed to assess this. The cooperative principle depends on identification of the 'accepted purpose or direction of the talk exchange'

(Grice, 1989, p. 26), but it is not clear how interlocutors are supposed to go about doing this. It is also not clear how brief, informative, or unambiguous a contribution needs to be to satisfy the CP.

Sperber and Wilson aim to avoid these criticisms by dispensing with the CP and maxims and instead proposing two key principles of relevance. The first principle is known as the **cognitive principle of relevance** and describes how we process information in general. The second principle is known as the **communicative principle of relevance** and deals with information that is deliberately communicated to us. The principles of relevance, as we will see in this chapter, are designed to capture generalisations about our cognitive processes, rather than laying down rules about how good communicators should or should not behave. Alongside these principles, Sperber and Wilson have developed a specific definition of what it means for something to be relevant. This definition allows us to compare inputs and their relative relevance for different individuals and in different contexts, and Sperber and Wilson make specific claims about what levels of relevance a hearer can expect. According to relevance theory, when information is communicated to us, we can expect that it will be optimally relevant. It is this expectation of **optimal relevance** that, according to relevance theory, drives interpretation. Whereas for Grice, the quality of a speaker's contribution hinges on whether it is true, for relevance theory, the key factor is not truth, but relevance.

It is important to end this introductory section with a key point to keep in mind when comparing the Gricean and relevance-theoretic approaches to pragmatics. Relevance theory is often, quite understandably, presented as in direct opposition to Grice. Indeed, it departs from the Gricean approach in some important and significant ways. Relevance theory is driven by principles, rather than maxims, and it does not assume that speakers will be cooperative, truthful, or informative. It only assumes that they will try to be relevant. Despite these differences, relevance theory owes a huge amount to the insights of Grice. Theoretical theories and frameworks very seldom, if ever, come into being fully developed. Research is a process and theories are tested and refined over time. Relevance theory was developed in part to address some of the issues with the Gricean approach and has itself changed and developed since it was first proposed in 1986. Meanwhile, as we saw in Chapter 5, Grice himself was aware of issues with his work and he commented on the need to revisit these areas and develop the ideas further. We should, therefore, see relevance theory as developing out of, and influenced by, Grice's work on meaning and communication, rather than as set in direct opposition to it.

6.1.2 Relevance and Cognition

Relevance theory is a theory of pragmatics and a theory of communication, but it is also a theory of cognition. It makes claims about how we, as humans, acquire, process, and manipulate information. To fully understand how relevance theory can be used to analyse pragmatic processes, we need to take a step back and think about how we process information more generally. Utterances, as we will see, turn out to be just a special type of information that we process.

To understand relevance theory as a cognitive approach to pragmatics, and to be able to talk about the processes involved in communication from this perspective, we need to define some terms. Relevance itself is defined in more precise detail in Section 6.2.3. However, broadly speaking, a new piece of information is relevant if it changes what we think and how we view what is true about the world. In relevance theory terms, an input is relevant to an individual if it has a **cognitive effect** on the assumptions that make up that individual's **cognitive environment**.

At any given time, as we move about our lives, we hold a range of assumptions about ourselves, about other people, and about how things are in the world. These assumptions are simply beliefs that we hold to be true, and they are sometimes referred to as **contextual assumptions**, because, as we shall see, they make up the context in which we process new information. These assumptions may include philosophical beliefs about where we come from and how the world operates, but they will also include everyday, mundane, and seemingly trivial beliefs about the way things are. For example, as I write this, I hold the assumption that it is Thursday and that I am in London, England. I also hold the assumption that I have enough milk left in the fridge to make coffee tomorrow morning. At any point in time, we each hold a range of assumptions, and we hold these assumptions with varying degrees of certainty. For example, while I am quite confident that I know which day of the week it is, I am less certain about the amount of milk that is currently in my fridge. It is, for example, possible that I have misremembered or that somebody else has drunk some of the milk without my knowledge. Therefore, I hold that particular assumption with a lower degree of certainty. Many of these assumptions take the form of propositions that can be either true or false, as in (1) and (2).

(1) It is Thursday today

(2) I have enough milk in my fridge to make coffee tomorrow morning

However, assumptions may also take the form of conditional statements, using an *if ... then* construction. For example, I am fairly sure that if I catch the early train to work, then I will be in the office by 8:30am. That is, I hold the assumption in (3).

(3) If I catch the early train to work, then I will be in the office by 8:30am

In relevance theory, assumptions are talked about as being manifest, and they can be more or less manifest. The notion of **manifestness** can be difficult to grasp, and it is perhaps most easily introduced, as Sperber and Wilson (1986/95) do, using an analogy with vision.

Imagine that you are sitting in a doctor's waiting room. Think of all the things that are around you in your field of vision: the other people in the room, the furniture, the notices on the walls, the walls themselves. All these things are visible to you, and they are in your visual environment, even if you do not look at them or see them. Just as your visual environment is made up of things that you are capable of seeing, so your cognitive environment is made up of assumptions that you are capable of holding. It is made up of assumptions that you are capable of representing mentally and accepting as true or probably true. We say that the things that we can see are visible, and we say that the assumptions that we can hold are manifest.

Assumptions can be more or less manifest, and again the vision analogy can help us here. Imagine that as you sit in the waiting room, you barely pay attention to a man sitting quietly in the corner. He is visible to you, even though you have not really looked at him. Suddenly, he asks you the time, and you turn to look at him. He is now much more prominent in your visual environment. In a similar way, a whole range of assumptions may be manifest to us, but a new input can cause them to become more manifest. For example, as you are sitting in the waiting room an assumption about what the time is is manifest to you. That is, you are capable of representing mentally what time it is, even if you are not actively thinking about it. However, when the man asks you for the time, your attention becomes focused on this assumption, and it becomes more manifest to you.

The set of assumptions that is manifest to an individual at any one time makes up that individual's cognitive environment. It is possible for two individuals to share a physical environment but have different cognitive environments. Imagine that we are holding a conversation while sitting in a coffee shop, and as we talk, I notice that a mutual friend has entered the shop and sat down at a table that is out of your line of vision. I have access to this new information but you do not. Once I have processed the visual input of the friend walking into the shop, I hold an assumption about the world that you do not hold. I hold the assumption that the mutual friend is in the coffee shop with us. You and I share a physical environment, but our cognitive environments are different. This notion of cognitive environment is key to the relevance-theoretic approach to cognition and communication. Communication, as we will see, is an attempt to change another person's cognitive environment. When an input has an effect on the assumptions that make up an individual's cognitive environment, we say that that input is relevant.

6.1.3 Relevance and Context

As we discussed in Chapters 1 and 2, pragmatics is the study of language in context. Therefore, any pragmatic theory must have a definition of what is meant by the term *context*. Many previous approaches to pragmatics have assumed that the context of an utterance includes information from the physical environment in which the utterance is produced and information from the surrounding discourse. However, relevance theory, as a cognitive theory of utterance interpretation, extends the notion of context to include any assumptions that the hearer might use when interpreting the utterance. This could include 'expectations about the future, scientific hypotheses or religious beliefs, anecdotal memories, general cultural assumptions, [and] beliefs about the mental state of the speaker' (Sperber and Wilson 1986/95, pp. 15–16). In short, according to relevance theory, the context of interpretation for an utterance is made up of all the assumptions that the hearer uses when interpreting that utterance. Consider, for example, the conversation in (4).

(4) John: Have you seen the new Pedro Almodóvar movie?

     Paula: I don't like reading subtitles

To interpret Paula's utterance in (4), John must use a range of information that is neither available from the physical context nor from the immediate discourse. For example, he must use the assumption that Almodóvar's movies are usually in Spanish, and that Paula does not speak Spanish. He must also use the assumption that in the United Kingdom foreign language movies tend to be subtitled rather than dubbed, along with the more general assumption that people usually avoid doing things that they do not like. These assumptions allow him to link what Paula says to his question, and from that he can infer an answer. In this case, the most likely interpretation is that, no, Paula has not seen the new Pedro Almodóvar movie.

    In the rest of this chapter, we will discuss how assumptions are used in the interpretation process. However, at this point it is enough to say that, according to relevance theory, a context is 'a psychological construct, a subset of the hearer's assumptions about the world' (Sperber and Wilson, 1986/95, p. 15). This subset of assumptions is not something that is determined or set before the utterance is produced. Rather it is constructed as part of the process of interpreting an utterance, and the process of constructing the context is itself driven by the search for relevance.

6.2 Defining Relevance

6.2.1 Cognitive Effects

Our cognitive environments change from moment to moment as we encounter new information. For example, when I saw my friend enter the café in the example above, the visual input that I received provided me with new information and changed my cognitive environment. Similarly, if my flatmate tells me that she has drunk all the milk that I thought was in the fridge, then this new information will affect my assumption about whether I have enough milk for tomorrow's coffee. When new information interacts with the assumptions that we hold and leads to a change in our cognitive environments, we say that it has had a cognitive effect. Relevance theory recognises three types of cognitive effect: strengthening, contradiction and elimination, and contextual implication.

To illustrate the three types of cognitive effect recognised by relevance theory, consider the following scenario. Deirdre is a tennis enthusiast. She enjoys watching and playing tennis, and she is a fan of Roger Federer. Federer is playing very well lately, and Deirdre is confident that he will win the men's singles title at the Australian Open tennis tournament this year. We can say that she holds the assumption in (5) with a reasonable degree of confidence.

(5) Federer will win the men's singles title at the Australian Open this year

Of course, Deirdre cannot be completely sure that Federer will win and so she follows coverage of the tournament closely. She lives in the United Kingdom and so the time difference means that she must check the news headlines each morning to follow Federer's progress. On the second day of the tournament, she wakes up and eagerly checks the news. She sees the headline in (6).

(6) Federer breezes past first round opponent in straight sets

Based on this new information, Deirdre is now more confident that Federer will progress to the final and ultimately win the tournament. We can say that the new information in (6) has strengthened her assumption in (5). Strengthening of an existing assumption is the first type of cognitive effect recognised by relevance theory. The information in (6) is relevant to Deirdre in this context because it leads to the strengthening of an assumption that she already holds.

The tournament continues, and Deirdre continues to check for updates each morning. As the tournament enters the second week, Federer prepares to play his quarter-final match. As usual, Deirdre wakes up the following morning and checks the sports news. She reads the headline in (7).

(7) Federer loses quarter-final match in straight sets

The new information in (7) contradicts the assumption that Deirdre held in (5). It is not possible for both (5) and (7) to be true at the same time. As Deirdre has no reason to mistrust the information in the newspaper, she accepts that (7) is true, and doing so necessarily eliminates her assumption in (5). This illustrates the second type of cognitive effect identified by relevance theory: contradiction and elimination of an existing contextual assumption.

The year progresses, and the Wimbledon tennis tournament approaches. Deirdre has always wanted to see a match at Wimbledon, and the week before the tournament begins, she decides that this is the year that she will finally go. She does not have a ticket, but she has heard that on the first few days it is possible to queue in the morning for a day ticket. She wants to try this, but she does not want to stand for hours in a queue in bad weather. This leaves her with the assumption in (8).

(8) If the sun is shining on Monday, I will go to the tournament

Notice that, in this example, Deirdre's assumption takes the form of a conditional statement. Monday arrives and Deirdre wakes up. As she looks out of the window, she sees the new information in (9).

(9) The sun is shining

The new information in (9) combines with the assumption in (8) to yield a new assumption that Deirdre did not previously hold. That new assumption is given here in (10).

(10) I will go to the tournament

Notice that Deirdre did not know whether she would go to the tournament until she received the new information in (9), and the new information in (9) did not have any consequences until it was combined with the conditional assumption in (8). This illustrates the final type of cognitive effect recognised by relevance theory: contextual implication. Contextual implications are new assumptions that were not available on the basis of existing assumptions or new information independently, but which result from the combination of the two.

According to relevance theory, a piece of information or an input to our sensory systems is relevant if processing it leads to at least one cognitive effect. The greater the cognitive effects that an individual can derive from an input in a context, the more relevant that input will be for that individual in that context. We can therefore compare inputs in terms of their cognitive effects, and this allows us to make comparative judgements of relevance. However, the number and size of the cognitive effects is not the only factor that determines how relevant an input will be in a particular context. Relevance also depends on **processing effort**.

6.2.2 Processing Effort

Processing new information and deriving cognitive effects require mental effort. Some new inputs are easier to process than others. Imagine, for example, that you are a fluent speaker of English, but you have been learning Spanish for several years. You have a reasonable level of fluency when reading Spanish, but you have to concentrate carefully, and you need to stop to look up new words fairly regularly. You are also very interested in world politics, and you try to keep up to date with the latest events each day by reading the news. The same information is available to you via English language and Spanish language online newspapers. As the information is the same, the cognitive effects that you can derive will be the same, regardless of whether you read the English or Spanish version. However, your fluency in the two languages means that reading the English newspaper demands a lot less mental processing effort of you than reading the Spanish equivalent. The information is the same, but the form in which it is presented affects how easy it is for you to access.

The form in which information is presented is just one factor that can affect the effort involved in processing new information, and it is not limited to choice of language. A typed note might be easier to read than a scribbled handwritten note, for example, or a freshly painted road sign might be clearer than one which is dirty and faded. Regularly processed inputs demand less effort from us than those which we come across infrequently. Similarly, if we have just been talking about a topic, assumptions related to that topic will be highly accessible and will be quick and easy to retrieve. If we use a word or talk about a topic frequently, the effort involved in processing related input will be less than it would be for talking about something that is new or rarely discussed. Finally, the linguistic or logical complexity of an input will affect how much processing effort it demands of us. Compare, for example, the utterances in (11) and (12).

(11) Sumaiyah is well today

(12) Sumaiyah is not unwell today

Logically, both these utterances provide the same information. However, the utterance in (12) demands more effort to process. To access the information, we must process two negative elements. As we will see, there may be instances in which the version in (12) is preferable, just as there may be times when you choose to read the Spanish, rather than English newspaper, even though it is more difficult for you to do so. Less effort is not always necessarily better. However, the level of processing effort directly affects the relevance of the input. The more processing effort required to process an input, the lower the relevance of that input. Finally, it is important to note that, in relevance theory, processing effort is always computed from the perspective of the hearer. When utterances are discussed in terms of demanding more or less processing effort, it is the processing effort of the hearer, not the speaker, which is significant. With this in mind, let us move on to the definition of relevance itself.

6.2.3 The Definition of Relevance

This brings us to the relevance theory definition of relevance as devised by Dan Sperber and Deirdre Wilson. Relevance depends on two factors, cognitive effects and processing effort, and the relevance of an input in a context is defined as in (13).

(13) (a) Other things being equal, the greater the cognitive effects, the greater the relevance

(b) Other things being equal, the smaller the processing effort required to derive those effects, the greater the relevance

The notion of relevance that is used in relevance theory does not give us an absolute or definitive measure of relevance. Rather, it defines relevance comparatively. An input that leads to more cognitive effects is more relevant than one that leads to fewer, so long as the processing effort involved is the same. Likewise, if two inputs lead to the same cognitive effects, but one demands less processing effort than the other, then that input will be more relevant. In this way we can compare the relevance of the same input in different contexts and different inputs in the same context.

Let us consider how this might work with some examples. Imagine that there is a bus stop just outside my house. I often see the sight of a bus approaching the bus stop as I leave home each day. Although every time I see the bus I am processing more or less the same visual information, the information will be more relevant to me on some occasions than on others. The relevance of the information will vary from day to day depending on the context in which I process it. For example, one Friday morning I leave the house to travel to an important meeting. I hold the assumption that to get to the meeting on time, I must catch the bus. In this context, the sight of the bus approaching the bus stop is relevant to me. I can infer that I have not missed the bus and that I am likely to make it to my meeting on time. However, on Saturday morning I leave my house for a casual stroll around the neighbourhood. Again, I see the bus approaching the bus stop. On this occasion, the same information has little or no relevance for me. In this context, I hold no assumptions with which it can interact.

An input is relevant when processing that input yields cognitive effects. Cognitive effects result when new information interacts with assumptions and in doing so alters a cognitive environment. As everyone has their own cognitive environment made up of all the assumptions that they hold, the relevance of an individual piece of information will be relative to each individual.

Consider the following scenario. I am walking through a park with my friend. A bee flies past us, and we both see this, and process it as new information. For me, this new information has little relevance. Perhaps I derive a few weak cognitive effects relating to the time of year or the weather. However, unbeknownst to me, my friend is allergic to bee stings. A single sting could be life-threatening. My friend holds many assumptions about how the presence of a bee could affect her and what she might have to do, and so there are many more ways in which the new information leads to cognitive effects for her. In short, the new information that there is a bee nearby is more relevant to my friend than it is to me.

In this example, the difference in relevance comes from the difference in the cognitive effects that the individual derives. However, the relevance of an input is also affected by the mental effort that is required to process it, and this too can vary from individual to individual. Recall the example from Section 6.2.2 where a reader has the choice between a Spanish and English language newspaper. For a fluent English speaker, the English language source is more relevant in that, compared to the Spanish version, it leads to the same cognitive effects for less processing effort. However, the situation will be reversed for a fluent Spanish speaker who is learning English. Similarly, if I use a particular technical term or vocabulary item on a daily basis, it will be easier for me to process that term than it will be for someone who has, perhaps, not come across it before or does not use it regularly.

A precise definition of what it means for something to be relevant should also help us to explain why some things are not relevant. Again, according to relevance theory, a piece of information is not relevant to an individual in a particular context if it fails to produce any cognitive effects for that individual in that context. Consider whether there are any assumptions that you hold with 100 per cent certainty. Perhaps you are 100 per cent sure of what your name is, for example. What effect would someone telling you what your name is have on that assumption? It is not possible to strengthen an assumption that we already hold with 100 per cent certainty, and so even when this information comes from a trusted source, it is irrelevant to us. Similarly, if your friend tells you that your name is not what you thought it was, but is actually something different, you are unlikely to accept this information, and so it will have no effect on the assumptions that you hold. For an assumption that we hold with as much certainty as we do about our own names, the say-so of a friend will not be enough to contradict and eliminate our beliefs. If the information came from a different source, perhaps a parent or close relative, for example, then the outcome might be different. We evaluate the information that we process, and something will only be relevant if we accept it as true or likely to be true and if we update our assumptions on this basis.

While the definition of relevance is comparative in nature, relevance theory does not claim that, as speakers and hearers, we are consciously comparing actual utterances with potential utterances. Rather, Sperber and Wilson suggest that, as humans, we are sensitive to effort and effect levels when processing information, just as we are sensitive to muscular effort and physical effect when we move our bodies. We do not have to compute, compare, or consciously control the processing. Our cognitive processing proceeds automatically, guided by a general cognitive principle of relevance. This principle, along with the second, communicative principle of relevance, will be introduced in the next section.

6.3 The Principles of Relevance

6.3.1 The Cognitive Principle of Relevance

Having established a definition of what it means for an input to be relevant, we move on to discuss the role that relevance plays in utterance interpretation. Central to the relevance-theoretic pragmatic framework are two principles of relevance. The first principle of relevance, also known as the cognitive principle of relevance, is concerned with our human cognitive systems, and it does not, in and of itself, have anything to say about communicative acts. However, it provides a crucial foundation for explaining how we process information. The cognitive principle of relevance is given in (14).

(14) Human cognition is geared to the maximisation of relevance

As we move around the world, we pay attention to different stimuli in our environment. Some sounds, sights, or smells may draw our attention, whereas others may be barely noticed. As I write this, I can hear my colleague across the office typing, I can hear the photocopier in the corridor whirring, and I can hear traffic outside my office window. In general, these are the sorts of sounds to which we pay very little attention. Paying attention to them is unlikely to lead to cognitive effects. However, when my colleague suddenly sneezes, I find my attention is immediately drawn to the sound, and I react with a conventional 'Bless you!' The sounds of the typing, the photocopier, the traffic, and the sneeze are all auditory stimuli, and yet I react to them very differently. Why do these different inputs to my auditory system provoke such different reactions? The reason, according to relevance theory, is a combination of their relevance in the context and a natural tendency for us to pay attention to those inputs that are most likely to lead to relevance. That is, we invest cognitive resources into inputs that are likely to provide us with cognitive effects.

The relevance of an input is determined by the cognitive effects to which it leads and the amount of mental effort that is required to process it. However, whether we pay attention to an input will also depend on the context in which we encounter that input. Something that barely draws our attention in one context, may be relevant in another. Imagine that you are working on an important document with a tight deadline. The room in which you are working has an open window and you can hear the birds singing outside. While your focus is on the task you are trying to complete you will pay very little attention to the birdsong, and you may not even consciously notice it. Your cognitive resources are focused elsewhere. Now imagine the same input in a different context. You might, for example, be taking a relaxing stroll along a country lane. You have nothing particular on your mind, and nothing pressing to attend to. In this context, you may notice and pay attention to the sound of birdsong, and it may lead to some general cognitive effects about the time of year or the beauty of nature. The same input may be processed differently in different contexts. We are constantly seeking to maximise relevance and so we pay attention to an input in a context where it is the most relevant stimulus, but we ignore it when other inputs seem likely to lead to greater relevance.

6.3.2 Ostension and Intentional Communication

So far, we have seen that according to relevance theory, we tend to pay attention to and allocate processing resources to inputs and stimuli which are likely to be relevant, and we go about processing these in a relevance-maximising fashion. New information can come to us via a number of different routes and from different sources. We might see or hear something in our physical environment, for example. We also get new information from other people, and this can be transferred to us in different ways.

First, we have situations in which **accidental information transmission** takes place. We may, for example, accidentally transmit information about how we are feeling when we speak or interact with another person. If someone with a fear of public speaking has to give a presentation to a large and important group, they may accidentally transmit information about how they are feeling to the audience. Their voice or hands may shake, for example. They certainly did not intend to transmit this information, and, on the contrary, most likely wanted to avoid doing so. The information is transmitted, nonetheless. In a related example, information might be transmitted incidentally. A stranger stops me in the street to ask me for directions. As soon as she starts to speak, I notice her Scottish accent. It was not her intention when speaking to me to communicate that she is from Scotland, but, again, this information has been transmitted to me, nonetheless. It may or may not be relevant to me. Perhaps I hold the assumption that Scottish people are usually friendly. Given this assumption and the new information I have just processed, I can derive the conclusion that this woman is likely to be friendly. If, however, I hold no particular assumptions about Scottish people, the new information will not be relevant to me. Whether the information is relevant or not, it was not the woman's intention to transmit it to me.

On other occasions, there may be cases of **covert intentional information transmission.** In these cases, a communicator intends to communicate something to an audience, but does not want the audience to be aware of this intention. Imagine, for example, that you are coming towards the end of a long work meeting and your colleague is talking at length about a topic that you feel has already been covered in sufficient detail. You are keen to end the meeting and get back to your work. As the colleague looks in your direction you glance at your watch, hoping that he will see this and realise that he should wrap up his point. You do not want him to know that you want him to see you do this. You intend to convey the information, but you wish your intention to do so to remain hidden or covert. In relevance theory terms we say that this communicator has an **informative intention** but does not have a **communicative intention**.

An informative intention is the intention to inform an audience of something. In cases of accidental information transfer there is no informative intention. However, in cases of covert intentional information transmission, the communicator does intend to inform an audience of something. The behaviour is covert because the communicator does not wish the audience to recognise that she has an informative intention. That is, she does not have a communicative intention. The communicative intention is the intention to inform an audience of one's informative intention. These definitions are summed up in (15) and (16).

(15) The informative intention: The intention to inform an audience of something

(16) The communicative intention: The intention to inform an audience of one's informative intention

If a communicator has both an informative intention and a communicative intention, then we have a case of what relevance theory refers to as **ostensive communication**. The communicator not only wants to communicate some information to the audience, but she also wants the audience to recognise that this is what she intends to do. She is communicating intentionally, and she is open with her audience about this intention.

This notion of ostensive communication as communication that is overt and intentional is crucial for understanding a key premise of relevance theory. According to relevance theory, ostensive communication is special and different. It triggers expectations that are not triggered by accidental or covert information transfer. These expectations are captured in the second principle of relevance, also known as the communicative principle of relevance.

6.3.3 The Communicative Principle of Relevance

Relevance theory recognises ostensive communication as a special case of information transfer. In Chapter 4, we saw that Grice viewed communication as a cooperative activity where two interlocutors work together to achieve understanding. He likened communication to working together to bake a cake or fix a car. Relevance theory views communication differently. An ostensive stimulus may be an utterance, but it may also be a gesture, a facial expression, or some other ostensive act. According to relevance theory, when a communicator produces an **ostensive stimulus**, she is offering her audience information.

Offers create expectations. Imagine that you have thrown a birthday party, and one of your friends walks in with a gift-wrapped box and offers it to you. You are likely to have expectations about the sort of item that you will find in the box. If you unwrap the box and open it to find a single, solitary jellybean inside, you might feel disappointed. You would likely feel that the gift did not live up to the expectations that had been created by the offer of a birthday gift. Similarly, if a friend offers us a cup of coffee, we will have certain expectations about the quality of the drink that they are offering us. We would probably expect it to be freshly made, handed to us in a suitable drinking vessel, and either hot or ice cold, depending on the circumstances.

Ostensive acts of communication are offers of information. They too create expectations. According to relevance theory, they create expectations of relevance. Recall that according to the cognitive principle we have a natural human tendency to try to maximise relevance. In communication, however, while we might hope for maximal relevance, we cannot expect it. What we can expect, according to relevance theory, is optimal relevance. The definition of optimal relevance is given in (17).

(17) An utterance (or other act of ostensive communication) is optimally relevance, if and only if:
   (a) It is relevant enough to be worth the hearer's processing effort
   (b) It is the most relevant one compatible with the speaker's abilities and preferences

This definition allows for the fact that both a communicator and addressee are involved in the communicative process. When a communicator produces an ostensive stimulus, she is demanding the addressee's attention. The addressee is therefore entitled to expect that giving his attention to the stimulus will result in enough worthwhile effects to justify doing so. This is formalised in clause (a) of the definition of optimal relevance. An utterance (or other ostensive stimulus) is optimally relevant if it is relevant enough to be worth the addressee's effort to process it. This clause sets the lower limit on what we can expect.

The second clause (b) sets the upper limit. While an addressee might hope for many effects for little effort, the second clause recognises that the communicator may be constrained in what she can offer. She may be constrained by her abilities and/or preferences. This is formalised in the second clause of the definition of optimal relevance, (b), which states that an utterance (or other ostensive stimulus) is optimally relevant if it is the most relevant that it can be given the speaker's abilities and preferences. In short, a speaker may not be able to make her utterance more relevant, or she may not want to do so. Let us consider how this might work in practice.

Recall that the relevance of an input is determined by two factors: cognitive effects and processing effort. To make an utterance more relevant a speaker can increase the cognitive effects to which it leads, or she can reduce the effort that is required to process it. However, the speaker cannot be expected to do anything that she (a) does not want to do, or (b) is not able to do. Therefore, we have four combinations of factors which can limit the relevance of an input: the speaker's ability to create more effects; the speaker's preference to create more effects; the speaker's ability to reduce the effort; the speaker's preference for reducing the effort. Let us consider these in turn.

On some occasions, a speaker may simply not have the information that a hearer would find most relevant. Consider the exchange in (18).

(18) Robert: How do I get to the train station?

       Anna: Head in that direction

Presumably, the most relevant reply to Robert's question would be clear and precise directions to the train station. However, if Anna does not know where the station is, she cannot provide these. The relevance of her utterance is constrained by her ability. She has made her utterance as relevant as it can be. Now imagine the following scenario. I am walking along a street in Finland and a woman stops me and speaks to me. I do not speak Finnish and so I am forced to reply in English in the hope that she might understand. She does, and she asks me for directions to the railway station. I give her the directions in English. If I could have replied in Finnish, then this would have provided her with the same information while putting her to less effort. However, I was constrained by my ability to do so.

Even if we can produce a highly relevant utterance, there may be occasions on which doing so would go against our personal preferences. We may for example have information, but we may not wish to disclose it. Consider the conversation in (19).

(19) Archie: Why were you late this morning?

       Bertha: I had a problem

Presumably, Archie had hoped for some more detailed information and probably already held the assumption that Bertha had experienced some sort of problem. More detail would have been more relevant to him. However, if Bertha does not wish to disclose further information, then she cannot be expected to do so. Similarly, there may be occasions on which a speaker could make an utterance more economical but chooses not to. She may, for example, choose to use an unusual or complicated word to show off her vocabulary. A simpler choice would have put the hearer to less effort, but the speaker chooses not to do this.

Recall the situation described above where a friend offers you a gift-wrapped box at your birthday party. Perhaps what you would really hope to find when you open the box is the key to a new car or a ticket for an around-the-world-cruise. However, you cannot reasonably expect such a lavish present. It is likely that your guest could not afford to give you such a gift. That is, they do not have the ability to fulfil your hopes. Alternatively, it may be that while they could afford it, they would prefer not to spend that amount of money on a friend's birthday present. That is, they would prefer not to give you such a present. What we can expect to find in the box is a gift that is worth our while opening and receiving, while not causing your friend to either end up in debt or resentful of you. This optimal gift might be, perhaps, a book, an item of clothing, or a voucher for your favourite shop. Just as we have expectations about the value of a present that is offered to us, so we have expectations about the relevance of information that is offered to us. This is captured in the communicative principle of relevance, given in (20).

(20) Every utterance (or other ostensive stimulus) conveys a presumption of its own optimal relevance

The communicative principle of relevance, combined with the associated definition of optimal relevance, allows us to explain the inferences that hearer's draw when they process utterances (or other ostensive stimuli). Inferences arise not because we assume that our interlocutor is being cooperative, but because we assume that they are trying to be optimally relevant. We will consider the role played by each clause of the definition of optimal relevance in turn.

According to clause (a) the hearer will assume that an utterance will be at least relevant enough to be worth processing. This will lead the hearer to derive inferences to maintain this assumption. Consider Hilary's reply to Andrew's question in (21).

(21) Andrew: Shall I make some tea?
Hilary: There's milk in the fridge

To understand Hilary's utterance as a relevant answer to his question, Andrew must infer that the milk in the fridge is appropriate in quality and quantity for making tea. Strictly speaking, Hilary's utterance would be true if there were one or two drops of sour, out-of-date milk splashed on a shelf in the fridge. However, for her utterance to be relevant as an answer to Andrew's question, we must make these further inferences.

According to clause (b) of the definition of optimal relevance, the hearer will presume that the utterance is as relevant as it could be, allowing for the speaker's abilities and preferences. Therefore, an utterance that is not as relevant as the hearer might like will lead to the inference that the speaker was either unwilling or unable to make it more relevant. Consider the example in (22).

(22) George: Where did Arnold go for his holiday this year?

  Eleanor: Somewhere in Scotland

Eleanor's utterance provides an answer to George's question, but a more precise answer, such as the name of a specific location or city, would give him more information and would be likely to lead to more cognitive effects. George must reconcile the fact that Eleanor has not given him this more specific information with the presumption that she was aiming at optimal relevance. He is likely to infer that she either does not have any more precise information or, if she has it, she does not want to share this with George. This is one way in which relevance theory differs from the Gricean approach. If we assume that speakers are always cooperative, then they should only fail to give information when they do not have it. Relevance theory does not assume that speakers are always cooperative. It only assumes that they are always aiming to be optimally relevant. Clause (b) of the definition of optimal relevance introduces another reason for speakers to withhold information: their own preferences.

Now consider utterance (23).

(23) I wonder if you would possibly be so kind as to pass me the sugar, if it's not too much trouble?

If the speaker had simply wanted to communicate a request for the sugar to be passed, she could have simply uttered (24).

(24) Pass me the sugar

However, she has chosen to produce a longer utterance with more linguistic material and in doing so has put the hearer to more effort. By uttering the longer version in (23), the speaker is requiring the hearer to process more linguistic material and is therefore putting him to more effort. We can use the definition of optimal relevance to understand why this might be. First, we ask why the speaker might have chosen to use the longer version and in doing so put the hearer to more effort. An obvious answer in this case would be for social and politeness reasons. The speaker has chosen to include hedges and indirect language, and she has chosen to formulate the utterance as a question rather than as a demand. This reduces the imposition on her hearer and helps to maintain a polite social relationship. She had the ability to produce the shorter utterance but chose to prioritise politeness. Given this preference, we can understand the utterance to be the most relevant version that is compatible with the speaker's (social) preferences. To be optimally relevant the utterance must also be relevant enough to be worth the hearer's effort to process. The extra effects relating to politeness and the speaker's wish not to impose on her hearer offset the extra effort, and thus we can reconcile the utterance in (23) with the presumption of optimal relevance.

A further consequence of the communicative principle of relevance is that if someone communicates with an addressee ostensively, then they must think that what they are communicating is more relevant than anything else that the addressee may have been attending to at the time. They are communicating that they think it is worthwhile for the addressee to turn his attention to the communicated message. So, for example, if you see that I am reading a book, you will only speak to me if you think that what you have to say is more relevant in that moment than what I am reading. Again, this has implications in terms of communicating politeness and impoliteness. Interrupting someone, for example, communicates that you consider what you have to say to be more relevant than what they were saying.

6.4 The Relevance-Theoretic Comprehension Procedure

The communicative principle of relevance and the presumption of optimal relevance have several important consequences. These consequences lead us to a comprehension procedure that hearers follow when interpreting utterances (or other ostensive acts of communication). The first clause of the definition of optimal relevance states that the utterance must be worth the hearer's effort to process. This amounts to a ban on wasting the hearer's effort. The hearer is entitled to assume that he will not be put to any gratuitous effort, and so he will go about interpreting the utterance by testing the most obvious and easily accessible interpretations first. In relevance theory terms, he follows the **path of least effort**.

As we saw in Chapter 2, a hearer must perform a range of inferential tasks to interpret an utterance. These include reference assignment, disambiguation, and the derivation of implicatures. In each case, the hearer will carry out these tasks by testing the most obvious, most accessible interpretations first. Remember that the hearer who is assuming optimal relevance is seeking an interpretation, which gives him enough cognitive rewards to justify the effort that he has put into processing the input. Therefore, the first, most obvious interpretation will only be rejected if it does not provide enough rewards to justify the effort. The utterance must, in short, be worth the hearer's effort to process. Once the hearer has reached an interpretation, which satisfies his expectations of optimal relevance, he will assume that this was the interpretation that the speaker intended to communicate, and he will stop looking for further effects or different interpretations. This is all captured in the relevance-theoretic comprehension procedure, which is given in (25).

(25) (a) Follow a path of least effort in deriving cognitive effects: test interpretations (e.g., disambiguations, reference resolution, implicatures, etc.) in order of accessibility

(b) Stop when your expectations of relevance are satisfied

In Chapter 7, we will discuss in detail how this comprehension procedure drives inferential processes and how it can explain how some misunder-standings occur and how some jokes work. However, for now, consider the example in (26), as discussed in Chapters 1 and 4.

(26) Gemma: Did Luisa get the job?

Pauline: She looked happy

Gemma has asked Pauline a yes/no question, and so we might think that the most relevant answer to his question would be either *yes* or *no*. Pauline, how-ever, has provided an indirect answer to the question. At the level of explicit meaning, Pauline's answer tells us nothing about whether Luisa got the job or not. It only tells us that she looked happy. However, Gemma will assume that Pauline was aiming to make her answer optimally relevant. That is, she will look for a way in which Pauline's utterance could offer a relevant answer to her question. To do this, she will follow the path of least effort.

   Notice that Pauline has used the pronoun *she* in her answer. To process the utterance, Gemma must decide who Pauline intended to refer to by using this pronoun. While logically it could be felicitously used to refer to any female human being (with some other possibilities too), Gemma will resolve reference by following the path of least effort. Given that they are discussing Luisa, she will test an interpretation on which *she* refers to Luisa first. She now has the hypothesis that the explicit meaning of Pauline's utterance is that given in (27).

(27) Luisa looked happy

She will use this hypothesis as she continues her search for a way in which Pauline's utterance could be relevant as an answer to her question. Again, she will follow the path of least effort when doing this. Given the topic of the conversation, there is likely to be a range of assumptions that are highly accessible to Gemma at this point in the discourse. These are likely to be assumptions about getting jobs and about what makes someone look happy. These may include the assumptions in (28) to (30).

(28) Getting a job is good news

(29) People feel happy when they get good news

(30) When people look happy, they are feeling happy

Combining these highly accessible assumptions with the explicit content in (27) will allow Gemma to infer that Pauline thinks that Luisa looked happy because she got the job. Although Pauline's answer has put Gemma to more effort than a simple *yes* or *no*, it has provided her with more cognitive effects. Gemma is likely to infer that Pauline does not know for sure whether Luisa got the job but is providing as much information as she is able to on the topic. Pauline's answer is as relevant as it can be allowing for her abilities.

Let's now consider this exchange from the perspective of Pauline. Pauline knows that Gemma will follow a path of least effort when interpreting her reply. She must therefore construct her utterance in such a way that it leads Gemma to her intended interpretation. Pauline must put herself in Gemma's interpretive shoes and make predictions about what will be most accessible to her. It is reasonable that she would predict that Luisa will be the most accessible referent for Gemma for the pronoun *she*. Therefore, if Pauline meant to refer to someone other than Luisa in her utterance, she should have used a different referring expression. Perhaps she knows that Luisa and Nicola were competing for the same job. She recently saw that Nicola looked very happy and assumed that it was Nicola, and not Luisa, who got the position. If she wishes to use this information to answer Gemma's question, she should adjust her utterance accordingly, as in (31).

(31) Nicola looked happy

Similarly, if it is true that Luisa looked happy, but Pauline knows that this is because her favourite football team just won the national league, and that her happiness is nothing to do with whether she got the job or not, then she should not use the utterance in (26) to reply to Gemma's question. She should predict that if she were to do so, the path of least effort would lead Gemma to infer that Pauline thinks that Luisa got the job. While Pauline would not be lying, she would certainly be misleading Gemma.

6.5 Chapter Summary

In this chapter, we have looked at the main assumptions that underlie the relevance-theoretic framework for utterance interpretation. Building on some general and significant observations from Grice regarding the importance of intentionality and inference in communication, relevance theory is focused around a specific and technical notion of relevance. Whereas cooperation and truthfulness are central to Gricean approaches to pragmatics, relevance theory hinges on the notion of relevance. Relevance is defined in terms of cognitive effects and processing effort. Cognitive effects result when new information causes us to update our assumptions in one of three ways: strengthening, contradicting and eliminating, or contextual implication. These are the three types of cognitive effect recognised by relevance theory. We also saw that the mental effort involved in processing information affects how relevant that information will be.

Relevance theory is driven by two key principles: the cognitive principle of relevance and the communicative principle of relevance. According to the cognitive principle of relevance, human cognition is geared to the maximisation of relevance. Key to understanding how communication works within this framework is the idea that overt, intentional (ostensive) communication is special in that it creates expectations of relevance. This is captured in the communicative principle of relevance.

Finally, we saw that the presumption of optimal relevance has important consequences for how utterance interpretation proceeds. Hearers follow the relevance-theoretic comprehension procedure. This procedure is not stipulated independently but falls out naturally from the underlying principles of relevance combined with the definition of optimal relevance. Hearers follow a path of least effort when interpreting an utterance, and they stop the interpretation process once they reach an optimally relevant interpretation.

Exercises

6a   Think of four contextual assumptions that you hold right now. How strongly do you hold them? What new information would cause you to update these assumptions, and in what way? That is, what type of cognitive effect would the new information have?

6b   Look back at the Gricean maxims of quality, quantity, relation, and manner from Chapter 4. Each maxim covers general ways in which (cooperative) speakers behave. How are these patterns captured in the definitions and principles of relevance? What is the role played by effort and effect in each case?

6c   Patrick and Lucy are talking on the telephone and arranging dinner at a restaurant that evening. Patrick asks Lucy what time he should book the table for. Suppose that all the following answers are true. Which answer might be the most relevant to Patrick and why?

(i)   Book a table for 7:30
(ii) Book a table for 7:30 this evening
(iii) Reserve a table for 7:30
(iv) Reserve a table for some time after 8 o'clock
(v)   Reserve a table for ninety minutes after 6pm
(vi) I'm not sure what time I'll be able to get there

6d   Imagine that you are due to catch an aeroplane to go on vacation. You hold the following assumptions:

(i)   I will catch the bus
(ii) If I catch the bus, I will make it to the airport on time
(iii) If I don't catch the bus at 10:30. I will miss my flight

You receive the following pieces of information as inputs when you arrive at the bus stop. What effects (if any) will (iv) to (vii) have on your assumptions? Are the inputs relevant in the context of these assumptions? Explain why?

(iv) The bus indicator board shows that the bus is due to arrive in ten minutes.
(v)   The bus indicator board shows that the bus left ten minutes ago.
(vi) A poster on the bus shelter is advertising a new shampoo.
(vii) You notice that it has started to rain.

6e   Consider again the example in (i), which we first saw in Chapter 4. Consider how Sara answers Helen's question.

(i)   Helen: Has Dan read War and Peace?
      Sara: He doesn't like long books

Use the ideas from this Chapter to explain how Helen is likely to interpret Sara's answer. What assumptions does Helen have to access to process Sara's utterance? Do you think Dan has read War and Peace? How do you know? How does the relevance-based explanation differ from the Gricean explanation that we saw in Chapter 4?

Key Terms Introduced in this Chapter
accidental information transmission, 124
cognitive effect, 114

Further Reading

The relevance theory framework was laid out first and most thoroughly by Sperber and Wilson (1986/95). The postface in the later (1995) edition includes important updates and clarifications which have become central to the theory as it is applied. A shorter, and perhaps more accessible, summary of the key points of relevance theory is laid out in Wilson and Sperber (2004). Blakemore (1992) provides a highly accessible, entry-level introduction to pragmatics from a relevance-theoretic perspective and this is a very useful text for those new to pragmatics. For readers who are interested in a more comprehensive overview of relevance theory, Clark (2013) is a very useful text. It takes the reader from basic principles to more complicated discussions of topics in pragmatics and semantics from a relevance-theoretic perspective.

There are many more advanced academic texts which use relevance theory in their analysis or discussion, but which also include clear introductory chapters covering aspects of the basic theory. Examples include Carston (2002), Iten (2005), Wharton (2009) and Scott (2020).

CHAPTER 7

Applying Relevance Theory

In This Chapter ...

In this chapter, we discuss how the various assumptions and principles that underlie the relevance-theoretic pragmatic framework can be applied to the pragmatic processes and inferential tasks that were introduced in Chapters 1 and 2. We begin by introducing relevance as an analytical framework that is based on key assumptions about human cognition and communication. These assumptions have consequences, and they allow us to explain and predict how utterances are interpreted. We see how these consequences play out in a range of examples that are discussed in the rest of the chapter. We start by looking at implicitly communicated meaning, before considering where we might draw the line between implicitly and explicitly communicated meaning. According to relevance theory, inference plays a role, not only in working out what a speaker is implicating, but also in working out what she is explicitly communicating. We then look in more detail at the various inferential processes that contribute to a speaker's explicit meaning, and we think about how a hearer reaches a hypothesis about the speaker's overall intended meaning.

7.1 Relevance Theory as a Theoretical Framework

In Chapters 1 and 2, we saw that there is a gap between what a speaker says and what she means. We saw that sentence meaning underdetermines speaker's meaning. The goal of pragmatics is to explain how hearers bridge this gap and reach a hypothesis about what a speaker intends to communicate. To do this we must lay some groundwork. We must define relevant concepts and we must make explicit the assumptions that we are using. This allows us to approach the problem systematically and it guides us as we develop hypotheses and make predictions. This groundwork of definitions and assumptions is known as a **theoretical framework**. We discuss the role of theoretical frameworks in research in Chapter 10. As a theoretical framework, relevance theory provides us with a structure for analysing language in use. The definitions, assumptions, and principles that were outlined in Chapter 6 provide a structure which can be used to explore pragmatic questions and issues. We start this exploration in this chapter as we look at some of the key issues to which relevance theory has been applied as a framework, and we use it to understand how a hearer constructs a hypothesis about speaker's meaning.

As we saw in Chapter 6, relevance theory is based on two key principles. The cognitive principle of relevance states that all human cognition is geared towards maximising relevance. The communicative principle of relevance deals specifically with overt, intentional acts of communication, known as ostensive acts of communication. According to the communicative principle, whenever we communicate openly and intentionally, we communicate a presumption that our message will be optimally relevant. Several consequences follow from this assumption. We explore these consequences in this section before moving on to apply them to specific pragmatic tasks and issues in the rest of the chapter.

According to relevance theory, when she produces an utterance, a speaker will be aiming to make it optimally relevant for her addressee. This means that she will be trying to construct her utterance so that it achieves enough cognitive effects to be worth processing. In this way, she avoids demanding any unjustifiable effort from her hearer. Essentially, we can think of this as a ban on wasted processing effort. If you ask a hearer to put some effort in to processing a message, then he will expect to get some reward for that effort. The more effort you put him to, the more rewards he will expect to get. As a speaker, you should not put your hearer to any unnecessary effort. You should not ask him to do work without rewarding that work. The utterance that you produce should get your intended message across in a way that requires the least effort possible from your hearer.

We can think of interpretation as a set of finely balanced scales with cognitive effects on one side and processing effort on the other. The point at which both sides are balanced is the point of optimal relevance. This is the point at which the effort is rewarded with adequate effects. However, if we put more into the processing effort side of the scales, they become unbalanced. To balance the scales again, we must put more into the cognitive effects side. A hearer will assume that the speaker intended the scales to be balanced. That is, she intends the utterance to be optimally relevant. The hearer must continue looking for cognitive effects until the scales are balanced. Once they are balanced, the hearer will stop and look no further.

This brings us to the first consequence of the ban on wasted effort. The first satisfactory interpretation is the only satisfactory interpretation. That is, once the cognitive effects balance out the processing effort, the hearer will stop and accept the interpretation as the interpretation that the speaker intended. If the hearer were to go on looking for extra effects, the scales would become unbalanced again, and he would have no way to know when to stop. A hearer could, in theory, keep looking for extra effects forever, but this would make communication virtually impossible.

The second consequence of the ban on wasted effort is that if a hearer is put to more effort, then he can expect more effects. If more is put into the effort side of the scales, the hearer will expect there to be more effects so that the optimally relevant balance is restored. Extra effort results in extra effects. We can see the consequences of this if we look at cases of repetition. Compare the interpretation of (1) with the interpretation of (2).

(1)   It was a stupid thing to say

(2)   It was a stupid, stupid thing to say

The repetition of the word *stupid* in (2) appears to have an intensifying, emphatic effect. We might understand it as communicating something like (3).

(3)   It was a very stupid thing to say

Why should this be? After all, (2) contains no more information than (1). A word is simply repeated. We can use the concepts and assumptions from relevance theory to suggest an explanation. By repeating the word *stupid*, the speaker makes the hearer process it twice. She thus puts her hearer to additional effort. Extra effort must be offset by extra effects, and so the speaker must have intended to communicate more than if she had just uttered (1). The hearer will follow the relevance-theoretic comprehension procedure when looking for what those extra effects could be. A highly accessible assumption is that the speaker thought that whatever was said was stupider than could have been communicated by uttering (1).

According to relevance theory, interpretation is driven by the search for an optimally relevant interpretation. This interpretation is not just a matter of what is explicitly communicated by the utterance, but also includes any intentionally implicated meaning. That is, relevance is assessed based on the speaker's **overall intended meaning**. As we have seen, a hearer must perform various inferential tasks if he is to construct a hypothesis about this overall intended meaning. We consider these tasks in turn, examining the processes that are involved in working out what a speaker is explicitly communicating, and the processes involved in deriving implicatures. We also briefly consider where the line between the two might be drawn, and where it lies according to the relevance-theoretic framework.

We start, however, in Section 7.2, by considering how implicit meaning is characterised and explained according to relevance theory. We think about what drives the formation of implicatures and we draw on a range of different examples to illustrate the roles that implicatures can play in utterance interpretation. In this chapter, we return to several of the examples that were introduced in Chapter 2. In this way, we show how a pragmatic framework can be used to explain the interpretations that were observed in the earlier chapter.

7.2 Relevance and Implicit Meaning

7.2.1 Explaining Implicatures

In this section, we consider how implicatures are derived according to the relevance-theoretic framework. To do this, we return to an example of an indirect answer to a yes/no question that we introduced in Chapter 2. It is repeated here as (4).

(4) Nuria: Shall I get you a coffee?

Mel: Coffee would keep me awake

As we saw in Chapter 2, Mel could be accepting or rejecting Nuria's offer of a coffee when she utters (4). Let us start by assuming that Mel intends to communicate that she does not want to stay awake, and that she is therefore politely turning down the offer of a coffee. How can we use relevance theory to explain the interpretation in this case? First and foremost, we start from the assumption that Mel is aiming at optimal relevance. That is, she intends for her utterance to be (a) worth Nuria's effort to process and (b) the most relevant it can be, allowing for her (Mel's) abilities and preferences.

Mel's reply does not provide a direct answer to the question. Indeed, if we assume that Nuria has a general level of knowledge about coffee and about how it affects the human body, we might well class Mel's utterance as communicating something that both already know. Nuria already knows that coffee keeps people awake. If she took Mel's utterance as simply intended to convey this piece of information, it would achieve no cognitive effects and would not be relevant. However, Mel has not produced this utterance as a standalone piece of information. She has not simply walked up to Nuria randomly and stated that coffee would keep her awake. She has produced the utterance as a reply to a specific question. Nuria must process the utterance relative to the discourse context in which it has been produced, and she must process it with the assumption that Mel was aiming at optimal relevance.

How might the proposition that coffee would keep Mel awake be relevant in this discourse context? Nuria must assume that the information in Mel's utterance will be useful in providing an answer to her question. Recall that one of the ways in which an input can produce cognitive effects is by combining with an existing assumption to yield implications. Imagine that Nuria holds the contextual assumptions in (5) and (6).

(5)   Mel wants to go to sleep soon

(6)   People who want to go to sleep soon will avoid anything that would keep them awake

The assumption in (5) is specific to the discourse context, and Nuria might hold it because she is aware that Mel has an early start in the morning, or perhaps Mel has already mentioned that she needs to go to sleep soon. The assumption in (6) is one of Nuria's general assumptions about the world and about how people behave in particular circumstances. Both these assumptions are likely to be accessible to Nuria at the time of the utterance, and they will be made more accessible by Mel's utterance and her reference to staying awake. These contextual assumptions constitute the context in which Nuria interprets Mel's utterance. The proposition expressed by Mel in her reply combines with these contextual assumptions to yield a relevant conclusion that answers Nuria's question, as summarised in Table 7.1.

Table 7.1 *Interpretation of 'Coffee would keep me awake' in Context 1*

Contextual assumptions	Mel wants to go to sleep soon.
	People who want to go to sleep soon will want to avoid anything that would keep them awake.
Input	Coffee would keep Mel awake.
Implicated conclusion	Mel will want to avoid coffee.

Table 7.2 *Interpretation of 'Coffee would keep me awake' in Context 2*

Contextual assumptions	Mel wants to stay awake.
	People who want to stay awake will want things that would keep them awake.
Input	Coffee would keep Mel awake
Implicated conclusion	Mel will want coffee

Notice that, if we change the contextual assumptions we also change the conclusion, and therefore the inference that Nuria will draw. Imagine, for example, a different scenario in which Nuria knows that Mel is very tired after staying up late the previous evening. Nuria also knows that Mel has urgent tasks to complete. If this is the case, the interpretation may well proceed as summarised in Table 7.2.

While this analysis explains how we would interpret Mel's utterance in different contexts, we also need to explain why a speaker would choose to use an indirect answer of this sort. The most straightforward way to answer a yes/no question would be to say *yes* or *no*. In (4), Mel has not done this. Given that, according to relevance theory, speakers are not supposed to put their hearers to gratuitous effort, we might wonder how we can explain this. After all, if all Mel had wanted to communicate was the information that she did not want any coffee, then the reply in (4) would not be optimally relevant. She should have chosen to simply say 'No'.

Given that every utterance carries with it a presumption of its own optimal relevance, we need to find a way to reconcile Mel's answer with the assumption that she is trying to be optimally relevant. It follows from the second clause of the presumption of optimal relevance that Mel must have intended to achieve some extra cognitive effects which could not have been achieved by simply saying 'No'. What could these be? Notice that, by mentioning that coffee would keep her awake, Mel not only refuses the coffee, but she also provides an explanation for her refusal. This extra information is likely to lead to other cognitive effects. Nuria might infer, for example, that this is a one-off refusal that is based on specific circumstances, rather than a refusal of coffee in general. Perhaps this might lead her to offer a non-caffeinated alternative, or she might repeat her offer of coffee later when Mel is not so tired. The extra information and extra cognitive effects that result from indirect answers are often also associated with politeness. Providing a reason for a refusal helps to avoid socially awkward misunderstandings. We return to this topic when we look more closely at politeness strategies in Chapter 9.

It is, of course, possible that Nuria holds no specific assumptions about whether Mel wishes to stay awake or avoid staying awake. In that case, it is likely that she will interpret Mel's utterance as a refusal. Mel's indirect reply is an explanation of her answer. Acceptances of offers do not usually require explanations, whereas refusals do. Therefore, without any further information about the specifics of Mel's current situation, Nuria is likely to draw on assumptions about when speakers provide explanations in response to offers and will infer that Mel is politely refusing.

In the analysis of (4), we saw implicatures in the form of **implicated conclusions**. An implicated conclusion follows from new information combining with existing contextual assumptions. However, implicatures can also be **implicated premises**. An implicated premise is an assumption that the hearer must infer to reach an optimally relevant interpretation. To illustrate, we return to an example which was briefly discussed in Chapter 2, and which is given again here as (7).

(7) Juliette: Have you read the latest novel by Ermintrude Brooks?
      Harriet: I don't read trash

To understand Harriet's utterance, Juliette must infer how the information in Harriet's reply is relevant to her question. Her reasoning is likely to be as summarised in Table 7.3.

Notice, that to make the information that Harriet provides relevant to the question that has been asked, we need to access a premise. This premise is not stated, and it need not be an assumption that the hearer previously held. We cannot, however, reach the implicated conclusion without it. In this example, we need to infer that novels by Ermintrude Brooks are trash in order to link the input with the conclusion. That is, we must infer a premise. Implicated premises are also implicatures. When Harriet utters her answer in (7), she is intending to imply not only that she has not read the latest novel by Ermintrude Brooks, but also that Ermintrude Brooks novels are trash. We have not fully understood the utterance if we do not derive both these implicatures.

Table 7.3 *Interpretation of 'I don't read trash'*

Input	Harriet doesn't read trash.
Implicated premise	Novels by Ermintrude Brooks are trash.
Implicated Conclusion	Harriet hasn't read the latest novel by Ermintrude Brooks.

Notice that we do not need to necessarily accept that implicated premises are true to derive the implicatures. Consider the exchange in (8).

(8) Archie: Have you seen *The Revenant*?

Bertie: I don't like Brad Pitt movies

Archie has asked a question about a movie which features Leonardo DiCaprio in the lead role. The movie does not feature Brad Pitt. Bertie's answer, however, references Brad Pitt. To make sense of Bertie's answer, Archie must look for an implicated premise which links Bertie's utterance with an answer to his question. He is likely to infer the premise in (9).

(9) Brad Pitt is in *The Revenant*

Even though Archie knows this premise to be untrue, he can still use it to reach a conclusion about whether Bertie has seen *The Revenant* or not.

7.2.2 Strong and Weak Implicatures

So far, the focus of this chapter has been the sort of utterances that we come across in ordinary, everyday conversation. Language is, of course, not just used for performing practical tasks and exchanging information about facts and figures. We also use language to entertain, to provoke thought, and to evoke emotions. In this section, we use another key idea from relevance theory to help us think about how poetic and literary texts might fit into the relevance-theoretic framework for utterance interpretation. This is the idea that implicatures can vary in strength.

Think about a poem you have read, the lyrics to a song you like, or a line from a book, play, or movie that struck you as particularly memorable or poignant. The chances are that your interpretation of this word, expression, or line might be different to that of somebody else. How do we account for literary texts where readers arrive at different interpretations and where the writer themselves may not have a fully determined intention for how their words should be interpreted?

According to relevance theory, the same underlying processes drive the interpretation of all ostensive acts of communication. As with everyday conversations, when hearers interpret literary texts they follow the relevance-theoretic comprehension procedure and assume that the speaker or writer was aiming at optimal relevance.

To understand how this might apply in cases of poetic and literary language, we must understand that implicatures can vary in strength. The more evidence a speaker provides for an implicature, the stronger that implicature will be. In Section 7.2.1 we saw examples of utterances that led to strong implicatures. When Harriet told Juliette in (7) that she does not read trash, she strongly implicated that she has not read any novels by Ermintrude Brooks. If Juliet does not recover this implicature, she will struggle to find relevance in Harriet's utterance. In cases like this an utterance achieves optimal relevance because it leads to one or two strong implicatures. However, in other cases, a speaker might provide less direct and determinate evidence for the assumptions that she intends to implicate. Consider the metaphorical description of Juliet that is uttered by Romeo in Shakespeare's *Romeo and Juliet* (Act 2, scene 2, line 4).

(10) Juliet is the sun

What does Romeo intend to communicate by this utterance? Can we paraphrase his meaning? It was fairly easy to put into words what Harriet was implicating in (7), and most hearers are likely to reach the same conclusion about what she was communicating. It is, however, much harder to paraphrase Romeo's meaning in (10), and different readers might interpret the meaning slightly differently. We might, for example, think that Romeo is communicating something along the lines of (11) to (13).

(11) Juliet is radiant
(12) Juliet lights up the scene like the sun lights up the world
(13) Seeing Juliet is like the dawning of a new day

It does not feel, however, as though any of these are direct and full paraphrases of Romeo's utterance. They each perhaps capture one possible aspect of his meaning, but they far from exhaust the possibilities. If we asked ten different people what they thought Romeo meant, we might well receive ten different answers. None of these would be wrong, but none of them would capture all the possibilities, either. There is a sense in which poetic language creates impressions, rather than determinate propositions. Relevance theory captures this via the notion of **weak implicatures**. When an utterance is compatible with a wide range of possible implicatures, the evidence for any one of them being specifically intended by the speaker is weaker. Poetic language often achieves relevance by communicating a wide range of weak implicatures.

7.2.3 Phatic Communication

According to relevance theory, utterances are relevant if they cause us to update our assumptions in one of three ways: strengthening an existing assumption; contradicting and eliminating an existing assumption; combining with an existing assumption to yield an implicated conclusion. In most of the cases that we have looked at so far, the relevance has come from the informational value of the utterance. The content of the utterance has provided a piece of information that leads to a cognitive effect. However, there is another type of utterance that achieves relevance not because of the informational value of the words and phrases, but because it is relevant in terms of social relationships. This type of utterance might be referred to as *small talk* and is also known as phatic communication.

Imagine (14) or (15) is uttered by one stranger to another as they wait at a bus stop on a glorious summer day.

(14) What beautiful weather we are having at the moment!

(15) I see the bus is late

When uttered in this discourse context, it is hard to see how the content of either of these utterances can lead to cognitive effects and therefore be relevant. It is obvious to both strangers that the weather is beautiful, and so the statement in (14) will not strengthen that assumption any further. Similarly, as both have been waiting together at the bus stop and the scheduled arrival time has come and gone, they both already hold the assumption that the bus is late. Therefore, it seems as though the proposition expressed by the utterance in (15) will also have no or very few cognitive effects.

How then can we explain the existence of such utterances in relevance-theoretic terms? How do hearers maintain the assumption that a speaker is aiming at optimal relevance when the propositional content of the utterance is so irrelevant? The answer lies in the presumption that if someone has done or said something that demands our attention, then they must have done so for a reason. We are entitled to look for that reason as part of our interpretation of their behaviour. This is the underlying scaffolding on which relevance theory is built. As the addressee of (14) or (15) will not find sufficient cognitive effects in the informational content of the utterance, he must assume that the relevance lies elsewhere. Optimal relevance is the fixed point around which interpretive processes revolve. In cases of phatic communication, the relevance lies in what the hearer can infer about the social relationship between himself and the speaker. That is, the relevance lies in the fact that the speaker has produced an utterance and thereby signalled that she is open to social interaction and further conversation.

Indeed, phatic communication is only successful if the content of the utterance does not lead to cognitive effects. Imagine how interpretation would proceed if a stranger uttered (16) to you while you were both standing at a bus stop.

(16) Excuse me! Your backpack appears to be open

As normal, you will follow the path of least effort when interpreting the utterance and, crucially, you will stop when you have an interpretation that is optimally relevant. The fact that your backpack is open in a public place is likely to be highly relevant to you. It is probably something that you did not know, and it will probably lead you to act, based on assumptions that you hold about likely scenarios. Perhaps you will check to make sure you still have all your belongings. You are also likely to close the bag to avoid anything falling out or being stolen. In short, the information that the stranger has given you is relevant. It is worth the processing effort to which you have been put, and so there is no need to look for any further relevance in the utterance to satisfy your expectations. Furthermore, you are likely to infer that the speaker was trying to be helpful about a specific issue, rather than trying to start a conversation or pass the time. Phatic communication works as phatic communication precisely because the content has little relevance. This drives the hearer to seek out cognitive effects arising, not from the content, but from the fact that the utterance has been produced.

7.3 The Explicit and the Implicit

A key theoretical issue in the field of pragmatics is the question of where the line between the explicit and the implicit should be drawn. When we communicate using language, how much of our message is said or stated and how much is implied or implicated? A reasonable first hypothesis might be that encoded meaning is explicitly communicated while everything else is implicit. This would amount to the distinction between saying and implying lining up with the distinction between semantics (encoded meaning) and pragmatics (inferred meaning). However, if we apply this to data, it soon becomes apparent that on this basis very few (if any) utterances can be said to explicitly communicate anything. Consider the example in (17).

(17) We saw her duck

Each of the words in (17) depends on the context for interpretation. The pronouns (*we, her*) depend on their referents for their meaning, and both *saw* and *duck* are ambiguous. We cannot tell which of the possible meanings is intended without further contextual information. If the explicit meaning of an utterance is determined only by decoding the semantics of the linguistic terms in that utterance, then we must accept that (17) does not communicate anything explicitly.

However, if we put this utterance into a context, we find that our intuitions perhaps do not align with this analysis. Imagine that (17) was uttered by a witness to a bank robbery, describing how the cashier reacted when the robber pointed a gun at her. In this context, the speaker has communicated that she (and the other witnesses) saw the cashier performing a ducking motion. Furthermore, it feels intuitively as if this is a proposition that she has stated, rather than implied. Even though inferential processes (disambiguation and reference assignment) have been involved, it feels as though this proposition has been explicitly communicated. We look more closely at reference assignment in Section 7.4.1 and at disambiguation in Section 7.4.2.

Grice distinguished two layers of communicated meaning: 'what is said' and what is implicated. His notion of 'what is said' is the closest we have to a notion of explicitly communicated meaning according to the Gricean approach. For Grice, 'what is said' is derived by decoding the linguistic meaning of the utterance and then performing the inferential tasks of disambiguating any ambiguous terms or structures and assigning reference. Grice (1989, p. 25) explained that he intended 'what someone has said to be closely related to the conventional meaning of the word (the sentence) he has uttered'. Applying this to the example in (17) gives us a proposition that seems to capture what the speaker is explicitly communicating. The witnesses saw the cashier perform a ducking motion. However, in other cases, the Gricean notion of 'what is said' appears to still underdetermine the speaker's explicitly communicated meaning.

Consider Christine's reply to Nuno's question in (18).

(18) Nuno: Would you like a Danish pastry with your coffee?
      Christine: I've had breakfast

When we decode the linguistic material, assign reference, and disambiguate we reach the proposition in (19).

(19) Christine has had breakfast [at some point in the past]

This is a truth-evaluable proposition. It will be true if and only if Christine has, at some point in her life, had breakfast. However, most hearers would take Christine to be asserting something more than simply that. Specifically, she would be taken to be asserting, not that she has had breakfast at some point in her life, but that she has had breakfast that morning.

It is this sort of example that led relevance theorists to propose that there is more involved in the derivation of explicitly communicated meaning than was suggested by Grice and by his notion of 'what is said'. Sperber and Wilson introduce the term **explicature** to refer to a proposition that is explicitly communicated by an utterance. Explicatures involve decoding and inference, but as (18) illustrates, the inferential processes that contribute to the explicature do not only include disambiguation and reference assignment. They may also involve pragmatic enrichment. We will look at other examples of pragmatic enrichment in Section 7.4.3. However, for now, let us focus on the example in (18) and consider what drives this enrichment.

According to relevance theory, the encoded meaning of an utterance will be enriched to a point where it can combine with accessible assumptions to yield relevant implicatures. We see this in (18) where Christine's answer is enriched to include the time frame in which she is claiming to have had breakfast. Notice that to fully understand what Christine is communicating by her reply in (18), we must infer how her statement might be relevant as an answer to Nuno's question. As we saw with the other examples of indirect answers in Section 7.2.1, we must look for assumptions with which the proposition expressed can combine to yield a relevant implicature. Let us first imagine that the only inferential processes that contribute to the derivation of explicit meaning are, as Grice suggested, disambiguation and reference assignment. In that case, we understand Christine to be asserting the proposition in (19), and we are looking for an assumption that can combine with this proposition to give us an answer to Nuno's question. However, it is difficult to see how having had breakfast at some point in her life could be relevant to the question of whether she would like a Danish pastry at this moment in time.

According to relevance theory, interpretation is driven by expectations of relevance. In Section 7.2, we saw how these expectations play a role in the derivation of implicatures. These same expectations drive the process of deriving the explicitly communicated meaning as well. Without further enrichment, Christine is only asserting that she has had breakfast at some point in her life. Very little follows from this. Nuno probably already assumed that this was the case with a high degree of confidence, and furthermore, it is not relevant in the context of his question. He will therefore not accept this as the intended interpretation. It does not satisfy his expectations of optimal relevance. However, consider what happens when we further enrich the proposition, along the lines illustrated in (20).

(20) Christine has had breakfast in the last few hours

This enriched proposition can then combine with the assumptions in (21) and (22) to yield the relevant implicatures in (23) and (24).

(21) If someone has had breakfast in the last few hours, they will not be hungry

(22) If someone is not hungry, they will not want anything else to eat

(23) Christine is not hungry

(24) Christine does not want anything else to eat

Thus, by enriching the explicit meaning of *to have had breakfast*, to mean 'to have had breakfast recently', we reach an overall interpretation which answers Nuno's question and is optimally relevant.

This brings us to another key consequence of the relevance-theoretic approach to utterance interpretation, and of the way in which explicit and implicit meaning is characterised on this approach. A key assumption of relevance theory is that what is assessed for optimal relevance is the overall interpretation. To form a hypothesis about the overall intended meaning of an utterance, hearers form hypotheses about the intended explicit meaning (explicatures) and the intended implicit meaning (implicatures). However, hearers do not necessarily work out what a speaker is explicitly communicating first and then use that to work out the implicitly communicated meaning. These processes happen in parallel, and they affect one another.

In the example in (18), working out what Christine is intending to implicate plays a role in working out what she is explicitly communicating, and vice versa. In relevance theory terms this is known as **parallel mutual adjustment**. This also explains why we do not usually spell out every part of our message explicitly. We will leave implicit everything that we can be confident that our hearer will be able to infer from the assumptions that they hold. We may be even more concise in our utterances when we communicate with close friends, because we are confident that we share many assumptions with them. Conversely, legal texts spell everything out as explicitly as possible. Ideally, there should be no room for inference in the interpretation of the law.

Finally, there is an aspect of speaker's meaning that seems to fall between the proposition expressed and the implicatures of an utterance, and which completes the relevance-theoretic picture of explicit and implicit meaning. Recall that in Chapter 2, we discussed the idea that information about a speaker's attitude and emotions can also be part of what is intentionally communicated. We also saw that to work out what a speaker is intending to communicate, we must work out what speech act they are intending to perform. In relevance theory, these aspects of speaker's meaning are captured by the notion of **higher-level explicatures**. In higher-level explicatures the proposition expressed (or basic level explicature) is embedded within a more complex proposition that describes either the speech act being performed or the speaker's attitude to the embedded proposition. These higher-level explicatures are, as the name suggests, part of what is explicitly communicated by the speaker, and they too can combine with assumptions to yield implicatures. We discuss higher-level explicatures in more detail in Section 7.4.4.

7.4 Relevance and Explicit Meaning

In Section 7.2, we focused on the role that inference plays in working out what a speaker is implying or implicating. In Section 7.3, however, we saw that inference is also involved in working out what a speaker is explicitly communicating. In this section, we look more closely at the inferential processes that we undertake when we form a hypothesis about the explicit meaning of an utterance. We start from the assumption that the linguistic content of most sentences is compatible with more than one truth-evaluable proposition expressed. This assumption was discussed in more detail in Chapters 1 and 2. To interpret an utterance, a hearer must form a hypothesis about which of the compatible meanings the speaker intended to convey. To fully understand how speakers do this, we must answer two questions. First, what determines the order in which possible interpretations are tested? Second, by what criterion is an interpretation selected as the one that the speaker intends to communicate? Unless we can answer these questions, we will be unable to explain how a hearer settles on a hypothesis about the interpretation. Relevance theory offers answers to these questions, and, as such, it makes predictions about how interpretation will proceed.

Recall that according to the relevance-theoretic comprehension procedure (see Section 6.4), hearers follow a path of least effort when interpreting an utterance, and they stop when their expectations of relevance are satisfied. Following a path of least effort means testing interpretations in the order in which they occur to you. More accessible interpretations will occur to you first and will require the least effort to construct. We will see how this plays out with examples in the next sections when we turn our attention to specific processes. However, for now we can answer the first question by saying that the possible interpretations of a word, phrase, or structure are tested in order of accessibility. Therefore, the most accessible interpretation will be tested first.

Once we have an interpretation, how do we then assess it and decide whether it is the interpretation that the speaker intended? According to relevance theory, the criterion against which interpretations are tested is optimal relevance. The first interpretation that satisfies both clauses of the definition of optimal relevance will be taken as the intended interpretation. Recall, that to be optimally relevant the interpretation must yield enough cognitive effects to be worth the processing effort that it demands. It must also be compatible with the speaker's abilities and preferences. As soon as these requirements are met, a hearer will stop looking any further. They will have their optimally relevant interpretation, this will satisfy their expectations of relevance, and they will accept it as the intended interpretation.

A key consequence of this is that we do not consider all interpretations and then choose between them. We test interpretations in order of accessibility, and if the first interpretation is optimally relevant, then other possibilities will not even be considered. We often do not notice that there was another possible interpretation until something goes wrong, or until it is explicitly pointed out. We will see how this can happen with jokes, puns, and word play in Section 7.4.2.

Having outlined this general approach, we now look more closely at the pragmatic processes that contribute to explicitly communicated meaning: reference assignment, disambiguation, and pragmatic enrichment.

7.4.1 Reference Assignment

As we saw in Chapter 2, reference assignment is a key inferential task, which contributes to what is explicitly communicated when a speaker produces an utterance. We will not be able to assess whether an utterance is true or false unless we can work out who or what the speaker is referring to. How then, does relevance theory explain the reference assignment process? As we have just seen, according to the relevance-theoretic comprehension procedure, a hearer will test interpretations in order of accessibility. Consider the utterance in (25).

(25) I saw Cris at the weekend. He owes me £25

To understand what the speaker is intending to communicate by uttering (25), the hearer must assign reference to the pronoun *he*. To do so, he will test the most accessible interpretation in the discourse context first. By virtue of just having been mentioned, Cris will be highly salient at this point. It is therefore likely that the hearer will test out an interpretation on which the speaker is communicating that she saw Cris at the weekend and that Cris owes her £25. If, given the discourse context, this results in an interpretation which is optimally relevant, the hearer will assume that this is what the speaker intended to communicate, and he will settle on this interpretation.

Now consider example (26).

(26) I saw Cris at the weekend. The scoundrel owes me £25!

Here we must work out who the speaker is intending to refer to when she uses the phrase *the scoundrel*. Again, the hearer will test interpretations in order of accessibility, and again, Cris is likely to be the most salient candidate. Therefore, the hearer will test out an interpretation on which it is Cris that owes the speaker £25.

Although reference has been assigned in the same way in (25) and (26), the utterance in (26) demands more effort from the hearer. The definite description *the scoundrel* is longer and less frequently used than the pronoun *he*, and so it will take more effort to process. Remember that, according to relevance theory, extra effort must be rewarded with extra effects. As he has been put to more effort, the hearer will look for more cognitive effects to justify this extra effort. Those extra effects come from the information that the speaker thinks that Cris is a scoundrel. The two utterances may be describing the same scenario in so far as it is Cris who owes the speaker £25 in both cases. However, from (26), we can confidently draw more conclusions about the situation and about how the speaker feels about it than we can from (25). The extra effort is rewarded with extra effects.

Remember that when we are looking for an optimally relevant interpretation, we must keep the speaker's abilities and preferences in mind. An optimally relevant interpretation is an interpretation that is compatible with the speaker's abilities and preferences. Consider example (27).

(27) Amy: Bryan is moving to Spain

Imagine that you are Amy's friend and work colleague. Both of you work with a colleague called Bryan. You know him, but you do not work with him particularly closely. The news that he is leaving would be interesting but not hugely significant for you. However, unbeknownst to Amy, your brother is also called Bryan. Let us consider how reference is resolved in this case, and how the relevance-theoretic comprehension procedure and the search for optimal relevance play their parts.

According to the relevance-theoretic comprehension procedure, you will test interpretations in order of accessibility. Given the scenario described, your brother might well be the most accessible referent for you for the name Bryan. It is therefore likely that the first interpretation that you might test is one on which Amy is referring to your brother. The news that your brother is moving to Spain would be likely to be highly relevant to you. The news would lead to many cognitive effects. Should you therefore accept this as Amy's intended interpretation? Recall that the end point of the relevance-theoretic comprehension procedure is an optimally relevant overall interpretation. Optimal relevance is not just about cognitive effects and processing effort. An optimally relevant interpretation must also be compatible with the speaker's abilities and preferences. Thus, when we are assessing this first potential interpretation, we must decide whether this interpretation is compatible with Amy's abilities and preferences.

Given that Amy does not know that your brother is called Bryan, we must reject this interpretation as not compatible with her abilities. We then continue to follow the path of least effort and test the next most accessible interpretive hypothesis, keeping Amy's abilities and preferences in mind. This time we are, perhaps, likely to test an interpretation on which the name Bryan refers to your work colleague Bryan. This interpretation does not lead to as many cognitive effects, but it is compatible with Amy's abilities and preferences. It may not be the most relevant interpretation, but it is the optimally relevant interpretation, and so we accept it as the interpretation that Amy intends.

Now consider the following situation and utterance, adapted from an example first discussed by Katz (1972).

(28) Donald Trump is a liar and a cheat

Imagine that Bob writes the utterance in (28) on a placard and then stands outside the White House in Washington DC holding the placard. Bob is arrested for libel and he is challenged to prove that Donald Trump, the forty-fifth President of the United States of America, is a liar and a cheat. Bob defends himself by saying that he was not, in fact, referring to former President Donald Trump, but rather to his neighbour Donald Trump who recently had an affair with Bob's wife and lied to him about it. That is, Bob is claiming that the truth of his utterance should be judged according to whether his neighbour is a liar and a cheat. His utterance, he claims, is nothing to do with former President Donald Trump.

Should this explanation and defence be accepted? Is it reasonable? Most people agree that Bob's explanation is not acceptable. As Katz (1972, pp. 449–50) explains:

> It seems clear that such a defense would probably fail. … The court would reason that the speaker must have known or can be assumed to have known that a national audience would inevitably take the occurrence of [*Donald Trump*] to refer to the [former American President], and thus he ought to have employed a qualifying expression [e.g., *my neighbour*] to make the statement that he says he intended to make.

Relevance theory offers us an analysis of why this should be, and why Bob's defence seems unreasonable.

When Bob constructs his utterance, he is aiming at optimal relevance. That is, he should construct his utterance in such a way that when the addressees follow the relevance-theoretic comprehension procedure they reach the intended interpretation. Let us assume that Tom is walking by and reads Bob's sign. What interpretation can Tom reasonably be expected to reach? Bob is standing outside the White House, the official residence of the president. His sign is visible to strangers. Those strangers cannot reasonably be expected to have knowledge about the name of Bob's neighbour. Those strangers (and anybody else who is interpreting his utterance) will also be familiar with scenarios in which protests are carried out in places that are relevant to the issue at hand. It is easy to construct a context in which someone who is protesting about the former president might stand outside the White House. It is less easy to construct a context in which someone who is protesting about their neighbour would stand outside the White House. That is, a context in which the name *Donald Trump* refers to Bob's neighbour is less accessible than a context in which it refers to the former president. Interpretations are tested in order of accessibility. We can therefore predict that Tom, or anyone else passing and reading the sign, would test out an interpretation on which former President Donald Trump is the referent for the name on the placard first. This interpretation leads to enough effects to justify the effort that has been expended. Various cognitive effects are likely to follow from the statement that the former president is a liar and a cheat.

Furthermore, Tom is unlikely to have any reason to think that this interpretation is incompatible with Bob's abilities and preferences. Therefore, Tom is entitled to take the interpretation on which Bob is asserting that former President Donald Trump is a liar and a cheat as the intended interpretation. If Bob had genuinely wished to refer to his neighbour Donald Trump, he should have anticipated Tom's interpretation and reformulated his utterance to avoid it. He could, for example, have written (29) on his placard instead.

(29) My neighbour (not the former president!) Donald Trump is a liar and a cheat

Although this is longer than the original version, the extra effort involved in processing the extra content is justified because it guides the hearer away from an otherwise highly accessible and highly relevant interpretation.

Misunderstandings are a failure to communicate the intended message and are costly. If Tom genuinely intends to refer to his neighbour, then (29), or something similar, is the optimally relevant way to do so. Misunderstandings do, of course occur. It is possible that certain assumptions are more accessible for some people than others, and it is also possible that we might misjudge how accessible those assumptions are for a particular person or at a particular moment. This may well lead to misunderstandings and miscommunication.

7.4.2 Disambiguation

As we saw in Chapter 2, disambiguation is an inferential task that contributes to the proposition that is expressed by an utterance. Sentences can be lexically and/or syntactically ambiguous. Consider example (30) which includes the lexically ambiguous word *bat*.

(30)   Matthew always takes his bat to baseball practice

This utterance has (at least) two possible interpretations which are compatible with the linguistic content. These might be paraphrased as (31) and (32).

(31)   Matthew always takes his piece of equipment for hitting balls to baseball practice

(32)   Matthew always takes his pet flying mammal to baseball practice

We might reasonably assume that the intended interpretation is (31), but how do we explain this? Both meanings are associated with the same lexical form, and there is nothing in that form itself to point us to one meaning rather than another. How then do we reach this interpretation?

Clearly, the hearer must form a hypothesis about which of the possible meanings is intended. According to relevance theory, he does not, however, do this in isolation. He is not simply disambiguating a word. He is looking for an overall interpretation. More specifically, he is looking for an overall interpretation which satisfies his expectations of relevance. Disambiguation is just one part of that process. Constructing an overall interpretation also involves constructing a hypothesis about the intended context. As we saw in Chapter 6, we can think of a context as a set of assumptions against which we interpret an utterance.

According to relevance theory, contexts are constructed rather than given. A hearer must select assumptions to form a context against which to interpret the utterance. He does so by assuming that the utterance was intended to be optimally relevant and then selecting a context which justifies that assumption. This construction of the context, as we saw in Chapter 6, is part of the interpretation process, and as such it proceeds according to the relevance-theoretic comprehension procedure. That is, the hearer follows the path of least effort and tests interpretive hypothesis in order of accessibility.

Let us suppose that assumptions about the world are stored in a sort of mental encyclopaedia. We have mental files for each concept, and those files contain information that we associate with that concept. We may, for example, have a conceptual file under the heading BASEBALL. That file will contain everything we know about or associate with baseball. Furthermore, we do not store mental information as a simple list of facts. Rather, encyclopaedic information is organised into chunks, also known as schemas, frames, or scenarios. These chunks are likely to contain frequently used, stereotypical information associated with typical, normal, or expected objects, events, or attributes. Thus, the use of the word *baseball* in (30) will make assumptions about baseball and how it is typically played highly accessible to the hearer.

One of these assumptions is likely to be that baseball is played using a baseball bat, and assumptions about baseball, sports, and the way in which they are typically played are likely to be highly activated in the hearer's mind when he interprets (30). If the hearer interprets *bat* to mean baseball bat, the resulting overall interpretation will call up a very stereotypical scenario in which someone takes a baseball bat to baseball practice. Use of the word *baseball* in the same utterance makes the hitting instrument sense of the word *bat* highly accessible so that it will be tested first. This interpretation is likely to be relevant, and so the hearer will accept it as the intended interpretation.

The flying mammal sense of *bat* is unlikely to consciously occur to Matthew in this context. We could, of course, invent a more elaborate context in which he has a pet bat, and he exercises it by throwing baseballs for it to chase through the air. However, this takes some effort of imagination and is much harder to construct. It is not part of any easily accessible schema or scenario.

Contrast the interpretation of the word *bat* in (30) with the likely interpretation of (33).

(33) John loved to watch the bats at the zoo

Just as the mention of baseball activated assumptions about sports and typical scenarios associated with playing baseball, so the mention of *zoo* in (33) will activate a schema or frame about what might happen at a zoo, and perhaps what sort of exhibits they are likely to have there. The animal sense of *bat* will be more accessible and will be tested first.

As we discussed in Chapter 2, we may only become aware of the process of disambiguation when it goes wrong or when it is exploited for the purposes of humour. Recall the pun that we discussed earlier, repeated here as (34).

(34) Two goldfish in a tank. One says to the other 'How do you drive this thing?'

We are now able to explain, using relevance-theoretic assumptions, how and why puns like this work. Use of the word *goldfish* will activate the hearer's encyclopaedic knowledge of goldfish, along with stereotypical assumptions about what goldfish are like, how they behave, and where they live. Thus, when we form a hypothesis about the intended meaning of the ambiguous word *tank*, we are likely to test the tank of water sense first. This sense is compatible with a typical schema where goldfish live in tanks of water. However, as the utterance proceeds, we are forced to revisit this hypothesis.

The hearer must assign reference to the phrase *this thing*, and information in the rest of the utterance guides him in this process. The referent of *this thing* must be something that you can drive. At this point, the hearer must reassess his interpretation of the word *tank*. We know that the goldfish are in a tank, and while we assumed this meant a water tank, we know that tanks are also a type of vehicle. Thus, we are suddenly jolted out of our initial interpretation into a different one, and this seems to be where the humour lies. We are led towards one meaning, and then that interpretation is flipped on its head.

In puns of this sort, it might seem that the hearer is put to gratuitous effort. He is, after all, led towards one interpretation, only to discover that that interpretation is wrong. However, remember that interpretation proceeds from the assumption that the hearer will not be put to gratuitous effort. There is, as we have seen, a ban on wasted effort. The speaker must, therefore, have intended to mislead the hearer. In Section 7.2.3, we saw examples where the relevance of an utterance comes, not from the information that is encoded, but from the social implications of producing the utterance. Puns function in a similar way. The information about the goldfish is not, in and of itself, relevant. The relevance of a pun lies in the humour that arises from realising that our first interpretation was misguided. The effort is then rewarded by the range of weak implicatures that are likely to follow from this and from the fact that we have been fooled.

7.4.3 Pragmatic Enrichment

As we saw in Section 7.3, the derivation of an explicature is, like the other aspects of interpretation, driven by considerations of relevance. A hearer must use both decoding and inference to form a hypothesis about the proposition that the speaker intends to express. This will often involve disambiguation and reference assignment, but it will also often involve further development or enrichment of the content of the utterance. In (18) ('I've had breakfast'), we saw that the content was enriched to include information about the time that the event took place. Indeed, most of the examples that we have looked at so far involved some element of enrichment beyond reference assignment and disambiguation. For example, when Nuria asks Mel if she should get her a coffee in (4), we understand her to be offering to get the coffee now, rather than at some unspecified time in the future. We also probably understand her to have asked for a cup of coffee, rather than a pot or urn, and we understand that she is asking for coffee in its liquid, drinkable form, rather than a bag of coffee beans. Each of these specific details of the request is inferred by the hearer and is a pragmatic enrichment of the decoded information.

We also saw further examples of pragmatic enrichment in Chapter 2, Section 2.4. We can now revisit those examples and propose a relevance-theoretic analysis. Recall, that the sentence in (35) was uttered by Clare to her son Jacob as he is crying after having fallen over and hurt his knee.

(35) You're not going to die

To interpret her utterance, we assign reference to the pronoun *you* and we disambiguate the verb *to die* to mean 'pass away'. However, without further enrichment, (35) expresses the proposition that Jacob is immortal. As we saw in Chapter 2, this does not fit with our intuitions about what Clare is asserting. It also does not easily combine with an accessible assumption to yield a relevant implication. If, however, we enrich it to the proposition in (36), it can combine with the assumption in (37) to yield the implicated conclusion in (38).

(36) You [Jacob] are not going to die [pass away] [from this injury soon]
(37) If an injury is not going to cause you to die soon, you should stop crying about it
(38) Jacob should stop crying

Relevance theory acknowledges a range of other ways in which the content of an utterance can be enriched. Temporal and locational information may be added. Underdetermined or relative terms or expressions such as *near*, *enough*, or *large* will be enriched. The meaning of words can be narrowed to a more specific meaning or broadened to a more general meaning. For example, in (39) the meaning of *drink* is likely to be narrowed to mean drink alcohol, and in (40), the brand name *Hoover* might be understood to refer to any vacuum cleaner.

(39) You must not drink while taking this medication
(40) Could we borrow your Hoover?

We will return to examples like these in Chapter 8, when we consider figurative uses of language. In each of these cases of enrichment, the enrichment is both driven by and constrained by considerations of relevance.

7.4.4 Higher-Level Explicatures

Relevance theory attempts to account for everything that is intentionally conveyed when a speaker produces an utterance (or any other ostensive stimulus). As we saw in Chapter 2, the speaker's attitude can be part of this intentionally conveyed meaning. Also, to fully understand what a speaker intends to communicate, we must identify the speech act that she intends to perform. According to relevance theory, these aspects of the overall intended message are communicated as higher-level explicatures.

Higher-level explicatures are explicitly communicated propositions in which the basic level explicature is embedded under a description of some sort. Imagine that Frances utters the sentence in (41), but she does so with a broad smile on her face and using an excited tone of voice.

(41)   The sun is shining

We might reasonably infer that she intends not only to communicate that the sun is shining, but also that she is happy about this. We capture this as the higher-level explicature in (42).

(42)   Frances is happy that [the sun is shining]

Notice that the relevance of her utterance might lie in the higher-level explicature, rather than the basic explicature. If the addressee of (41) is in the same location as Frances, he probably already knows that the sun is shining. Therefore, this information will not lead to any cognitive effects on its own. However, the fact that Frances is happy about this may lead to cognitive effects and therefore be relevant.

Furthermore, when Frances utters (41), the addressee must work out what speech act she is performing. She could be asserting that the sun is shining, or she could be asking if the sun is shining. As we saw in Chapter 3, given the right context, (41) could also be used to place a bet, make a promise, or issue a threat. Assuming that Frances is making a simple assertion, we would capture this as the higher-level explicature in (43).

(43)   Frances is asserting that [the sun is shining]

If she uttered it with rising intonation, we might interpret her utterance as a question and construct the higher-level explicature in (44).

(44)   Frances is asking whether [the sun is shining]

In these examples, the attitudinal or speech act information is carried by the speaker's facial expression and tone of voice. However, sometimes information about the speech act or about the speaker's attitude or emotion can be linguistically encoded. We see this in examples (45) and (47). By using the expressions *sadly* and *I promise* the speakers help to guide the hearers towards the intended higher-level explicatures given in (46) and (48) respectively.

(45)   Sadly, you've failed your driving test
(46)   The speaker thinks it is sad that [you've failed your driving test]

(47) I promise that I'll be back on time

(48) The speaker is promising that [the speaker will be back on time]

Whether the speech act and/or attitudinal information is encoded or left implicit, the higher-level explicatures form part of the speaker's intended meaning.

7.5 Procedural Meaning

As we have seen, inference plays a role in the derivation of what the speaker is explicitly communicating as well as what she is implicitly communicating. The relevance of an input depends on two factors: cognitive effects and processing effort. While inferences can lead to cognitive effects, they also require effort. If, therefore, there were ways for speakers to guide the inferential processes of their hearers and thus reduce their processing effort, we might expect speakers to use them. Relevance theory identifies a range of devices which contribute to relevance in just this way, and they are understood as encoding what is known as **procedural meaning**.

The term procedural was first introduced by Diane Blakemore, who argues that some linguistic elements encode an instruction that guides the hearer in his inferential processes. To illustrate, compare the examples in (49) to (51)

(49) Korina is happy. She is going to the party

(50) Korina is happy. After all, she is going to the party

(51) Korina is happy, so she is going to the party

All three versions contain the same two conjuncts, and they will all be true if and only if Korina is both happy and going to the party. To work out the speaker's overall intended meaning, the hearer must infer what relationship (if any) there is between the two conjuncts. Is Korina's happiness the cause of her going to the party, or is the fact that she is going to the party, the cause of her happiness? In (49) we are given no further information, and we must infer the relationship from the discourse context alone. In (50), however, the use of the term *after all* guides the hearer to infer that the party-going is the cause of Korina's happiness. The use of *so* in (51) guides the hearer to infer the opposite causal relationship. In this case, Korina's happiness is the cause of her party-going. By guiding the inferences in this way, the speaker not only lowers the risk of misunderstanding, but she also reduces the hearer's processing effort. Remember that, when all other things are equal, the lower the processing effort, the greater the relevance.

In Chapter 4, we saw that Grice drew a distinction between conventional and conversational implicatures, and a further distinction between generalised and particularised conversational implicatures. Relevance theory makes no such distinction. Implicatures are the intended contextual assumptions (implicated premises) and intended implicated conclusions that arise during the interpretation process. They arise because we assume that the speaker is aiming to make her utterance optimally relevant. Those words and expressions which, according to Grice, encode a conventional implicature (for example, *but*, *however*, *nonetheless*) are accounted for within relevance theory by this notion of procedural meaning. They guide the hearer in the inferences that she makes and thus contribute to the relevance of the utterance.

This idea that some elements of an utterance contribute to interpretation by guiding inferential processes has been highly influential, and procedural analyses have been suggested for a range of linguistic expressions and communicative devices including discourse connectives, pronouns, syntax, intonation, and punctuation. In each case, the assumption is that guiding inferential processes reduces the risk of costly misunderstandings and reduces processing effort, thereby optimising relevance.

7.6 Chapter Summary

We started this chapter by thinking about relevance theory as a theoretical framework. Rather than analysing utterances and interactions in a vacuum, we use a theoretical framework to provide structure to our analyses. The principles of relevance theory can be thought of as assumptions about how human cognition and communication function. These provide a scaffold on which we can build analyses. The assumptions allow us to make predictions and generalisations.

We touched on some of the consequences of the relevance-theoretic principles, including the idea that the first interpretation that is optimally relevant can be taken as the intended interpretation, and the idea that more processing effort should be offset by more cognitive effects. We then moved on to see how these generalisations and consequences play out in practice, by looking at the various elements that make up speaker's meaning.

We then turned to implicit meaning, discussing a range of examples. The notion that implicatures may be strong or weak was introduced, and we saw how literary and poetic devices might be designed to lead, not to one strong implicature, but to a range of weak implicatures. We then considered cases of phatic communication, where the relevance of an utterance lies in its social implications.

Section 7.3 focused on the explicit–implicit distinction. We introduced the relevance theory notion of explicature and saw how inference is involved in constructing explicatures as well as implicatures. We then looked more closely at the pragmatic processes that contribute to explicature formation, discussing examples of reference assignment, disambiguation, and pragmatic enrichment, and we saw that speech act and attitudinal information can be captured as higher-level explicatures.

Finally, we briefly introduced the idea that some elements of an utterance function to guide the hearer's inferential processes. We can think of such elements as encoding procedural meaning, and they contribute to relevance by reducing the processing effort required to reach the speaker's overall intended meaning.

Exercises

7a   In Section 7.1, we saw that repeating a word can have an emphatic effect. The examples are repeated below. However, (ii) and (iii) are not completely equivalent. Can you use concepts and assumptions from relevance theory to explain why there is a difference?

  (i)   It was a stupid thing to say
  (ii) It was a stupid, stupid thing to say
  (iii) It was a very stupid thing to say

7b   For each of the examples, identify (a) the basic explicature, (b) any higher-level explicatures, and (c) any implicatures for Jasmine's utterance.

  (i)   Alex: Would you like a glass of wine?
        Jasmine: I don't drink
  (ii) Alex: Have you visited La Sagrada Familia?
        Jasmine: I've never been to Madrid
  (iii) Alex: Are you going to party tonight?
        Jasmine (sadly): I've got nothing to wear
  (iv) Alex: Do you want to order dessert?
        Jasmine: I've had enough
  (v)   Alex: Are you a good cook?
        Jasmine: I'm half Italian

7c   Choose a poem or a song lyric and think about what is being implicitly communicated? Can you paraphrase the ideas, thoughts, and feelings that are conveyed? Compare your interpretation with a partner.

Is the writer communicating one strong implicature, or do you find yourself constructing a range of weak implicatures?

7d   Look at the sentences in (i) to (v) and identify the ambiguity. What do you think is the intended meaning? Explain why this should be, using the ideas from relevance theory.

(i)   Can I borrow your pen? Mine is out of ink
(ii)   Could you call me a taxi please?
(iii)   John lost his bottle and ran away. [Hint: Think about possible meanings of the word *bottle* and associated phrases]
(iv)   Eating children can be messy
(v)   The spy checked the room for bugs

7e   Pay attention to the meaning that is communicated by the conjunction *and* in the following examples. How is it enriched in each case? Use the assumptions of relevance theory to explain how the enrichment comes about.

(i)   Pablo picked up the guitar and played
(ii)   I spent a year in Spain and learned to dance flamenco
(iii)   Tara took out her keys and opened the door
(iv)   Justin didn't study and failed all his exams
(v)   Paris is the capital of France and Madrid is the capital of Spain

Key Terms Introduced in this Chapter
explicature, 148
higher-level explicatures, 149
implicated conclusions, 142
implicated premises, 142
overall intended meaning, 139
parallel mutual adjustment, 149
procedural meaning, 160
theoretical framework, 137
weak implicatures, 144

Further Reading
The main reference text for relevance theory is Sperber and Wilson (1986/95). This sets out the approach in full and includes discussions of key areas in relevance theory and pragmatics more generally. Several other works include accessible introductions and overviews to the framework. These include Blakemore (1992), which adopts a relevance-based approach and provides

a clear overview of how we understand utterances. Clark (2013) provides a more detailed discussion of many of the ideas that have been introduced in this chapter, along with examples, discussion points, and exercises.

Robyn Carston has written extensively on the explicit-implicit distinction, arguing for the relevance-based position outlined in this chapter. Carston (2002) is a key text for any readers who would like to engage more with this debate and the nature of explicature.

The discussion of phatic communication in this chapter draws on work by Žegarac and Clark (1999). For more on how relevance theory can be used to explain poetic and stylistic effects, see Pilkington (2000) and Scott (2020).

To read more about the general notion of procedural meaning and the role that it plays in the relevance-theoretic framework, readers should start with the work of Diane Blakemore (1992, 2002). Papers by Wilson (2016) and Carston (2016) discuss how the notion of procedural meaning has developed since it was first proposed by Blakemore. Both discuss the range of procedural analyses that have been proposed and reflect on just how influential Blakemore's work has been in both semantics and pragmatics.

CHAPTER 8

Figurative Language

In This Chapter …

In this chapter, we take a closer look at figurative language from a pragmatic perspective. When we use words or phrases figuratively, we use them in a way that departs from their literal, conventionally encoded meaning. Traditionally, discussion of figurative language has been focused on a relatively small set of rhetorical tropes, including metaphor, hyperbole, irony, meiosis, and metonymy. Other devices that are sometimes included under the figurative umbrella include idioms, onomatopoeia, and similes. These tropes were traditionally analysed as rhetorical devices that could be used in the art of persuasion, and, as we saw in Chapter 2, figurative language is also often associated with literary language. However, as we shall see, from a pragmatic perspective, non-literal use of language extends far beyond the devices and tropes traditionally associated with rhetoric and poetry. The inferential processes that we employ to interpret metaphors, irony, and other figuratively used language, are part of a more general pragmatic system. Non-literal use of language is pervasive, and the processing of non-literal language plays a central role in utterance interpretation.

In this Chapter, we focus on metaphor, hyperbole, and irony, outlining several of the most influential pragmatic approaches to the analyses of these. The chapter opens in Section 8.1 with an overview of the Gricean account of figurative language. The field of lexical pragmatics is introduced in Section 8.2, and a range of examples are discussed to illustrate just how often we use language 'loosely'. It is not only in traditionally categorised cases of metaphorical and hyperbolic language use that we find words being used non-literally in this way. Pragmatic processes of lexical adjustment are introduced and discussed as a pervasive part of everyday communication. These processes are then applied to hyperbole, metaphor, and other loose uses to illustrate the role of lexical pragmatics in these figurative examples. In Section 8.3, the attention turns to irony, and two leading analyses are introduced and then compared: irony as pretence and irony as echoic use.

8.1 Grice and Figurative Language

As we saw in Chapter 4, according to Grice, figurative readings arise when a speaker flouts the maxim of truthfulness. Typical examples illustrating irony (1), metaphor (2), hyperbole (3), and meiosis (understatement) (4) are repeated here.

(1) (Uttered after dropping and breaking a vase): That's just what I needed!

(2) (Uttered on a hot day): My office is a greenhouse

(3) (Uttered by someone who skipped lunch that day): I'm starving!

(4) (Uttered after a serious argument has taken place): It's a little tense in here

In each case, the speaker has said something that is blatantly false, thereby flouting the maxim of truthfulness (or quality). The hearer assumes, however, that the speaker must still be being cooperative and must therefore intend to implicate something true. In the case of irony, the speaker is taken to have implicated the opposite of what she has said. The dropping and breaking of the vase in (1) is not at all what the speaker needed. When she utters the metaphor in (2), the speaker is implicating that her office is like a greenhouse in some way. In the hyperbole in (3), the speaker is not literally starving. The flouting of the maxim of truthfulness again triggers the search for a related proposition, and the hearer is likely to assume that the speaker is implicating something related to, but in this case weaker than, what she has said. The hearer will, we imagine, take the speaker to be communicating that she is very hungry. The understatement in (4) follows a similar pattern, but this time the implicated proposition is a strengthening of the speaker's literal statement. She is communicating that the atmosphere is more than a little tense.

On this Gricean approach to figurative language, each variety functions in more or less the same way. The speaker says something blatantly false, and this triggers a related implicature. However, this approach has faced several criticisms. For example, in each case, an implicature is triggered by the flouting of the maxim of truthfulness. However, it is not clear how a hearer knows that, on some occasions, the flouting should lead him to infer that the speaker means the opposite of what she has said, but that in other cases, he should take her to be communicating a weakening or strengthening of the literal meaning. That is, it is not clear how the hearer moves from the literal meaning to a figurative interpretation, and it is not clear how he knows which inferential path to follow.

As we saw in Chapter 4, Grice took communication to be a cooperative and rational endeavour. On this account, it is not, therefore, clear why a speaker would ever choose to speak non-literally. Indeed, in the case of irony, it could be viewed as downright uncooperative and irrational to utter the opposite of what you mean. Yet, irony (along with other forms of figurative language), appears to be universal across communities and cultures, and it appears to arise spontaneously wherever humans communicate with each other.

According to the Gricean account, all cases of figurative language are floutings of the maxim of truthfulness, and comprehension follows broadly the same inferential patterns of implicature derivation across the different varieties of non-literal language use. However, there is evidence that metaphor and irony have little in common. For example, children seem to develop the ability to use and understand metaphor earlier than they do irony. This is unexpected if they are interpreted using the same pragmatic processes. In contrast, metaphor and hyperbole appear to be very closely related. Indeed, it is not always easy to distinguish between them. For example, when a speaker utters (5) to mean that she found the movie boring and tedious, is she exaggerating or is she using a metaphor?

(5) That movie put me to sleep

An argument could be made for either analysis. Indeed, it is unlikely that the hearer will need to make a choice between the two to derive a relevant interpretation of the utterance in context. Either interpretation will lead the hearer to the implicature that the speaker did not enjoy the movie because she found it dull and boring, and this is the key point that she is intending to communicate. As we shall see, metaphor and hyperbole seem to also have characteristics in common with other non-literal uses of language such as the **loose uses** in (6) and (7).

(6) The room was silent

(7) The storm raged for an hour

It seems very unlikely that the room in (6) was silent, strictly speaking. That is, it is unlikely that there were no audible sounds at all within the room, no matter how quiet or insignificant. We are likely to accept the speaker as having said something true if nobody was speaking and there were no other significant or distracting noises in the room. Similarly, the utterance in (7) is likely to be judged as true, so long as the storm was roughly an hour. It need not have been precisely sixty minutes in duration and not a second more or less, for us to consider what the speaker has said as true. As we saw in Chapter 4, these types of non-literal language use do not seem to trigger implicatures in the way that metaphorical and hyperbolic utterances do. In these cases of so-called loose use, speakers say something that is not literally true. However, in doing so they do not seem to be flouting the maxim of truthfulness. Indeed, rather, they seem to have said something true or true enough. We revisit this category of non-literal utterance in Section 8.2.3.

Another issue for the Gricean account is that not all metaphorical uses of language can be straightforwardly understood as floutings of the maxim of truthfulness. Consider the negative metaphor (8) and the non-declarative metaphors in (9) and (10).

(8) Jacqui is not an angel

(9) Jacqui, be an angel

(10) Is Jacqui an angel?

In (8), the speaker states that Jacqui is not an angel. On most occasions of use this is, we assume, true. Jacqui is a human being, and not a supernatural creature often depicted with wings, a harp, and a halo. Therefore, the speaker has not said anything blatantly false, and there is no flouting of the maxim of truthfulness. As there is no flouting, there is nothing to trigger the search for a related implicature. However, in most circumstances this utterance would still be taken to be metaphorical. That is, we do not usually take the speaker of (8) to be asserting that Jacqui is not a literal angel. An exception to this might be if the question under discussion is whether Jacqui is playing the part of an angel in a play. However, on most occasions, we take the speaker to be asserting that Jacqui is not a metaphorical angel. Jacqui is not, we might assume, kind and well-behaved in the way that we might expect someone who is appropriately described as an angel to be.

We find a similar issue with the imperative in (9) and the interrogative in (10). Again, neither can be meaningfully said to be true or false, and so, again, there is no flouting of the maxim of truthfulness to trigger the search for a related implicature. However, once again, we find that the most usual interpretation for such utterances is metaphorical. The speaker of (9) is asking Jacqui to be kind, helpful, and well-behaved etc., and in (10) she is asking whether this is an appropriate way to describe Jacqui.

These examples pose an issue for the Gricean account, and, indeed, for any account that relies on the notion that the speaker has said something that is blatantly false.

It follows from the Gricean account that hearers will test out a literal interpretation of an utterance initially, and then only proceed to a figurative interpretation if the literal interpretation is blatantly false. We would therefore expect metaphorical interpretations to take longer to process than literal interpretations. The hearer needs to construct the literal interpretation, assess it against what he knows about the world, reject it, and then construct a related metaphorical interpretation. However, evidence from experimental studies suggests that metaphorical interpretations are derived just as quickly as literal ones. Again, this is not predicted by the Gricean analysis of metaphor.

Moving on to consider the Gricean account of irony, we find similar issues. Grice himself pointed out a problem that is faced by any account of irony that relies solely on the notion that a speaker is saying the opposite of what she means. It is simply not always possible to be ironic simply by stating the opposite of something that is clearly true. Grice (1989, p. 53) discusses the example in (11) to illustrate this. Imagine that two people are walking down a street and they see a car with broken windows. One points to a car and utters (11).

(11) Look, that car has all its windows intact

If it were possible to be ironic simply by saying the opposite of what we mean, the utterance in (11) should be successful as an instance of irony. However, as Grice points out, it is not. Furthermore, (11) seems to be an absurd thing to say in the discourse context. The issue here, Grice (1989, p. 53) suggests, is that irony is 'intimately connected with the expression of a feeling, attitude, or evaluation'. Irony 'is intended to reflect a hostile or derogatory judgement or a feeling such as indignation or contempt' (p. 54). Alternative accounts of irony are outlined in Section 8.3, and we shall see that attitude is central to these accounts, in line with Grice's observation.

Given the undoubted influence that Grice has had on pragmatics as a discipline, along with the various issues and questions that arise from his account, it is perhaps not surprising that post-Gricean analyses of figurative language have emerged. In the rest of this chapter, we look at some of these alternative accounts. Broadly speaking these have been developed as attempts to avoid the problems and criticisms that are faced by the Gricean approach. However, as with most work in cognitive and linguistic pragmatics, they remain indebted to Grice's groundbreaking ideas and observations about the role of intentions and inference in the communication of meaning.

8.2 **Metaphor and Lexical Pragmatics**

8.2.1 Words and Concepts

Lexical pragmatics is a subfield of pragmatics which explores what is communicated by words when they are used in context. This is in contrast with **lexical semantics** which is concerned with what is encoded by words. The field of lexical pragmatics is key to the relevance-theoretic account of figurative language, and, in particular, to its account of metaphor.

When words are used metaphorically, the concept that they communicate is different to the concept that they encode. A concept can be understood as anything about which we can have thoughts. We can think about people, places, and things. We can also think about emotions, colours, and ideas. We can have thoughts about groups of things or groups of people, and we can think about fictional or imaginary people, places, and events. For each of these, we will have a concept, and for each concept we have what we might think of as a mental or conceptual file. That file contains all the information that we have about the concept. For example, we might assume that most humans will have a concept MOON. When we are writing about concepts, we distinguish between words and concepts by presenting the concepts in small capital letters. Each individual's conceptual file for MOON will contain all of the information that they have about moons and the moon. This is likely to vary slightly between different people. Some people may know a lot of information about the moon. Others may not know many facts, but they may associate the moon with a particular painting or poem. Others still might think that the moon is made of green cheese. In each case, the information that the individual has will be stored in their MOON mental file. If you are an English speaker, your conceptual file for MOON will also include the information that we refer to this concept by using the label *moon*. If, however, you are a Spanish speaker, your label for this conceptual file will be *luna*. While the labels, associations, facts, and details of different individuals' MOON files will differ, there is also likely to be a core meaning that we all agree on. This is the information that we might give if asked to define what the word *moon* means, and we might think of this as the literal meaning of that word.

With this characterisation of concepts in mind, consider again the metaphorical utterance from (2), repeated here.

(2) My office is a greenhouse

The word *greenhouse* encodes the concept GREENHOUSE. An individual's concept GREENHOUSE consists of a conceptual file containing all the information that they know about greenhouses, along with various grammatical and logical pieces of information. The literal concept GREENHOUSE will probably be associated with a range of features and qualities including those in (12).

(12)   Hot; humid; full of plants; made almost entirely of glass

Notice, however, that when the speaker uses the word *greenhouse* metaphorically in (2), she uses it to communicate a concept that is somewhat different to the literal concept in (12). She uses it to communicate something like (13).

(13)   Uncomfortably hot; stuffy; airless; unpleasant place to work in

While the concept that is communicated is related to the concept that is encoded, it is not identical. We would not, for example, usually take the speaker of (2) to be communicating that her office is entirely made of glass, nor that it is full of plants. This metaphorical use is an example of the communicated meaning of a word being different from the encoded meaning of a word. A hearer's task is to infer the speaker's intended meaning, and words are a clue to this. Using words to communicate their literal meaning and no more or no less is limiting, and this will not always be the most efficient way to guide the hearer to the intended meaning. As we shall see, as speakers, we very frequently use words to communicate something different to or beyond the meaning that they encode. Thus, the issue of how to analyse figurative language is not just relevant to those occasions on which we speak metaphorically, or on which we use hyperbole or irony. It is central to lexical pragmatics and to understanding a speaker's meaning. We explore some instances of this in the next section.

8.2.2 Ad Hoc Concepts

Consider what the work *drink* communicates when it is produced as part of the utterance (14) in different discourse contexts.

(14)   She's not allowed to drink this evening

First, imagine that Rosa is hosting a party. Sue and Maria arrive together, and Maria goes to put their coats away in another room. While they are waiting for her to return, Rosa asks Sue whether Maria would prefer to drink red wine or white wine. Sue utters (14) as an answer to Rosa's question. It seems likely that in this discourse context, Sue is using the word *drink* to communicate the concept DRINK ALCOHOL. Even though the literal meaning of Sue's utterance is that Maria is not allowed to consume any liquids during the evening, we would not usually take that to be her intended meaning. Rather we would take her to be communicating the proposition in (15).

(15) Maria is not allowed to drink alcohol this evening

Now imagine that the discourse context is not a party. Instead, Rosa and Sue are visiting Maria in hospital the night before she is due to have surgery. They are discussing the preparations that she is undergoing, and Sue utters (14). In this case, the meaning of Sue's utterance is much closer to the literal meaning of the sentence than it was in the party context. This time, we draw on accessible contextual assumptions that we hold about what happens before a surgical operation when interpreting Sue's utterance. This leads us to interpret *drink* to mean 'drink any liquid'.

The same word *drink* has communicated different concepts in different discourse contexts. In the party context, the meaning of the word *drink* has undergone a process of **narrowing** to communicate something more specific than the concept that it literally encodes. This narrowed concept forms part of the explicature. In the party context, Sue's utterance will be true if and only if Maria is not allowed to drink alcohol this evening. When (14) is uttered in the hospital context it forms part of a different explicature. In the hospital context, Sue's utterance will be true if and only if Maria is not allowed to drink any liquids at all this evening. These different explicatures interact with contextual assumptions to lead to different implications and implicatures. For example, in the party context, it follows from Sue's utterance that Maria is not allowed to drink beer or vodka that evening. However, it does not rule out that she can drink water or lemonade. In contrast, it would not be appropriate to offer Maria water or lemonade in the hospital discourse context.

Next, consider the utterance in (16).

(16) Paula and I met for coffee last week

The word *coffee* literally encodes a concept representing a particular substance that can be made into a particular drink. We can roughly represent this as the concept in (17).

(17) COFFEE = Caffeinated drink that is usually served hot and is made from roasted and ground beans

However, in this utterance and in particular discourse contexts, the word *coffee* can be used to represent any hot drink, or perhaps just any drink that one might purchase at a café or coffee shop. Imagine that it was later revealed that Paula and the speaker had met last week but one had drunk a cup of tea and the other had consumed hot chocolate. It would not, in most cases, feel as though a lie had been told. In this example, the concept communicated by the word *coffee* has undergone a process of **broadening**, and it now includes drinks that would not fall under the literal definition of coffee. Uses that include broadening are sometimes referred to as loose uses.

Narrowing and broadening are both processes of **lexical adjustment** that play a role in the construction of meaning. The concepts that are communicated when a word is used in context may be broader and/or narrower than the literally encoded concept. We indicate that a concept has been adjusted by adding an asterisk to the conceptual label. In the party discourse context, the work *drink* communicates the concept in (18) and in the example in (16), the word *coffee* communicates the concept in (19). The asterisk is read aloud as 'star', and so DRINK* would be pronounced 'drink star'.

(18) DRINK* = drink alcohol

(19) COFFEE* = any drink that you might buy at a coffee shop

These adjusted concepts are known as **ad hoc concepts**. They are created ad hoc and on the fly as part of the interpretation process. As we shall see, ad hoc concept formation is central to the relevance-theoretic account of metaphor and hyperbole. However, ad hoc concepts play a much more extensive role in the communication of intended meaning. Understanding words in context almost always involves ad hoc concept formation. Relevance theory does not have a maxim of truthfulness and there is no expectation that we will use language literally. Words are clues to the speaker's intended meaning. The concepts that are encoded by lexical items are modified in context to satisfy expectations of relevance.

Imagine that words could only convey their literally encoded meaning, and the speaker of (16) was not, therefore, able to use the word *coffee* to communicate the concept COFFEE*. She would be forced, instead, to produce a much longer and more complicated utterance, such as (20) or (21).

(20) Paula and I met for a hot drink in a café last week

(21) Paula and I met for tea and hot chocolate last week

While these are both perfectly grammatical sentences of English, they are longer than the utterance in (16) and they provide more detailed information. They therefore demand more processing effort from the hearer, and the hearer will look for extra meaning to offset this effort. If something relevant follows from the fact that it was tea and hot chocolate (rather than some other drink) that Paula and the speaker consumed during their meeting, then (21) is likely to be a preferred version. However, if nothing follows from these details, then it would be putting the hearer to gratuitous effort to include them. The version in (16) is sufficient so long as it leads to an explicature that can combine with accessible assumptions to generate a relevant overall interpretation.

Ad hoc concepts are occasion specific, and they depend on the context in which an utterance is produced. While the word *coffee* may communicate the concept COFFEE* in some contexts, in others it will convey a concept that is much closer to, or identical with, the lexicalised concept COFFEE. Imagine that (16) is uttered, not as part of a general discussion, but during a conversation about the fact that Paula has claimed to have given up caffeine. For (16) to be relevant in that context, the use of *coffee* must be taken to communicate the concept COFFEE.

In this section, we have seen that words are often used to communicate a concept that is narrower or broader than the concept that they literally encode. Although such cases are not usually thought of as figurative uses, the speaker uses a word to convey a meaning that is different from the strictly literal sense. Over the next three sections, we see further examples of this same process of lexical adjustment in action, culminating in a lexical pragmatic analysis of metaphor.

8.2.3 Approximations

Lexical pragmatics recognises that the meaning that is communicated by a word when it is used in context may not be the same as the meaning that is lexically encoded by that word. We can represent the communicated concept as an ad hoc concept, and this helps us to understand how language can be used loosely. In Sections 8.2.4. and 8.2.5 we see how this offers us a way to understand hyperbole and metaphor. However, first it is useful to consider **approximations** as a further, and very commonly occurring category of loose use. Approximations involve a broadening of the lexicalised concept encoded by a word. They are, however, much less often discussed than metaphor and hyperbole, and, indeed, are often not even noticed or recognised as cases of non-literal use. Typical examples of approximations are given in (22) to (26).

(22)   That guitar cost me $2,000

(23)   The children sat in a circle around the campfire

(24)   Madrid is south of London

(25)   The water in the kettle was still boiling hot

(26)   The glass on the table was empty

As (22) illustrates, rounding is often applied to numbers to give an approximate value or price. Imagine a friend used this utterance to tell you the price of her guitar, and then later you found out that she had in fact only paid $1,999.99 for it. You could claim that your friend had uttered something untrue in saying (22). However, you are unlikely to feel as though you have been lied to. Again, if we think about the overall communicative aim of the speaker, we can start to understand why this might be, and why in some discourse contexts, literal truth seems to matter, while in others, it does not.

According to relevance theory, there is no maxim of truthfulness. There is no expectation that an utterance will be true. There is only an expectation that the speaker will be aiming to make her utterance optimally relevant. Relevance is determined by two factors: the cognitive effects that follow from the input, and the effort required to derive those effects. If the speaker is contributing to a general discussion about the price of musical instruments, it is very unlikely that the strictly true utterance in (27) would lead to any more cognitive effects than the approximation in (22).

(27) The guitar cost me $1,999.99

Most implications that follow from a guitar costing $2,000 will also follow from a guitar costing $1999.99. The utterance in (27), however, is likely to demand more processing effort from the hearer than the one in (22). The hearer of (22) has a shorter numerical expression to decode, and rounded numbers are, in general, easier to process. This means that overall, the utterance in (22) is more relevant. The effects are the same for both, but the effort that is required to access those effects is less for the approximation in (22). We return to this idea in Chapter 10, when we see experimental evidence for the relevance of rounding numbers.

We see similar cases of approximation in (23) to (26). Approximations may be used with geometric shapes, as in (23), geographic terms, as in (24), as well as for scientific terms, as in (25), and negatively defined terms, as in (26). We might think of the speaker of (23) as claiming that the children sat in a CIRCLE* around the campfire. CIRCLE* is an ad hoc concept which includes any shape broadly recognisable as a circle and close enough to being a circle to be relevant in the context. The same process can be followed with the interpretation of *south*, *boiling*, and *empty* in (24) to (26).

That is not to say that the literal truth never matters. Producing an utterance that represents a literally true state of affairs matters, according to relevance theory, when the literal truth is needed for the communication of an optimally relevant interpretation. If a loose use leads the hearer to an interpretation which is optimally relevant, then it should be the preferred option. In cases of approximation, the concept that is communicated is broader than the concept that is encoded, but this broadening is minimal. If the extent of the broadening is increased, we find cases that would normally be classified as hyperbole, and we turn our attention to these next.

8.2.4 Hyperbole

Consider the hyperbolic utterances in (28) to (30), repeated from Chapter 2.

(28) There were a million people at the party

(29) I was starving when I got to the restaurant

(30) The room was boiling hot

In each case, the speaker exaggerates for dramatic or emphatic effect. We can probably assume that there were not literally a million people at the party described in (28), and that the speaker of (29) was, in fact, far from being in a state of starvation. Similarly, we do not seriously entertain the notion that the room temperature described in (30) is so hot that water would be boiling. Notice, however, that these are not approximations. We do not assume that there were roughly a million people at the party, or that the speaker was close to being starving. Neither do we understand the speaker to be communicating that the room was realistically anywhere near boiling point. The optimally relevant interpretation of these utterances involves a greater degree of broadening than we find in the approximation cases. There are more people at the party in (28) than we might otherwise have expected, the speaker of (29) is very hungry, and the room in (30) is very hot. The concepts have been broadened to a greater extent and are further from the literal truth. Compare the concept that is communicated using *boiling* in (30) with the concept that is communicated in the approximation in (25).

(31) The water in the kettle was still BOILING* hot

(32) The room was BOILING** hot

In both cases, the word *boiling* is used non-literally, and in both cases the concept that is communicated is broader than the lexicalised concept. However, the precise features of the communicated concept are different. The ad hoc concept BOILING* (= roughly at 100 degrees Celsius) is different from the ad hoc concept BOILING** (= very hot, too hot for comfort). Thus, we can understand hyperbole as a loose use in which the derivation of the ad hoc concept involves a significant degree of broadening.

8.2.5 Metaphor

According to the relevance-driven, lexical pragmatics account, metaphors are not exceptional. They are interpreted using the same inferential adjustment processes that are used to interpret other loose uses of language, including approximations and hyperbole. Metaphors sit on a continuum with these other loose uses of language, and arguably represent the furthest departure from the lexically encoded literal meaning. Consider the example in (33), which was first introduced in Chapter 2.

(33) My office is a sauna

In this utterance, the speaker uses the word *sauna* as a clue to her meaning. As the word is used as part of an ostensive stimulus (in this case, an utterance), the hearer will assume that the speaker was aiming at optimal relevance and will look for what her intended meaning could be. The lexicalised concept SAUNA is likely to include a range of information associated with saunas. This might include, for example, the characteristics in (34).

(34) SAUNA = hot, humid room, usually made largely of wood; heated by hot rocks or coals; often used to relax after exercise; used by people wearing bathing suits; popular in Scandinavia; often found in gyms or leisure centres

When the speaker produces the utterance in (33), her use of the word *sauna* will activate a number of these associations and assumptions, and it will make a range of implications accessible to the hearer. Some of these assumptions and implications will apply even though the office is not literally a sauna and will be relevant in the context in which the utterance has been produced. For example, use of the word *sauna* might activate assumptions that the office is hot and humid. This can then combine with assumptions associated with the concept OFFICE, including perhaps that offices are places where people spend extended periods of time, and where work takes place. This then leads to the implication that the heat and humidity in the office means it is a difficult place to spend extended periods of time and is not a suitable work environment. From this, the hearer will infer that the speaker intended to communicate that her office is a SAUNA*. SAUNA* represents a concept 'which is close enough [to being literally a sauna] to yield the implications that make the whole utterance contextually relevant' (Wilson and Sperber, 2012 p. 107). SAUNA* can be taken to communicate something like 'hot, humid, uncomfortable space'. From this, the hearer might then infer that the speaker is unhappy with her current working conditions and needs to take regular breaks outside to get fresh air. He will take the speaker to have been complaining about her working conditions, and this is likely to be relevant enough to satisfy the hearer's expectations of relevance. The hearer is not, however, likely to infer that the speaker wears a bathing suit in her office or that she uses it as a place to relax after exercise. Nor will he assume that the office is a small room made largely of wood.

This ad hoc concept SAUNA* is arrived at by a process of lexical adjustment which in this case includes both narrowing and broadening of the lexicalised concept. It is narrowed in that SAUNA* includes only functioning saunas that are in use, and not, for example, saunas that have fallen into disuse and are now only used as storage cupboards. However, the concept is also broadened to include all hot, humid places, and not just actual saunas. According to Wilson and Sperber (2012, p. 111), this combination of narrowing and broadening is a common feature of metaphors, although not a defining feature. Some metaphors involve only broadening.

Notice that certain very common qualities of saunas are not part of the meaning of the communicated concept SAUNA* (walls made of wood, heated by rocks and coals, etc.). Meanwhile, other features that emerge as part of SAUNA* are not part of the meaning of the lexicalised concept SAUNA. Neither are they part of the lexicalised concept OFFICE. A SAUNA*, for example, is uncomfortable and would be an unpleasant place to spend time. Actual saunas, of course, are designed for relaxation and to be comfortable, pleasant environments. This phenomenon of **emergent features** is a common characteristic of metaphors. The process of ad hoc concept construction helps us to understand how a feature like 'uncomfortable' might emerge in this case. The ad hoc concept SAUNA* is a place that is hot and humid in the way that saunas are. Any office that was hot and humid in this way, would, we might infer, be uncomfortable.

A key consequence of this account is that the interpretation of metaphors does not require any special inferential processes. Metaphorical interpretations are reached via the same pragmatic processes of lexical adjustment as the other loose uses that we have seen, including hyperbole and approximation. Indeed, the standard view within relevance theory is that these different uses sit on a continuum. As we move from literal at one end to metaphor at the other, we see a greater and greater level of adjustment being made to the lexicalised concept. Approximation, for example, involves only a slight broadening. Hyperbole involves a further degree of broadening. Finally, metaphors involve further broadening again, along with narrowing in some cases. While we may think of each of these as a separate category with a different label, when it comes to actual examples and utterances, the line between where one ends and the next begins can often be blurred.

8.3 **Irony**

Two key approaches to irony have emerged in response to Grice's work. First, a number of analyses have been proposed which share the assumption that irony is a type of **pretence**. A second, alternative account argues that irony is **echoic** in nature. Both approaches build on key insights from Grice by positioning the attitude of the speaker as central to the analysis. However, as we shall see, they vary in their detail, and they make different claims about which quality is ultimately decisive in determining whether an utterance is ironic. Pretence theorists allow that many instances of irony involve an echoic element. Similarly, those who argue for the echoic account also acknowledge that there may be an element of pretence involved in some ironical utterances. Where the two accounts differ is which of these two characteristics, (involving pretence or being echoic), they claim to be the defining quality of irony. Pretence theorists argue that we cannot have irony without pretence. Those arguing for the echoic account claim that, by definition, all ironic utterances must be echoic.

8.3.1 Pretence Accounts of Irony

Grice suggests that when a speaker produces an ironic utterance, she is pretending to say something and intending that her pretence be recognised. Pretence accounts of irony are designed to build on this suggestion while overcoming or avoiding the issues faced by the Gricean approach. According to such accounts, when a speaker produces an ironic utterance, she is not actually performing the speech act in question. Whether the utterance she has produced appears to be a statement, a question, a command, or any other speech act, she has, in fact, only pretended to perform that act. That is, she has pretended to make a statement, ask a question, or issue a command. The speaker then uses this act of pretence to communicate a negative attitude either towards the sort of people who might produce such utterances sincerely, or towards the sort of people who might interpret them as sincere.

For example, when the speaker looks out of her window at the pouring rain and utters (35), she is pretending to be the sort of person who would describe such weather as beautiful.

(35) What beautiful weather!

The weather clearly is not beautiful, and so the speaker can use this act of pretence to mock, ridicule, or otherwise criticise the person or sort of person that she is imitating. According to this analysis, irony is the act of pretending to hold a defective view, belief, or opinion. The speaker is pretending to be the sort of person who would say a clearly ridiculous thing sincerely, and she is also pretending that the hearer is the sort of person who would accept her utterance as sincere. Both speaker and hearer are aware of the pretence, and both are, therefore, in on the joke. The target of the irony might be the pretend speaker, the pretend hearer, or perhaps both.

According to this account, verbal irony involves two audiences. One audience who is in on the irony, and another who is not. The second of these can be either real or imagined. This, it has been claimed, provides us with a link between verbal irony and dramatic irony. In cases of dramatic irony, the audience for the literary work sees meaning and consequences that are not accessible to the plot-internal characters. In verbal irony, both speaker and hearer are assumed to see meaning and consequences that are not accessible to the pretend interlocutors.

8.3.2 The Echoic Account of Irony

Deirdre Wilson and Dan Sperber (Wilson, 2006, 2013; Wilson and Sperber, 2012) propose an alternative account which treats irony as echoic in nature. We will unpack precisely what that means in a moment, but broadly speaking we can say that the echoic account treats the speaker of an ironic utterance as using a free indirect quotation to communicate a negative attitude about the ideas that she is quoting. Although Sperber and Wilson position their account of irony within the relevance-theoretic pragmatic framework, it is possible to accept an echoic account of irony without necessarily buying into the other claims of relevance theory. According to this approach, various conditions need to be in place for an utterance to be ironic. We will discuss these one-by-one, and, in doing so, we will draw out some important distinctions between utterances and their meaning. This will lead us to the echoic account of irony.

A first key distinction is between what are known as **descriptive uses** of language and what are known as **attributive uses** of language. When a speaker uses language descriptively, she is describing a state of affairs in the world. For example, when Mel utters the sentence in (36) descriptively while talking to Andy, she is describing a state of affairs in the world in which she (Mel) is not talking to you (Andy).

(36) I'm not talking to you

When a speaker uses language attributively, however, she is using it to represent either a thought or an utterance that she attributes to someone else (or perhaps that she attributes to herself at a different time). To illustrate, imagine that the sentence from (36) is uttered as part of the exchange in (37).

(37) Andy: What did Paula say when you invited her to the party?

     Mel: I'm not talking to you

We now have two possible interpretations of Mel's utterance. The first is the descriptive interpretation that we have seen already. On this interpretation Mel is telling Andy that she is not talking to him, and Mel is making a truth-evaluable claim about the world. Her utterance will be true if and only if Mel is not talking to Andy. However, another interpretation is possible. It is possible that Mel is using her utterance to represent what Paula said to her. Although Mel is uttering the words, she is attributing them to Paula. On this interpretation Mel is not making a claim about who is talking to whom.

Rather, she is making a claim about what Paula said. On an attributive reading, Mel's utterance will be true if Paula uttered the words 'I'm not talking to you' to Mel when she was invited to the party. She is representing Paula's description of the world. In Paula's description, Paula is not talking to Mel.

Attributive uses of language need not be direct quotations and they can represent thoughts as well as actual utterances. To be successful they need only resemble the attributed thought or utterance in some way. Imagine that Ryoko has just watched a televised speech by a politician when Phil walks into the room. Phil asks Ryoko what the politician said, and she utters the reply in (38).

(38) The economy is booming, and the people have never been happier

Here, Ryoko has provided a summary of the politician's speech. She is not herself making a claim about the state of the economy or the satisfaction levels of the people. Rather, she is attributing the claims in her utterance to the politician. Whether or not the politician used these precise words or phrases in her speech is of no matter.

The attributive nature of an utterance can be overtly signalled by the speaker. In (37), for example, Mel could have indicated that she intended the content of her utterance to be attributed to Paula by producing the version in (39). Similarly, Ryoko could have indicated the attributive nature of her utterance by producing (40).

(39) She said, 'I'm not talking to you'
(40) According to the prime minister, the economy is booming, and the people have never been happier

However, as we saw in (37) and (38), the attributive nature can also be left unspoken (or **tacit**), for the addressee to infer. This brings us to the echoic account's first key claim about irony. Irony is a tacit attributive use of language. Ironic utterances do not, it is claimed, describe the world. Rather they attribute a thought or utterance to someone else (or to the speaker at another time).

There are various possible motivations that could drive a speaker to use an utterance attributively. She might be reporting what someone has said, as in the attributive reading of (37). She might be summarising somebody else's discourse or opinions, as in (38). However, she might produce an attributive utterance simply to indicate that she has heard and understood what has been said. Imagine that Tom has asked Gemma for directions to the local post office, and they have the exchange in (41).

(41) Gemma: There's no post office in this village
      Tom: Hmm. … There's no post office in this village

Consider Tom's contribution to the exchange. He does not repeat the information to communicate the content of the utterance to Gemma. Gemma clearly already has this information, and so there would be little to be gained for her in terms of cognitive effects if Tom were to do this. Rather, Tom's utterance achieves relevance because it communicates to Gemma that he has heard and understood the information. Tom might also use his utterance in (41) to communicate his attitude to the information he has just received. Perhaps he is disappointed or surprised. When an attributive utterance is used to communicate the speaker's opinion of the attributed thought or utterance, we say that the utterance is echoic. Echoic uses of language are attributive utterances that communicate the speaker's attitude. It is important not to assume that echoic simply means echoed. Repeating something is not enough to make something echoic. In relevance theory, echoic is a technical term, and it means that the utterance is attributive in nature and that at least part of its relevance lies in the attitude that the speaker is communicating.

The speaker's attitude can be positive or negative. She can endorse what the other speaker has said, or she can dissociate herself from it. In (41), the most accessible interpretation is that Tom feels negatively about the news that there is no local post office. However, imagine that Gemma's reply to his inquiry is more positive, and he communicates his positive attitude to this via an echoic utterance, as in (42).

(42)   Gemma: There's a new one just around the corner

Tom: There's a new one just around the corner!

Ironic utterances are echoic. They achieve relevance because they communicate the speaker's attitude towards the attributed thought or utterance. Irony must, however, involve a negative, dissociative attitude of some sort. The speaker might be mocking or poking fun at the original thought or utterance or she might be communicating her scorn, disgust, or contempt. For an utterance to count as ironic, the attitude must be dissociative in some way.

Finally, the speaker's dissociative attitude must be left tacit for the hearer to infer, rather than being spelled out explicitly as part of the utterance. In echoic utterances more generally, the speaker's attitude can either be explicitly communicated or left tacit. In (41) and (42) the hearer must infer how Tom feels. However, he could have uttered (43) to explicitly communicate his frustration, or (44) to convey his excitement at the news.

(43)   It's absolutely ridiculous that there's no post office in this village

(44)   It's brilliant that there's a new one just around the corner

In the case of irony, however, the speaker's dissociative attitude must be left tacit. This is the final component in the echoic account of irony. Irony is a tacit echoic use of language with a tacit dissociative attitude.

Wilson and Sperber argue that this echoic account avoids the issues and problems that were faced by the classical and Gricean approaches. As we saw in Section 8.1, Grice himself pointed out that it was not possible to simply say something that is blatantly untrue and by doing so produce irony. The echoic account explains why we cannot simply point at a car without broken windows and ironically utter (11) ('Look, that car has all its windows intact'). Irony, according to the echoic account, involves an attributive use of language. In (11), the utterance has no easily accessible attributive reading. Notice, however, that if (11) were to be uttered in a discourse context that provides an accessible attributive interpretation, irony emerges. As Wilson and Sperber (2012) outline, we might imagine a discourse context in which a friend has been telling you how safe their neighbourhood is. Despite your worries, they have reassured you that when you come to visit, you will be able to leave your car parked overnight without worrying that it will be stolen or vandalised. You arrive to visit, and you notice that the car down the street has broken windows. You point at the car and utter (11). In this discourse context, you are not simply saying the opposite of what you see. Rather, you are echoing the reassurance that the friend gave you earlier and expressing a mocking, perhaps cynical, dissociative attitude towards it. With this context, the utterance is ironic.

A criticism that is often levelled at the echoic account is that in many cases it is not clear what thought or utterance is being echoed. For example, I wake up in the morning, open my curtains and see that it is pouring down with rain. I utter (45). Or imagine that you go shopping and when you are about to pay, you realise that you have left your wallet or purse at home, so you utter (46).

(45) What beautiful weather we're having!

(46) Brilliant. Just brilliant. I'm so organised!

In these examples, it is not immediately obvious what the echoed utterance or thought might be, and such examples have been raised as an issue for the echoic account by various critics. Wilson and Sperber (2012) and Wilson (2017) have responded to these criticisms by arguing that these examples can be understood in terms of our 'normative bias'. Irony, they note, is most often used to criticise, or to complain. That is, irony usually involves saying that something is positive or pleasing when it clearly is not. Examples of irony where a speaker says that something is bad, when it is clearly good are less common. This, Wilson and Sperber claim, is because we often use irony to complain about things not living up to norm-based expectations about how they should be. For example, we expect people to be polite and respectful, and so when they are not, we can ironically echo this norm-based expectation. Similarly, we have an expectation, or at least a hope, that the weather will be pleasant, and so when it isn't, we can again ironically echo this expectation. Normative bias, therefore, explains both an asymmetry in the type of things we tend to be ironic about, and the cases where no actual thought or utterance is being echoed.

8.3.3 The Ironic Tone of Voice

The pretence accounts and the echoic account of irony each seek to explain how ironic utterances convey meaning. One characteristic of verbal irony that might help us to choose between the two accounts is the so-called **ironic tone of voice**. It is, of course, perfectly possible to be ironic in written language. Therefore, while intonation cues may be helpful in guiding a hearer to the speaker's intended meaning, they are not essential. However, there are two intonation patterns that are often associated with verbal irony: a flat deadpan monotone tone of voice, and an overly enthusiastic, emphatic pattern with exaggerated pitch changes. The first of these is what is most commonly referred to as the ironic tone of voice. Wilson and Sperber (2012) argue that this tone of voice is linked to the attitudinal dimension of irony. The reason that we have intonation patterns associated with irony, but not, for example, metaphor, is that the communication of an attitude is key to irony, but not to other forms of figurative language use. The deadpan monotone pattern reflects the speaker's dissociative attitude towards the attributed thought or utterance, and, as Wilson and Sperber note, it is closely related to the intonation patterns that are associated with disgust and contempt.

In their proposal that irony be treated as pretence, Clark and Gerrig (1984) note that speakers often mimic, exaggerate, and caricature another person's voice when pretending to be that person. This, they suggest, explains the overly enthusiastic, emphatic pattern that we sometimes find used in spoken irony. Recall that according to the pretence accounts, speakers use irony to mock certain people or certain types of people by pretending to be them. The overly enthusiastic tone of voice is perhaps expected on such an account. The speaker is mimicking and mocking the vocal patterns of the sort of person who would say such an obviously ridiculous thing. Imagine that Stella has had an awful day. Everything has gone wrong for her. She was late for work, all her meetings went badly, and she was completely soaked in a rain shower during her lunch break. When she arrives home, her housemate asks her how her day was. She replies ironically using the utterance in (47).

(47) Oh, I've had the best day ever! I'm so glad I got out of bed this morn-
       ing. I wouldn't have missed this day for the world

If produced with an overly emphatic intonation pattern with exaggerated
pitch changes, we might interpret Stella to be caricaturing an overly positive and relentlessly enthusiastic sort of person. Analysing irony as pretence, Clark and Gerrig (1984) claim, explains this sort of example.

In response, Wilson and Sperber suggest that the mimicking and caricaturing of tone of voice is a feature not of irony, but of parody. When she
utters (47), Stella is parodying the overly enthusiastic person. Parody can,
of course, be used to communicate an ironic attitude, and in such cases
pretence and irony combine. When ironic utterances are uttered with the
overly enthusiastic tone of voice, we have, they claim parodic irony, which
involves both echoing and pretence.

A key argument in favour of an echoic account is, however, that not all
irony uses this mimicking tone of voice. Ironic utterances which are produced with the deadpan intonation pattern are perhaps unexpected on the
pretence account. Imagine Stella were to utter (47) using the monotone,
deadpan intonation pattern. The hearer is still likely to interpret her utterance as ironic, and yet her intonation patterns reflect her own attitude,
rather than the attitudes of someone she is pretending to be. Thus, Wilson
and Sperber argue, the key to irony is the communication of a dissociative
attitude to an attributed thought, rather than pretence. All irony is echoic,
they suggest. Some may also involve elements of pretence, but this is not a
defining characteristic.

8.4 Chapter Summary

The chapter opened with a discussion of the Gricean approach to figurative language, with a focus on the criticisms that it has received and
the counterexamples that are often discussed. This set the groundwork
for the exploration of post-Gricean analyses of metaphor, hyperbole, and
irony. This exploration began with an introduction to the field of lexical
pragmatics. Words, it is argued, are very often used to communicate something different to their literally encoded meaning. The ad hoc concepts that
words are used to communicate may be narrower or broader than their
encoded meaning. We see this at play in cases of approximations, and ad
hoc concepts underlie the relevant account of hyperbole and metaphor.

In the second half of the chapter, two key approaches to irony were
outlined. Pretence accounts characterise irony as an act of pretending.

The echoic account of irony, on the other hand, treats irony as an attributive use of language communicating the speaker's dissociative attitude. Irony is often associated with distinctive intonation patterns. We finish the chapter by considering how these patterns might help us to choose between the two approaches to understanding and analysing irony.

Exercises

8a   Consider the concept that the word *red* communicates in examples (i) to (x). How do the concepts that are communicated differ? Think about the shade of red that you picture for each example. What part of the object is red in each case?

(i)   His face was red
(ii)   His eyes were red
(iii)   His hair was red
(iv)   His jumper was red
(v)   The sky was red
(vi)   The traffic lights were red
(vi)   He saw a red squirrel
(viii) He gave her a red rose
(ix)   He ate a red apple
(x)   He ate a red watermelon

8b   Consider the utterances in (i) and (ii). What (if anything) might it mean for the speaker to be using the utterances (a) literally, (b) as an approximation, (c) as hyperbole, and (c) as a metaphor? Can you think of contexts for each interpretation? Are they all possible?

(i)   The horror movie made me sick
(ii) I'll be back in two minutes

8c   Examples of so-called category extension illustrate another non-literal use of words and expressions. Consider the examples in (i) to (v) below. Suggest an analysis of them based on your understanding of lexical pragmatics and ad hoc concepts.

(i)   (Uttered while on a picnic, pointing to a flattish rock): That's a table (Wilson and Sperber, 2012, p. 106)
(ii) (After having looked up information using the DuckDuckGo search engine): I have Googled the answer for you

(iii) Let's talk on Zoom soon (followed by an invitation to a Microsoft Teams meeting)

(iv) (Headline in a fashion magazine): Pink is the new black

(v) (From a magazine article April 2010): Lady Gaga is the new Madonna

8d Think of as many different interpretations of the sentence in (i) as you can. What does *pig* mean in each case? Can you note down the features that form part of the ad hoc concepts that are constructed in each case? Which are part of the literal concept encoded by *pig*, and which are emergent?

(i) Simon is a pig

8e Consider the following scenario (adapted from examples discussed in Wilson (2006)). William and Kate have just played a game of tennis. William's brother Harry is watching. Kate won easily. After the game, William says (i) to Harry (seriously).

(i) I nearly won

Imagine that Kate then utters one of the following.

(ii) The poor fool thinks he nearly won

(iii) He's a fool if he thinks that

(iv) He thinks he nearly won

(v) He nearly won

For each of Kate's possible utterances (ii) to (v), answer the following questions:

- Is the utterance used descriptively or attributively?
- If it is an attributive use, is this explicitly indicated or left tacit?
- Does the speaker communicate a dissociative attitude?
- Is the attitude explicitly indicated or left tacit?

Based on your answers, which of Kate's possible utterances would count as irony (according to the echoic account)? Does this align with your intuitions about which (if any) are ironic?

Key Terms Introduced in this Chapter

Further Reading

There is a wealth of literature on non-literal language use. Figurative language, and in particular metaphor, can be analysed from a range of perspectives. We have focused on a pragmatic perspective here, but a more semantics-focused overview is available in Valenzuela (2017). This text also includes an accessible introduction to Conceptual Metaphor Theory (CMT). Those readers who want to explore CMT in more detail should read Lakoff and Johnson (1980).

To read more about lexical pragmatics and the ad hoc concept approach to metaphor, readers are encouraged to explore the work of Deirdre Wilson and Robyn Carston, both of whom have written widely on the subject (separately and together). Experimental studies into the processing of metaphors compared to literal utterances can be found in Gibbs (1994) and Glucksberg (2001). A full account of category extension (see exercise 8c) can be found in Wilson and Sperber (2012).

Wilson and Sperber (2012) discuss Gricean, pretence, and echoic accounts of irony in their chapter *Explaining irony*, and their chapter *A Deflationary account of metaphors* in the same book, discusses and outlines the ad hoc concept approach to metaphor. Wilson (2017) explores the difference between irony and other seemingly similar figures of speech, including hyperbole, banter, understatement, jokes, and rhetorical questions. The pretence theory of irony is outlined and argued for by Clark and Gerrig (1984) and by Currie (2006), amongst others. Wilson (2006) compares the echoic and pretence accounts, arguing for the relevance-based echoic account. Meanwhile, Currie (2006) responds to criticisms of the pretence account and outlines his own account of irony as pretence.

CHAPTER 9

Politeness

In This Chapter ...

In this chapter, we turn our attention to the role that pragmatics plays in the study of social interaction. When we communicate, we do not simply exchange information. We also manage relationships. As speakers, we can choose to be more or less direct, more or less formal, and more or less attentive to our hearers. The decisions that speakers make are often motivated by concern for how their hearers will react to the utterance, and by the effect that this might then have on the relationship. Perhaps the most influential work in this area of pragmatics is Brown and Levinson's (1987) model of politeness. The first half of this chapter provides an overview of their framework and the politeness strategies that they propose. In the second half of the chapter, we discuss some recent developments that have arisen in response to Brown and Levinson's work. These include analyses of impoliteness, consideration of how cultural variation might be incorporated into the pragmatics of interaction, and a shift to focus less on politeness and more on a broader notion of the relational work that speakers perform.

9.1 What Does It Mean to Be Polite?

When we interact with someone, exchanging information is rarely our only concern. Consider the examples in (1) to (5) as different ways in which we might perform the act of asking for a glass of water.

(1) Could I have a glass of water please?

(2) Can I have a glass of water?

(3) Give me a glass of water

(4) Water. Now

(5) I'm a bit thirsty …

In each case, the speaker is hoping to achieve the same thing. She is hoping that the hearer will give her a glass of water. However, the way she goes about achieving this is different in each case, and we might imagine each of these utterances being appropriate in different social contexts. The difference between these utterances lies, not in the speech act that is being performed or the information that is being conveyed, but rather in the social relationship between the speaker and hearer(s).

In Chapter 4, we discussed Grice's CP and maxims, and we saw how these were very much focused on the 'effective exchange of information' (Grice, 1989, p. 28). When we communicate, however, we are often also concerned with maintaining the social relationship between us and our interlocutor(s). When we communicate, we may, for example, be trying to influence our interlocutor in some way. We may be keen that they form a good opinion of us, or that they know that we have a good opinion of them. These more socially oriented objectives will affect what we say and how we say it.

Grice (1989) briefly acknowledged that there is a need to take social motivations into account when interpreting utterances. He suggested that, in addition to the maxims that he identified, there might be other maxims, which are 'aesthetic, social, or moral in character' (p. 28) and which govern this more social aspect of communication. While this was not his key focus, Grice suggested that 'Be Polite' might be just such a social maxim. This idea was then taken up and developed by Robin Lakoff (1973). She considers why, if the maxims are rational and cooperative rules of conversation, they are so frequently violated. The reason, she suggests, is that 'in most informal conversations, actual communication of important ideas is secondary to merely reaffirming and strengthening relationships' (p. 298). The speaker of (5), for example, has taken an indirect approach to asking for a glass of water. This might be less brief and perspicuous than the maxim of manner suggests is optimal. However, it may help maintain a harmonious relationship between the speaker and the hearer. We will look more closely at why this might be and how this might occur as the chapter progresses.

Lakoff proposed that there are two basic rules of pragmatic competence: (1) be clear, and (2) be polite. In some cases, these two rules work in the same direction. There are occasions on which being clear also means being polite. For example, when giving instructions, we might try to be extra clear to avoid confusing the hearer or wasting his time. In such cases, politeness and clarity coincide. On other occasions the two rules might be in conflict. Perhaps, for example, the clearest way to issue an order is to do so directly. This might not necessarily be perceived as polite. The utterance in (3) is, perhaps, the clearest of the options, but, in certain cultural and social contexts, would be considered less than polite. The speaker must then decide which of the two rules to prioritise. Should she compromise on clarity to maintain politeness, or should she make clarity her priority? The answer will, of course, depend on the context in which she is speaking and on her relationship with her hearer.

Having proposed these two rules, Lakoff then further breaks down what it means to be polite. She proposes that there are three rules of politeness: (R1) don't impose, (R2) give options, and (R3) make [the addressee] feel good – be friendly. The more a speaker can avoid imposing on her hearer, the more she can give him options. The better she can make him feel, the more polite her utterance will be. These rules are presented as universal in nature. However, how they are applied in practice will vary according to cultural and custom specific expectations and assumptions. Lakoff's insights generated an ongoing interest in the issue of politeness in language and communication, and this led to the development of hugely influential work by Penelope Brown and Stephen Levinson (1987). Brown and Levinson's work draws heavily on the concept of **face**, and, as this has become central to the discussion of politeness, we introduce it next.

9.2 Face

The notion of face was first established by sociologist Erving Goffman in the 1950s and 60s. He characterised face as a person's positive self-image, and as something that can be enhanced, maintained, or threatened during interactions. This notion became the basis for Brown and Levinson's influential politeness theory. While their conception of face is derived from Goffman's (1967) work, it is also connected with non-technical notions of face. We might, for example, describe someone who is feeling humiliated or embarrassed as having lost face, or someone might do something to save face. Face is a person's public self-image, and the need to maintain both your own face and, usually, the face of your interlocutor, drives a speaker to perform politeness work.

According to Brown and Levinson, the need to take face into consideration during communication is universal. However, just as Lakoff acknowledges in her work on politeness, cultural values and priorities may affect how this plays out in practice. Therefore, we may expect to find cross-cultural variation in how speakers behave. According to Brown and Levinson, however, the underlying principles and motivations remain the same. We return to consider cultural aspects of face and politeness in Section 9.6.1.

Brown and Levinson divide their notion of face into two aspects: **positive face** and **negative face**. We outline these in the next section, but first it is important not to be misled by these labels. It is easy to assume that positive face might be something that we should strive to cultivate, while negative face should be avoided. However, this is to misunderstand these terms. Each and every one of us, according to Brown and Levinson, has a positive and a negative face which we want to protect. They are aspects of our public self-image, and there is, as we shall see, often a tension between the two. Both our positive and negative faces can be threatened, maintained, or enhanced. Interactions inevitably involve threats to our face, and politeness is about mitigating those threats so that, ideally, the faces of both conversational partners will be maintained, or even enhanced through the interaction.

Positive face can be thought of as our positive self-image. It is our desire to be liked, admired, and approved of by others. It may also involve our desire to be connected to others and to be accepted as part of a group. Our positive face will be threatened when we are caused to think less positively about ourselves, and it will be enhanced when our self-image is enhanced.

Negative face, on the other hand, can be thought of as our desire to act freely and without imposition. Our negative face will be threatened when an outside force limits our freedom to choose or to control our actions. When we are not able to do whatever we please, our negative face is threatened, and it will also be threatened when something is imposed on us, or when we are expected to do something or other.

Notice from these definitions that there is an almost inevitable conflict between the two faces. If we do exactly as we please without taking other people into consideration, then we are likely to annoy or inconvenience others, and therefore, they are likely to think less of us. On the other hand, if we always prioritise what other people think of us, then we are unlikely to be able to act freely and without imposition. There is therefore a tension between the two faces, and whenever we interact with others, we must negotiate that tension. Brown and Levinson characterise the tensions that arise from interaction in terms of **face-threatening acts**, and we look more closely at these in the next section.

9.3 Face-Threatening Acts

Whenever we interact with someone, face-threatening acts (FTAs) are likely to take place. That is, during any interaction, there is the possibility that our positive sense of ourselves (positive face) may be damaged, and/or that we may feel that our freedom from imposition (negative face) has been constrained in some way and/or an imposition put upon us. Once again, we must not be misled by the terminology into thinking that all FTAs are due to negative, hostile, or threatening behaviours. Any communicative act can be an FTA, including, as we shall see, those which are well intentioned, generous, and/or friendly.

According to Brown and Levinson (pp. 74–7), the relative seriousness of an FTA is determined by three social factors or variables. First, there is the social distance between the hearer and the speaker. This will depend on how frequently the hearer and speaker interact, and the kind of interactions and exchanges in which they are involved. Politeness is, Brown and Levinson claim, more important when the speaker and hearer have a more distant relationship. The second variable is the relative power of the speaker and the hearer. If the hearer is of a higher status than the speaker and/or has some sort of power over her, the seriousness of the speaker's FTA will be greater, and more mitigating actions will be appropriate. Finally, the seriousness of the FTA will be affected by the extent to which it imposes on the hearer. For example, asking someone to tell you the time will place a relatively small imposition on the hearer. Asking someone to lend you money, however, is likely to impose on the hearer to a greater degree.

Each of these variables are context-dependent and independent of each other. Imagine that a stranger asks you to keep an eye on their bag while they go to the bathroom during the interval of a theatre performance. You have never met this person before and so there is a relatively large social distance between you. However, there is no power difference between you, as you are both simply members of the audience, and the imposition is relatively small. The FTA is therefore likely to not be considered very serious.

Now imagine that you decide to ask your boss for a pay rise. You interact with her regularly, so the social distance between you is small. However, as your manager, she is relatively high status, and she holds some power over you in a work context. Following your request, your manager must either find the funds to fulfil your request, and then process the necessary paperwork, or she must justify why she cannot fulfil your request. Asking for an increase in wages is therefore likely to place a significant imposition on her and constitutes a serious face-threatening act.

As well as assessing the seriousness of an FTA, we can categorise FTAs according to the face that is threatened (positive or negative) and according to whether it is the face of the hearer or of the speaker that is being threatened. From this, we can identify four categories: threats to the hearer's positive face, threats to the hearer's negative face, threats to the speaker's positive face, and threats to the speaker's negative face. During any interaction, both conversational partners will perform FTAs, and both will also have their faces threatened. An interaction is like a dance, as both interlocutors try to protect their own faces and, assuming that they value the social relationship, also try to mitigate the risks to their partner's faces.

As we go through the categories of threats, it will be apparent that there are also overlaps between them. Some acts may threaten both the positive and negative face, and/or they may constitute a threat to the speaker and to the hearer at the same time.

9.3.1 Threats to the Hearer's Positive Face

A hearer's positive face will be threatened by any act that might make him feel less positively about himself. Most obviously this will include acts where a speaker communicates a negative evaluation of the hearer, such as a criticism, a reprimand, or an insult. It will also include acts in which a speaker contradicts or challenges the hearer, or in which she ridicules or makes fun of him. These acts indicate that the speaker disapproves of the hearer in some way. They all have the potential to damage the hearer's positive face, and so they are face-threatening acts.

The hearer's positive face may also be threatened by other acts which are perhaps less direct, but which, nonetheless indicate that the speaker is not concerned about the hearer's positive face (his self-image). According to Brown and Levinson, this might include mention of inappropriate or controversial topics or of bad news. Bringing up these topics in conversation sends the message that the speaker is willing to risk causing the hearer distress or is willing to risk causing a difficult or uncomfortable atmosphere. Non-cooperative conversational behaviour is also a threat to the hearer's positive face. If a speaker interrupts the hearer, abruptly changes the subject, or simply shows that she is not paying attention, this will indicate that she does not value the hearer's opinions and viewpoints, and again, this is an FTA. Imagine how you feel if you are interrupted or if someone is obviously distracted during your conversation. You are likely to feel that you are not valued, and this, in turn, is likely to affect your own sense of self-worth, even if only fleetingly.

Finally, Brown and Levinson consider incorrect use of address terms or status markers as posing a threat to the hearer's positive face. The address terms that we use often reveal status or power relationships, and failure to use a particular term can send the message that the speaker does not feel the hearer deserves the associated status or regard.

9.3.2 Threats to the Hearer's Negative Face

The hearer's negative face will be threatened when the speaker performs an act that impedes on the hearer's freedom of action, or at least indicates that the speaker is not trying to avoid doing so. These will include speech acts in which the speaker puts some pressure on the hearer to do something. Orders and requests indicate that the speaker wants the hearer to do (or not do) something. Questions, as a request for information, also impose on the hearer, thus threatening his negative face. When a speaker makes a threat or issues a warning, she is communicating that something negative will happen if the hearer does not comply. Even some positively intended acts like offering advice or giving a suggestion threaten the hearer's negative face. By suggesting or advising, the speaker is communicating that the hearer ought to do something. In all these cases, pressure is put on the hearer to comply, and in this way his freedom of action is imposed upon. The very act of communicating involves a request for the hearer's attention, and this imposes on the hearer, threatening his negative face.

Brown and Levinson identify two further categories of acts that may threaten the hearer's negative face. These are, perhaps, a little less intuitive in terms of understanding how they place an imposition on the hearer. First, we have offers and promises. According to Brown and Levinson, when we make an offer or a promise, we put pressure on our hearer to accept or reject it. By doing so we require a decision from the hearer that they would otherwise not have had to make. This is an imposition, even when welcome. Furthermore, we may feel that when someone offers us something or promises us something we incur a debt to them. Perhaps someone has offered to buy you a coffee, and you feel that you must remember to offer them one back in the future. This is an obligation that you did not have before they made their initial offer. Notice, as mentioned above, that an FTA that threatens the hearer's negative face need not be negative in nature. A generous and well-intentioned offer or promise may still constitute a threat to the hearer's negative face by placing an imposition on him.

This brings us to the final group of acts that Brown and Levinson identify in this category: compliments, expressions of envy or admiration, and expressions of strong negative emotions such as hatred or anger. It is important to separate out the two faces in these cases. The acts in this final group are also likely to interact with the hearer's positive face. Expressions of negative emotions such as hatred or anger will be a threat to the hearer's positive sense of himself. Compliments or admiration, on the other hand, may enhance the hearer's positive face. However, according to Brown and Levinson, each of these acts poses a threat to the hearer's negative face. When a speaker expresses envy or admiration, or gives a compliment, the hearer may feel obliged to respond by giving something to the speaker in return. He could feel obliged to give the object of desire itself or he may feel that a corresponding compliment or expression of admiration is required. When a speaker expresses negative emotions such as hatred or anger, the hearer may feel that he, or his belongings, are in danger and that he needs to take protective action. In each case, the act gives the hearer reason to think that he may need to do something that he was not otherwise required to do. This is an imposition on his freedom and thus a threat to his negative face.

9.3.3 Threats to the Speaker's Positive Face

There are some acts which, when performed, constitute a threat to the face of the speaker herself. The speaker's positive face will be threatened by any act which might cause her to reflect on her own self-image and find herself wanting. Some of these may be things that she has control over such as issuing an apology or admitting guilt. When a speaker apologises, she acknowledges that she has done something wrong or inappropriate. Confessions, or admissions of guilt are, likewise, acts in which the speaker admits to some wrongdoing or other. In each case, this is likely to damage the speaker's positive face as she confronts her own weaknesses and imperfections.

Other acts that threaten the speaker's positive face are beyond her immediate control. According to Brown and Levinson, when we lose physical control over our bodies, our positive face is likely to suffer damage. This could be what they call 'emotion leakage' (p. 68), when one is unable to control tears or laughter, or it could be a physical mishap, such as tripping over or stumbling. In either case, a physical act has taken place that we would have preferred to have avoided or prevented. This constitutes a loss of control over our own self-image and therefore over our positive face.

9.3.4 Threats to the Speaker's Negative Face

A speaker's negative face will be threatened when the act she performs places an imposition on her that was not previously there. In the examples discussed by Brown and Levinson, this imposition often takes the form of a debt, with the implication being that that debt must be paid at some point in the future. For example, when a speaker expresses thanks, she acknowledges a debt to the hearer. This is also the case when a speaker accepts an offer. By accepting an offer, she puts herself in debt to the hearer (who has made the offer). We saw in Section 9.3.3 that apologising poses a threat to the speaker's positive face. However, accepting an apology is also an FTA. According to Brown and Levinson (p. 67) when a speaker accepts an apology, or indeed, when she accepts an expression of thanks, she may, as part of that acceptance, feel obliged to downplay the significance of the situation. This is illustrated in the interactions in (6) and (7).

(6) Fan: Thank you so much for covering my shift last week
    Beth: No problem. It was nothing at all. Any time
(7) Fan: I'm really sorry about missing the meeting
    Beth: Don't worry. It wasn't very important anyway

First, let us consider the FTA associated with Fan's utterances. In (6), by expressing her thanks, Fan acknowledges a debt to Beth, and in doing so she damages her own negative face. There is an expectation that debts will be paid, and this expectation imposes on Fan's freedom of action. In (7), Fan is issuing an apology, and as such she is admitting a transgression. This time, the act of doing so damages her own positive face, as we saw in the previous section. Beth's replies in (6) and (7) both offend her own negative face. Accepting thanks, as in (6), or accepting an apology, as in (7), often involve downplaying the impact of the original act. Beth may feel obliged to respond in this way, regardless of the actual impact of Fan's actions. As soon as an interlocutor is placed under an obligation, there is a threat to their negative face. The exchanges in (6) and (7) illustrate the complexity of the dance of FTAs that we perform when interacting. Fan thanks/ apologises, damaging one of her own faces. This, in turn, places a face-threatening obligation on Beth to accept the thanks/apology, and when she does so, she offends her own negative face by downplaying the imposition.

Finally, if a speaker makes a promise or an offer, she commits herself to some future action, and this is an imposition which offends her negative face. Again, it is important to notice that these acts which damage or offend the negative face of a speaker or hearer, are not necessarily inherently negative acts. They can be well-intentioned, generous, and cooperative acts. They become an FTA when they place some sort of imposition on one or both of the interlocutors.

9.4 Politeness Strategies

When we interact with other people, it is inevitable that we will be faced with FTAs. As we have seen in Section 9.3, many everyday interactions, including promises, offers, requests and expressions of gratitude, involve FTAs. Assuming we want to maintain the social relationship between ourselves and our interlocutors, we must consider the impact of these FTAs and make decisions about how best to manage them. Brown and Levinson outline a number of strategies that we employ to navigate interactions while minimising the threats to the faces (including our own) of the interlocutors.

The diagram in Figure 9.1 (adapted from Brown and Levinson, 1987, p. 69) shows how the various strategies relate to one another. We can think of each branching point as a choice that the speaker must make. The decisions that she makes lead her to one of the following strategies: don't do the FTA; do the FTA off record; do the FTA **on record** without **redressive action** (**bald on record**); do the FTA with redress using positive politeness; do the FTA on record with redress using negative politeness.

The choices we make are determined by the relative importance (in the discourse context) of what Brown and Levinson describe as 'three wants' (adapted from Brown and Levinson, 1987, p. 68):

(a)   The want to communicate the content of the FTA

(b)   The want to be efficient or urgent

(c)   The want to maintain the hearer's face to any degree

The relative degree of these 'wants' determines the most appropriate strategy for doing the FTA. We examine these in turn, and we discuss some of the linguistic strategies that are associated with each.

First, the speaker must decide whether to perform the FTA or not. She may decide that the disadvantages of performing the act outweigh the advantages. That is, the want to communicate the content of the FTA may not be great. You might, for example, choose not to tell your dinner companion that they have spinach in their teeth, because you know that it will embarrass them, and because you know that they will notice it next time

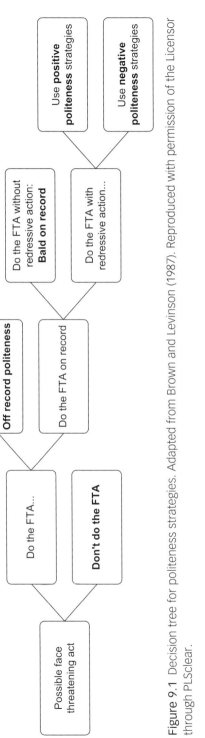

Figure 9.1 Decision tree for politeness strategies. Adapted from Brown and Levinson (1987). Reproduced with permission of the Licensor through PLSclear.

they go to the bathroom. The gain from performing the FTA does not outweigh the risk to your dinner companion's face.

If, however, we cannot, or do not want to, avoid doing the FTA, we have options about how we go about mitigating the risk to our own and our interlocutor's face. The first choice we must then make is whether to perform the FTA directly or indirectly. That is, should we do the act on record or off record?

9.4.1 Off Record Politeness

A speaker performs an FTA **off record** when she does so in such a way that she could deny that the FTA was her intention. The utterance that she produces will usually be compatible with more than one interpretation, and so she avoids committing herself to any one of the possible meanings. The hearer must decide how to interpret the utterance.

There are two overarching approaches to performing an FTA off record. The speaker can perform the FTA via an implicature, or the speaker can perform it by being vague and ambiguous. Brown and Levinson identify a range of strategies associated with each of these approaches, and we consider them in turn.

Throughout this book we have seen various examples of indirect utterances. In the case of indirect requests, the speaker does not explicitly ask for anything, but rather implies that a course of action might be desirable. For example, we might imagine a speaker uttering (8) as an attempt to get the hearer to open a window.

(8)   It's getting a bit stuffy in here

Here, the speaker is performing an FTA, but she is doing so off record. Notice, that she could later deny that she wanted the window open. She was, she could claim, merely commenting on the air quality in the room. In other cases, a speaker might choose to make a general statement with the intention that the hearer take the statement as relevant to his own situation and respond accordingly. Examples of this are given in (9) and (10).

 (9)   Those windows need to be cleaned

(10)   Thoughtful people call if they are going to be late

In these cases, the speaker has only gone on record with a general statement and not a specific FTA.

A speaker may use understatement or overstatement to perform an FTA off record. Consider the criticisms that are implicated by the understatement in (11) and the overstatement in (12).

(11)   Maybe that wasn't the best idea in the world

(12)   You are never on time!

The figurative language that we discussed in Chapter 8 can be employed to perform an FTA off record. In cases of either irony or metaphor, a hearer must infer what the speaker means, and as soon as there is inference, there is room for the speaker to deny that a particular interpretation was what she intended to communicate. As Brown and Levinson note (p. 212), a speaker is unlikely to get very far if she tries to claim she meant the utterance literally. However, the nuances of the interpretation are deniable. Consider the examples in (13) and (14), where (13) is a metaphor, and (14) is uttered ironically.

(13)   Adam is a devil

(14)   What a fantastic idea! Let's definitely do that!

The metaphor in (13) could be used to convey a range of propositions, from the notion that Adam is a little mischievous and cheeky, through to him being genuinely unkind or malicious. By leaving it to the hearer to infer precisely what was intended by her use of the metaphor, the speaker avoids committing herself to any particular proposition. Similarly, by using irony in (14), the speaker can convey her criticism indirectly. In this way she stays off record, at least superficially. Other strategies which allow a speaker to perform her FTA indirectly include speaking a necessary truth (tautology), as in (15), or a contradiction, as in (16). In each case, the FTA is implicated rather than directly performed.

(15)   You have to do what you have to do

(16)   I like him, and I don't like him

The search for an intended interpretation that is either relevant (in relevance theory terms) or cooperative (in Gricean terms) triggers an implicature, and it is via this implicature that the speaker performs her FTA.

Finally, Brown and Levinson note that rhetorical questions, such as (17), can be used to perform an FTA off record.

(17)   Why would you think that was a good idea?

While the speaker of (17) is not likely to expect an answer to her question, by asking it she implies that she does not think it was a good idea. On the surface, however, she simply asks a question. Thus, the FTA is performed indirectly.

As Brown and Levinson note (p. 212), for many of these off record strategies, it is likely that the hearer will be aware of the speaker's underlying intention. Indeed, it would not be a rational strategy to pursue if the hearer was not likely to reach the conclusion that the speaker intended.

However, if the surface form of the utterance affords the speaker the room to deny that intention, we can say that the FTA was performed off record.

9.4.2 Bald on Record

Once we decide to perform the FTA directly (what Brown and Levinson call 'on record'), we have the option to do so with or without redressive action. That is, when we perform the act, we can choose to modify the way we do it to try to mitigate the face threat, or we can do it without any modifications. Performing the FTA without face-saving mitigations or redress is known as the bald on record strategy. When adopting this strategy, the speaker will perform the FTA in the most direct, clear, and concise way possible. This strategy will be appropriate in situations where the urgency and efficiency of communicating the message (want (b)) override the desire to maintain the hearer's face (want (c)), and Brown and Levinson identify three categories of cases where this might occur.

First, we have cases where the urgency of the context outweighs concerns about face. Imagine, for example, that you see a friend reaching out to pick up a very hot saucepan. You realise that he does not know that it is hot, and he will burn his hand if you do not act quickly to stop him. It would be appropriate to adopt a bald on record strategy in this situation by uttering (18).

(18) Stop! Don't touch that!

This is a direct imperative, and there is no attempt to mitigate any FTAs. However, the urgency of the situation makes this the best strategy to adopt. Imagine if you uttered (19) instead.

(19) I'm sorry to interrupt you, but I think it might be the case that the saucepan is hot, and you probably shouldn't touch it

In this version, you have taken redressive action to mitigate the FTA (we shall see what sort of action this is in the next sections), but your friend will have hurt himself by the time the message is conveyed. Or imagine that you have called someone to give them important information but the battery on your mobile phone is low and about to run out. You would probably be forgiven for speaking more directly than usual, as the need to convey the information in the limited time available is more pressing than the need to take redressive action.

The second category of acts in which the bald on record strategy may be appropriate is those acts which pose very little threat to the hearer's face, and, indeed, may be in the hearer's interest, even if they are not urgent. For example, Brown and Levinson suggest that imperatives such as (20), when used to make a request or offer, pose little threat to the hearer's face, and so do not require redressive action of any sort.

(20)   Come in! Sit down!

Finally, there are cases where the speaker's desire to maintain the hearer's face (want (c)) is small. This may be because the speaker occupies a position of authority or power over the hearer, or perhaps, the context is such that the speaker does not care about maintaining face. An invigilator at the end of an examination might utter (21).

(21)   Put your pens down. Leave the room without talking

In this case, the speaker is in a position of power, and she is not invested in any social relationship with the hearers. It is easy to think that by adopting a bald on record strategy we are being impolite. However, as these examples illustrate, there are discourse contexts in which a direct, on record and without redress utterance is the most appropriate way to communicate.

9.4.3 On Record with Redress

In some cases, the wish to maintain the hearer's face outweighs the need to be efficient or to perform the FTA urgently. In these cases, the speaker is likely to take redressive action to mitigate the risk to face. Brown and Levinson identify a range of general and specific strategies that the speaker might adopt, and they classify them according to whether they contribute to the maintenance or enhancement of the positive or negative face. Redressive strategies which are directed towards the positive face are classified as **positive politeness**. Those strategies which are directed towards the negative face are classified as **negative politeness**.

   Negative politeness strategies are associated with showing respect to your hearer (Brown and Levinson, 1987, p. 129), while positive politeness strategies are about communicating closeness and a sense of shared perspective. Positive and negative politeness strategies interact with FTAs in ways that are slightly different to one another. Negative politeness strategies are generally intended as redressive action for a specific FTA, and that FTA will be a threat against either the speaker's or the hearer's negative face. We discuss a range of these strategies in Section 9.4.5. Positive politeness strategies, on the other hand, are not necessarily related to a specific FTA. Rather, they are designed to enhance the speaker's and/or the hearer's positive face by highlighting connections and shared values, goals, and assumptions. Therefore, a speaker might adopt a positive politeness strategy, even if the FTA that is being performed is a threat against negative face. As we shall see, positive politeness strategies tend to be focused on

203

highlighting connections and common ground and on making your conversational partner feel valued. We will also see that there is some overlap. Some strategies, including, for example, hedges, offer redress to both positive and negative faces.

Finally, before we look more closely at these strategies, it is important to remember that negative politeness strategies are not a lack of politeness. Neither are they somehow worse or less valuable than positive politeness strategies. The word *negative* in the label refers to the fact that they are strategies which are employed to minimise or mitigate the threat to the hearer's negative face by reducing the sense of imposition.

9.4.4 Positive Politeness Strategies

Positive politeness strategies are politeness strategies which are intended to maintain or enhance the hearer's positive face. Our positive sense of our own self-image is likely to be enhanced if we feel that others share our perspectives, values, and goals, or if we ourselves feel valued by others. Brown and Levinson identify a range of strategies which a speaker might use to attend to her interlocutor's positive face.

9.4.4.1 Pay Attention to Your Hearer

Several of the positive politeness strategies can be understood as means by which a speaker claims common ground with her hearer and conveys a sense of shared perspective and experience. The speaker might, for example, communicate that she is paying attention to the hearer. Imagine that you want to ask a friend for a favour. As in (22), you might decide to comment positively on the friend's new haircut or on an item of clothing before you do so.

(22) That's a lovely shirt! Is it new? … Could I borrow £20 until next week?

By showing an interest in him and paying him some attention, you enhance your hearer's positive face. You could also do this by anticipating his needs, and offering him something before he asks for it, as in (23).

(23) You've had a long journey. Would you like a glass of water before we start the meeting?

In both (22) and (23) the speaker is performing an FTA that threatens the hearer's negative face. She is asking to borrow money in (22), and in (23), she is indicating that she wants to start the meeting. In each case, she is placing an imposition on her hearer. Even though it is the hearer's negative face that has been threatened, the speaker can use positive politeness strategies to redress the FTA. Regardless of the face that has been threatened, paying attention to hearers and their needs is a positive politeness strategy. Politeness strategies are defined in terms of the face that they maintain or enhance, rather than the FTA that they redress.

A speaker might attempt to convey common ground by showing exaggerated interest in the hearer and his circumstances. She might, for example, use emphatic or superlative adjectives as in (24).

(24) That's the worst possible news! You must be devastated!

Similarly, there is a range of strategies that a speaker might use to intensify her utterance and draw the hearer in, making him feel more involved. These include use of the historic present tense (or 'vivid present' as Brown and Levinson call it), as in (25), use of hyperbole as in (26), use of tag questions, such as (27), and use of directly, rather than indirectly, quoted speech, as in (28).

(25) So, I walk up to my manager, and I tell him that I want a pay rise

(26) Everyone I've ever met was at the party

(27) It was a reasonable thing to do, wasn't it?

(28) He said, 'Speak to me again at the end of the week'

These strategies all function to draw the hearer into the conversation and thus establish shared perspective and common ground.

9.4.4.2 Indicate In-Group Membership

As Brown and Levinson (1987, p. 103) note, positive politeness strategies may be used, not only to redress an FTA, but also 'as a kind of social acceleration'. These sorts of strategies build intimacy and contribute to the formation of in-group relations. Feeling part of an in-group enhances one's positive face.

In-group membership is also key to the next positive politeness strategy that Brown and Levinson identify: the use of in-group markers. There are various ways in which we can signal in-group membership. We might, for example, use an informal term of address, such as *mate*, *buddy*, or *guys*. Alternatively, we might signal membership of an in-group by the language, dialect, or vocabulary that we use. In multilingual contexts, one language may be associated with intimate and domestic contexts, and use of that language may signal to hearers that they are considered to appropriately fall within that context. Similarly, speakers may use in-group jargon or slang to signal that they consider their interlocutor to be a member of their group. Finally, speakers may use more ellipsis and contracted forms to signal in-group membership. By leaving certain elements of an utterance implicit, the speaker is indicating that she considers herself and the hearer to share common assumptions. She is signalling that she is confident that the hearer will be able to infer her meaning on this basis and therefore does not require any more explicit information.

9.4.4.3 Seek Agreement

A speaker may also try to establish common ground with a hearer by seeking agreement and by avoiding disagreement. She may, for example, start a conversation by raising a topic that she knows her hearer is likely to agree with her on. This may well be something general like the weather or an uncontroversial news item. In Chapter 7, we saw examples of phatic communication where an utterance is designed to establish or maintain a social relationship. The same sort of utterances can be used to establish common ground and thereby enhance the hearer's positive face. Again, they have little relevance in their own right, but serve an important social function. Speakers may also signal agreement by repeating something that their interlocutor has said. This also has the benefit of indicating that the speaker has been paying attention to the hearer, which, as we have seen, is another positive politeness strategy.

There are also various ways in which a speaker can try to avoid disagreement and thereby indicate that she shares common ground with the hearer. She may, for example, focus on aspects of topics that she and her hearer agree on, while skipping over possible points of disagreement. She may also use a strategy that Brown and Levinson call 'token agreement'. This is where an utterance begins with what seems to be agreement before the speaker backtracks to reveal some degree of disagreement. This could be the classic 'yes, but ...' response, or something more subtle, as in Jasmine's response in (29).

(29) Amelia: Did you enjoy the movie?

Jasmine: Yes, I did! I mean, it was a little too long in my opinion, and the plot was pretty convoluted and unbelievable. I also didn't like the ending, but, yes, it wasn't bad

A speaker may also seek to enhance her hearer's positive face and mitigate an FTA by spending some time talking about trivial matters, gossiping, or by telling a joke. This can be used to establish a sense of common ground before the speaker moves on to ask a favour, raise a difficult point, or perform some other FTA. Alternatively, the speaker might choose to tell a white lie. If the matter is quite trivial, we may say something that is not true to avoid disagreeing or otherwise damaging the hearer's positive face.

A speaker may use a linguistic marker to indicate that she is assuming agreement. According to Brown and Levinson the words *then* and *so* may be used in this way. Consider the examples in (30) and (31).

(30) So, let's meet at 12:30

(31) You're going to speak to your boss, then?

The imperative in (30) and the question in (31) are functioning as suggestions. However, the use of *so* and *then* implies that they are suggestions based on a previously agreed plan of action. This gives the impression that the speaker is merely confirming arrangements, rather than suggesting something new, and this, in turn, creates a sense of common ground.

A speaker may seek to avoid disagreement by **hedging** her opinion. When she uses a hedging device, the speaker makes her claim or opinion vaguer, and thus less open to objections or contradictions. As we will see, hedges are also a feature of negative politeness, and we will explore them in more detail in Section 9.4.5.

9.4.4.4 Signal Cooperation and Collaboration

As well as claiming a sense of common ground, a speaker can attend to the positive face of her hearer by using strategies that present her and her hearer as collaborators who share a common goal. A key technique here is to use the inclusive first-person pronouns *we* and *us*. Imagine that a teacher utters (32) to her students when they have been distracted from a task at hand.

(32) Let's get on with the exercise, shall we?

The teacher is not herself doing the exercise, but by using the inclusive pronoun, she communicates the assumption that she and the students are all part of one cooperative group.

A speaker may also signal cooperation in a more general way by indicating that she understands and shares the hearer's wants and needs, and by assuming that the hearer understands and shares her wants and needs. This can be achieved in a variety of ways including being optimistic that a request will be fulfilled, as in (33), and presupposing the hearer's objections or concerns, as in (34).

(33) I've come to borrow a cup of milk

(34) I know you wanted to meet on Thursday, but I need to postpone until next week

Notice that (32) to (34) are further examples of positive politeness strategies used to redress a threat to the hearer's negative face.

9.4.4.5 Satisfy the Hearer's Wants

Finally, the speaker can try to enhance the hearer's positive face by giving him something that satisfies his wants. This could be by giving an actual gift, or it could be by giving attention, sympathy, understanding, or cooperation. By giving him something that he wants, the speaker demonstrates that she knows and respects the hearer's wants and that she is willing to help to satisfy them.

9.4.5 Negative Politeness Strategies

Negative politeness strategies are used to attend to some aspect of the negative face by acknowledging that the hearer has been imposed upon, and/or minimising or mitigating the imposition. According to Brown and Levinson, negative politeness strategies are those behaviours that are perhaps most obviously and stereotypically thought of as being polite and courteous in an everyday sense (pp. 129–30). They mirror the sort of advice that we might expect to find in guides to etiquette and good manners. Most often a negative politeness strategy is employed to mitigate a specific and particular FTA. However, they may also be used to create a sense of social distance between the speaker and the hearer. Next, we consider in turn the various negative politeness strategies discussed by Brown and Levinson.

9.4.5.1 Acknowledge the Imposition

One way for the speaker to mitigate a threat to the hearer's face is to communicate that she is aware of the threat and that she has taken it into consideration when deciding to perform the act. That is, she is communicating that she has not done the act lightly or thoughtlessly, and that the imposition is unavoidable and regrettable. The speaker can do this by directly acknowledging the imposition, as in (35), indicating reluctance to impose on the hearer, as in (36), or apologising and asking for forgiveness, as in (37) and (38). She might also provide the hearer with a reason as to why she is unable to avoid performing the FTA, as in (39).

(35) I realise this is a huge ask but …
(36) I hate to have to bother you, but …
(37) I'm really sorry, but …
(38) Excuse me, but …
(39) I wouldn't normally bother you, but I've tried everything else I can think of …

9.4.5.2 Impersonalise the FTA

According to Brown and Levinson, a speaker can implicitly communicate that she is reluctant to impose on the hearer by dissociating herself and/or the hearer from the FTA, and thereby impersonalising the interaction. There are various ways in which a speaker might do this, and often they involve avoiding the personal pronouns *I* and *you*. Notice, that in English, the most common imperative form is without the overt subject pronoun, *you*. Brown and Levinson (p. 191) suggest that using an overt second-person pronoun creates a more aggressive and direct imperative. Compare (40) with (41).

(40)   Stop it now

(41)   You stop it now

We might also avoid personal pronouns by using the passive, rather than the active voice. Compare (42) with (43).

(42)   You must wear a mask at all times

(43)   Masks must be worn at all times

Alternatively, orders or instructions might be impersonalised by being issued in the form of a general rule, as in (44) and (45), or using the first-person plural pronoun, as in (46).

(44)   Passengers must not speak to the driver while the bus is in motion

(45)   Customers must wait here to be seated

(46)   We don't eat with our mouths full in this family

A speaker may distance herself from the imposition inherent in her FTA by switching to the past tense, as in examples (47) and (48).

(47)   I was wondering if you could spare a few minutes of your time

(48)   I thought you might like to join us next week

This, according to Brown and Levinson, allows the speaker to distance herself from the here and now of the imposition, and thus mitigate the threat.

Notice that the phrases, 'I was wondering' in (47) and 'I thought you might' in (48) communicate that the speaker is not presuming that the hearer will agree. This is a key negative politeness strategy and can be achieved in various ways. We look at some of these next.

9.4.5.3 Hedging

As we saw in Section 9.3.2, threats against a hearer's negative face are often to do with asking something of the hearer, whether that be in the form of a request, a command, or an instruction. One strategy to mitigate this FTA is to avoid assuming or presuming that the hearer is willing or able to do the act. By doing so, the speaker, at least superficially, gives the hearer reasonable grounds to refuse the request or command, and in this way, she lessens the imposition.

A key strategy for mitigating the threat is to use hedges. A hedge can be thought of as anything that indicates a level of uncertainty or tentativeness. This might include the use of modifiers such as *rather*, *quite*, or *sort of*, or tag questions such as, *isn't it?* or *don't they?* Brown and Levinson discuss these and a range of other hedging expressions and techniques that can be used as negative politeness devices. As they acknowledge, these are only examples and those discussed do not exhaust the hedging possibilities. The same caveat applies to the discussions throughout this section. These are illustrations only, and there are likely to be other ways, linguistic or non-linguistic for a speaker to achieve the same effect. An example of a tag question is given in (49).

(49) Bring me another glass of water, will you?

Some hedging expressions communicate that the speaker is not entirely committed to what she is saying or that she is not taking full responsibility for it. A speaker can distance herself from the imposition by using an expression which indicates a degree of uncertainty, as in (50) and (51).

(50) I believe we need to stop now

(51) I don't think you're meant to do that

A similar effect can be achieved by using the conditional mood, as in (52) and (53), and indeed we may even hedge an offer in this way, as in (54), so as to not pressure the hearer to accept.

(52) If you don't mind, we will stop now

(53) If you are all ready, we'll begin

(54) There is tea in the pot if you'd like some

There are hedges which indicate that, perhaps, the speaker feels that although she is doing the FTA on record, this is somehow against her will or against her preference, and she feels it would be more appropriate off record. These include adding phrases such as *I hate to have to say this*, *I must say*, and, *I have to be honest with you*. By admitting the imposition, the speaker is seeking to, at least partially, redress it. Finally, the speaker might hedge what she is saying by using a tentative facial expression or tone of voice, or she may utter interjections associated with hesitation, such as *um* or *ah*.

9.4.5.4 Minimise the Imposition

Another related strategy is to use phrases that present the imposition on the hearer as being small or insignificant. In English this is often achieved by the use of the word *just*, as in (55), but we also see cases of understatement or minimising to achieve the same effect, as in (56) and (57).

(55) Just wait here

(56) I'll be back in two seconds

(57) I need a tiny favour

A speaker might also redress the FTA by acknowledging that by performing it she is placing herself in the hearer's debt, as in (58).

(58) If you could let me know by tonight, I would be ever so grateful

Use of expressions which encode status relationships may be used to mitigate the FTA by signalling that the hearer is in control of the situation, and, therefore, in some sense, free from the imposition. For example, in (59), a waiter in a restaurant might use the address term *Sir* to show deference to the hearer and thus mitigate the FTA.

(59) Please follow me to your table, Sir

Another negative politeness strategy is what Brown and Levinson (p. 174) call 'polite pessimism'. Here the speaker expresses doubt that the hearer can reasonably do whatever is being asked of him, and in doing so, she reduces the imposition. Consider the FTAs in examples (60) to (62)

(60) I don't suppose you could drive a little slower, could you?

(61) Perhaps you could wait a little longer

(62) Could you possibly lend me £10 until next week?

Notice that in each case the speaker uses the modal auxiliary *could*, rather than *can*, and by doing so makes a hypothetical, rather than direct, suggestion or request. In these examples, the speaker also uses expressions which mark possibility, rather than certainty: *suppose*, *perhaps*, and *possibly*. Finally, in (60) we have the use of a negative phrase along with a tag question. Each of these strategies communicates a pessimism on the part of the speaker.

9.4.5.5 Conventionalised Indirectness

As these examples illustrate, speakers often use more than one negative politeness device to reduce the sense of imposition on the hearer. This brings us to a final point to consider when we think about negative politeness. So far, many of the strategies that we have considered involve a degree of indirectness, and they mitigate the imposition by introducing an element of optionality or doubt. However, in most cases, the speaker still intends to perform the FTA on record. This creates a tension. There is, as Brown and Levinson describe 'a clash between the two wants' (p. 130). The want of the speaker to do the FTA on record encourages her to be direct. However, her want to avoid imposing on and therefore damaging the hearer's negative face pushes her towards indirectness. This tension is often resolved, according to Brown and Levinson, by **conventionalised indirectness**.

Conventionalised indirectness involves the use of phrases and sentences which have a conventionally accepted meaning that is different to their literal meaning. Consider the utterance in (63).

(63) Can you put the kettle on?

If taken literally, the speaker of (63) is asking about the hearer's ability to put the kettle on. However, as we saw in Chapter 3, Section 3.3.3, *can you* can be used to perform the speech act of requesting. The speaker is requesting that the hearer put the kettle on.

Phrases such as *can you* followed by a verb phrase have, it is claimed, become conventionally associated with indirect requests 'to the extent that there can be no doubt about what is meant' (Brown and Levinson, 1987, p. 133). Other phrases used in conventionalised indirect requests in English include *will you …, why don't you …,* and *can I ask you to …* (Ruytenbeek, 2019, p. 82). These expressions communicate the speaker's desire to be indirect and thus to attend to the hearer's negative face. However, they are conventionalised to the point that the FTA is recognised as being on record.

In this section we have seen the wide variety of strategies that may be employed to mitigate threats to the hearer's negative face. These strategies are usually targeted at a particular FTA, and they may be used in combination to achieve the speaker's aim. The strategies often involve indirectness of some sort, but they are all intended to reduce the sense that an imposition is being placed on the hearer.

9.5 Impoliteness

9.5.1 What Is (and Isn't) Impoliteness?

So far, much of the discussion around politeness and facework in this chapter has assumed that interlocutors enter into a conversation or interaction with the aim of maintaining and enhancing, as much as possible, their partner's faces. This is not always necessarily the case. Consider the examples in (64) to (67).

(64)   You useless rotten liar!

(65)   (Shouted) Go away and leave me alone. I never want to see you again!

(66)   John tries to speak to Mary, but Mary looks away and puts her hands over her ears

(67)   Get out now!

In each of these examples, the speaker (or in the case of (66), Mary) is actively trying to attack the addressee's face. When face is attacked in this way, we might say that the communicator is being impolite.

A common feature of impoliteness is that the same utterance or act attacks both the addressee's positive and negative faces at the same time. For example, the addressee of (65) is being ordered to go away. This order places an imposition on the addressee and thus threatens his negative face. However, at the same time, his positive face is likely to be damaged by the fact that the speaker does not wish to be in his company now, or perhaps ever. The same utterance attacks both his positive face and his negative face.

We also find that cases of impoliteness often involve extra-linguistic communication either alongside, or instead of, an utterance. Tone of voice, gesture, and facial expression often play a key role in impoliteness. In (65), for example, the damage to the addressee's face comes, not only from the words, but also from the fact that the speaker is shouting, and in (66), Mary's message is conveyed without using words at all. We might also consider someone to have been impolite, not because of what they have said, but because of what they have done. Imagine, for example, how we might feel if someone deliberately pushes in front of us in a queue or talks loudly in a movie theatre. These are impolite acts or impolite behaviours, and they need to be considered alongside impolite utterances.

Impoliteness, like politeness, is sensitive to the discourse context and to cultural norms and expectations. The utterance in (67) is likely to be judged as impolite if it occurs during an argument between two adults of equal status. However, if it is uttered by a firefighter during the evacuation of a building, it would not be impolite. If a parent utters it to a child, it is not impolite, but if a child utters it to their parent, then it might be considered so. A particular act or behaviour might be considered impolite in one cultural context, but neutral, or even polite, in another. Belching after eating, for example, might be taken as positive feedback on the food in some cultures, while being considered incredibly impolite in others. Cultural contexts can be highly localised, and it is easy to accidentally fall foul of behavioural expectations. Some people might, for example, consider it impolite for a guest to visit a home and not remove their shoes before entering, while others will not.

So far, the picture of impoliteness that is emerging is both complex and varied. Indeed, there is no generally agreed upon definition of what it means for an act or an utterance to be impolite. The politeness strategies that were discussed in Section 9.4 are focused on the mitigation of face threats. In the examples in (64) to (67), there is no attempt to mitigate any threats. Indeed, in such examples, there often appears to be an attempt to increase or boost the face threat. Impoliteness is not a simple lack of mitigation that we might be able to understand in terms of Brown and Levinson's strategies. Rather it is an active attempt to damage the addressee's face.

Jonathan Culpeper (1996, 2005) discusses what should and should not be classified as impoliteness, and he offers the following definition:

Impoliteness comes about when: (1) the speaker communicates face attack intentionally, or (2) the hearer perceives and/or constructs behavior as intentionally face-attacking, or a combination of (1) and (2) (Culpeper, 2005, p. 38).

As we can see, intentionality is central to this definition. The speaker must intend to attack the hearer's face, and/or the hearer must recognise or interpret the speaker's behaviour as intentionally face-attacking. Without intentionality, we are not dealing with impoliteness. Impoliteness is not simply a matter of failed politeness.

Imagine that a witness in a UK law court does not realise that she should address the high court judge as *My Lady*, and instead calls her *Ma'am*. This is a mistake. However, any damage to the judge's face was not intended by the witness. Provided that the judge realises that the witness has innocently misjudged what is appropriate, she is likely to interpret the witness as having made a mistake, rather than as having intentionally attacked her positive face. If, however, the witness is corrected, but then continues to use the inappropriate form of address, the judge may well interpret this as intentionally face-attacking, and it would count as impolite according to Culpeper's definition.

Incidental cases of face threat or damage may also occur, but again, these do not count as impoliteness if there is no intention to be impolite and/or if no intention is perceived by the addressee. Culpeper (2005) uses the example of a university tutor providing feedback to a student on their work. Constructive criticism may cause damage to the student's positive face if it makes them feel less positive about themselves. However, we assume that that was not the intention of the tutor. The face threat is an unavoidable side effect of the feedback process. Indeed, in practice, the tutor is likely to use politeness strategies to try to mitigate the effects of the FTA.

Mock impoliteness or **banter** is also not true impoliteness. Imagine the conversation in (68) taking place between two close friends.

(68) Frances: I'm being so clumsy today. I keep dropping everything!

Malcom: You're a total idiot! I don't know how you make it through the day in one piece!

While Malcolm's utterance is superficially insulting, it is not intended to be taken as true. Frances knows this and so her positive face will not be threatened by his reply. On the contrary, banter of this sort is associated with intimacy, and so by using insults with a good friend, Malcolm is communicating that they have a close relationship and that they understand and trust one another. Again, the key is intentionality. Malcolm does not intend to be impolite, and Frances does not perceive his intention as impolite, and so his utterances do not fall under Culpeper's definition.

As Culpeper discusses, impoliteness is also not the same as bald on record politeness. As we saw in Section 9.4.2, bald on record politeness strategies are adopted in situations where the need to communicate outweighs the need to mitigate the face threat, such as in emergencies. Somebody shouting 'help' after falling into a river would not be considered impolite. Impoliteness, on the other hand, involves an intentional face attack, and we are only likely to consider something to be impolite if the face threats that arise cannot be explained away by mitigating circumstances.

9.5.2 Models of Impoliteness

Brown and Levinson's model of politeness was not intended to account for impoliteness and face attacks. We therefore need another way to think about such utterances. Various models of impoliteness have been developed to understand how and why impoliteness arises, and various impoliteness strategies and tactics have been identified. In the rest of this section, we explore two influential models of impoliteness that have been influenced by Brown and Levinson's theory of politeness and which offer useful analytical frameworks for examining impoliteness data. First, we will look at the work of Jonathon Culpeper and we will outline the impoliteness strategies that he identifies. As we shall see, these broadly parallel Brown and Levinson's model for politeness. Then we will briefly outline how this work has been developed by Derek Bousfield, and we will look at the slightly simplified model that he proposes.

Culpepper proposes a model of impoliteness, consisting of impoliteness strategies which broadly parallel Brown and Levinson's politeness strategies (as discussed in Section 9.4). Impoliteness, Culpeper (1996, p. 355) says, is the 'parasite of politeness'. Whereas politeness strategies are about maintaining or enhancing face, impoliteness strategies are means by which the speaker can attack the hearer's face.

Bald on record impoliteness occurs when the speaker performs an FTA without any attempt at redress in a context in which maintaining the hearer's face would usually be considered relevant and appropriate. For example, if a school pupil uttered (69) to their teacher in a non-emergency situation it would usually be considered to be impolite.

(69) Be quiet!

The social and power relationships between pupil and teacher would normally dictate that the pupil should choose not to perform such an FTA, or at the very least should have employed redressive action to mitigate the threat to the teacher's face. Notice, once again, that context is key here. The same utterance would be considered bald on record politeness (rather than impoliteness) if produced in a different context. Imagine, for example, that the power relations are reversed and (69) is uttered by a teacher to a pupil. Now we have a case of bald on record politeness because the social context does not require redressive action in this case.

Positive impoliteness strategies are those which attack the hearer's positive face. They are designed to leave the hearer feeling less positively about themselves than they did before. This includes the use of insults, name-calling, and disrespectful terms of address. It also includes strategies to ignore, exclude or signal a lack of interest in the hearer.

Negative impoliteness strategies are those which are designed to make the hearer feel that they do not have freedom of action and that they are powerless in the situation. This could be achieved by physically or metaphorically invading their space and thus imposing on their freedom, or it could be achieved by being direct and explicit about a debt that is owed. An impolite speaker might attempt to frighten, mock, or belittle her hearer to emphasise her relative power over him.

In cases of off record impoliteness, the speaker performs an FTA by means of an implicature. That is, the offense is implied, rather than explicitly stated. However, as Culpeper (2005, p. 44) explains, the act is performed 'in such a way that one attributable intention clearly outweighs any others'. We see this, for example, in cases of sarcasm or mock politeness. In cases of off record impoliteness, speakers may produce an utterance that is superficially polite, but which is clearly intended insincerely. Imagine, for example, a sarcastic apology or expression of gratitude. Perhaps a speaker produces the utterance in (70) to someone who has just pushed past her roughly in a crowd.

(70) No please, after you. Don't let me get in your way!

On the surface the speaker has said something very polite, but it is clearly not intended sincerely in this discourse context. Rather, it is a case of off record impoliteness. Such uses are intended to damage the hearer's face and promote social disharmony. Finally, a speaker may be impolite by withholding politeness where it would otherwise be expected. Withholding thanks or an expected apology may be taken as a deliberate attempt to be impolite.

As we have seen, it is very difficult to define precisely what it means to be impolite. Derek Bousfield (2008) develops and builds on Culpeper's work, and he considers impoliteness to be behaviour that is intentionally face-threatening, and which is performed without mitigation and/or with deliberate aggression. Furthermore, according to Bousfield, for impoliteness to be successful, the speaker's intention to attack or damage the hearer's face must be recognised. He identifies some weaknesses in Culpeper's model and suggests some adaptations.

It is hard, Bousfield argues, to talk about individual impoliteness strategies as they are often used in combination and any one behaviour or strategy might target both positive and negative faces. There is also a wide variety of ways in which someone can be impolite, and this variety and variation is not, according to Bousfield, fully captured by Culpeper's model. For this reason, he suggests restructuring the model and simplifying it down to two key tactics for impoliteness: on record impoliteness and off record impoliteness.

Culpeper's bald on record, positive and negative politeness strategies fall under one tactic of on record impoliteness. When a speaker uses an on record impoliteness tactic, they explicitly attack the hearer's face. Off record impoliteness is, as with Culpeper's model, offence that is implied, rather than explicitly stated. Both sarcasm and withholding politeness where it might otherwise be expected fall under this category.

While we instinctively recognise impoliteness when we experience it, it is notoriously difficult to define what impoliteness is, and it is even harder to reduce it to a list of strategies. The work by Culpepper and Bousfield offers us models that we can use in data analysis. Their work is part of an ongoing conversation about how impoliteness is produced, perceived, and understood, and it feeds into a wider discussion around how we manage social interactions and relationships via the communicative choices that we make.

9.6 **Responses, Criticisms, and Developments**

Brown and Levinson's politeness theory has been hugely influential. As Locher and Watts (2005, p. 9) explain, it has 'towered above most others [theories] and has served as a guiding beacon for scholars interested in teasing out politeness phenomena from examples of human interaction'. Brown and Levinson's work is now considered to be what many refer to as the 'first wave' of politeness research. This first wave has been followed by second and third waves which have grown out of criticisms, critiques, and developments of Brown and Levinson's work.

As should be evident from the overview in this chapter, Brown and Levinson's approach focuses on the mapping of linguistic expressions and practices onto a range of strategies that mitigate face-threatening acts. Several issues with this approach have been raised and various limitations have been pointed out. This has led to some new approaches to the study of politeness and its role in interaction. In this section, we look at some of the key criticisms and responses to Brown and Levinson's work and explore some of the further directions that have emerged as a result.

9.6.1 Cross-Cultural Variation

As mentioned in Section 9.2, Brown and Levinson present their theory of politeness as universal. This claim has been the basis of much criticism of their work, and so it is useful to explore it in a little more detail and to consider some of the objections that have been put forward. Although Brown and Levinson claim to be presenting 'universals in language usage', this does not mean that they do not acknowledge or allow for cultural variation. They explain that 'quite specific universal principles can provide the basis for an account of diverse cultural differences in interaction' (p. 242), and they appeal to three social factors (relative power, social distance, and ranking of imposition – see Section 9.3) to do so. The significance of each of these social factors and the role that they play in interaction can, they suggest, vary from culture to culture. This helps us to understand some cross-cultural differences in interaction.

If, for example, within a certain culture, power differences are minimal, social distance is small, and impositions are not considered to be significant, Brown and Levinson predict that positive politeness strategies will dominate. That is, speakers and hearers will be most concerned with maintaining and enhancing the positive faces of their communicative partners. If the opposite is the case, then we might find relatively large differences in power and social distance, along with impositions being considered as significant. This will result in the emergence of a negative politeness culture where interlocutors focus on avoiding placing impositions on their partners. Similarly, Brown and Levinson suggest there may be cultural differences in the extent to which a particular act is considered to be face-threatening. They discuss, for example, the act of making an offer. In some cultures, they claim, making offers might be seen as placing the recipient under a 'tremendous debt' (p. 247). In others, however, offers may be treated as fairly insignificant in terms of the face threat that they pose.

Brown and Levinson acknowledge that such cultural generalisations can be, what they call, 'crass' (p. 245), and they propose that analyses should be refined both across and within cultures. However, they argue that, far from ignoring cultural differences, their model 'puts into perspective the ways in which societies are *not* the same interactionally' (p. 253). By incorporating the three social factors into their model, Brown and Levinson claim to be able to account for cross-cultural variation while identifying more general, underlying patterns associated with the use of politeness strategies. To strengthen this claim, Brown and Levinson discuss examples from a range of unrelated languages and cultures. Alongside US English, they draw extensively on data from Tamil (from South India) and Tzeltal (a Mayan language from southern Mexico) as well as from Malagasy, Japanese, and other languages.

Brown and Levinson's model of politeness assumes that 'all competent adult members of a society' (p. 61) have a positive and negative face, as defined in Section 9.2. This claim to the universality of face is, however, the focus of various other critiques of Brown and Levinson's work. Gu (1990), for example, claims that 'the Chinese notion of negative face seems to differ from that defined by Brown and Levinson' (pp. 241–2). As he describes, negative face in Chinese is threatened when someone cannot live up to something they have claimed or when they have done something that 'is likely to incur ill fame or reputation' (p. 242).

Matsumoto (1989) uses Japanese data to make a similar argument for the non-universality of face. She describes how in Japan self-image depends on an individual's position as a member of a group and on relations to other members of that group. Matsumoto explains that '[a]cknowledgement and maintenance of the relative position of others, rather than preservation of an individual's proper territory, governs all social interaction' (p. 405). She concludes that it is possible to develop a universal model of politeness, but only if that model allows for cultural variation in the characterisation of face. As she explains:

> In applying this framework to a particular culture and context, knowledge of the society would be required before the constituents of face in that culture could be determined (pp. 424–5).

Haugh (2018, p. 608) sums up the influence that such cross-cultural work has had on the study of politeness as follows:

> It is now widely acknowledged that while a concern for what others think of us may well be universal to the human condition, the ways in which we can use language to conceptualize such feelings, and the various linguistic practices by which we indicate appropriate levels of consideration for the feelings of others, is subject to considerable cultural diversity.

This shift to focus on the study of face and politeness from a cross-cultural perspective aligns with another key development in the study of politeness. Brown and Levinson's work, which has been described as 'first wave politeness' focuses mainly on identifying linguistic strategies which mitigate face-threatening acts. In the second wave of politeness work that has since emerged, the judgements and perceptions of participants are treated as central. We turn our attention to these developments in the next section.

9.6.2 Discursive Approaches and a Shift to Relational Work

The approach proposed by Brown and Levinson allows us, as observers, to evaluate behaviours against a theoretical model of politeness. Consider the utterances in (71) and (72), taken from Locher and Watts (2005, p. 15).

219

(71) Lend me your pen

(72) Could you lend me your pen?

Using Brown and Levinson's model we can compare these utterances in terms of the politeness strategies that are used, and this leads us to conclude that (72) is more polite than (71). However, this is only one way to understand what it means to be polite. An alternative is to classify behaviours as polite (or otherwise) based on the evaluations of the participants in the interaction. As Locher and Watts (2005, p. 15) point out, most people would judge the indirect request in (72) to be 'appropriate in a given social context', but not necessarily particularly polite. Likewise, the utterance in (71), is likely to be judged as direct, but not necessarily impolite. Furthermore, (71) and (72) might be considered equally acceptable in certain social contexts, such as between very close friends. Depending on how we conceive of and evaluate politeness, we can end up with very different analyses of what is and is not polite. We might also conclude that some utterances or behaviours are neither polite nor impolite, but simply appropriate.

An understanding of politeness as something that is evaluated by participants in the interaction is referred to as 'first order politeness' or 'politeness1'. When politeness is evaluated by observers applying a theoretical model, this is referred to as 'second order politeness' or 'politeness2'. This terminology helps us to distinguish between two different ways of understanding what politeness is and is not. Be careful not to confuse the first and second waves of politeness theory with 'first order' and 'second order' politeness. 'First wave' and 'second wave' are used to describe phases of politeness research. The second wave followed from the first wave. 'First order' and 'second order' politeness, on the other hand, describe the perspectives from which we evaluate the politeness (or otherwise) of an utterance or behaviour. 'First order' politeness is concerned with the evaluations of the participants, whereas 'second order' politeness focuses on the analysis of observers of the discourse. Brown and Levinson's work is concerned with 'second order' politeness ('politeness2') and constitutes the first wave of politeness theory. In the second wave of politeness research, the focus shifted to 'first order' politeness ('politeness1'), with assessment of politeness situated in a socially discursive context and taking into account the evaluations of the participants.

According to Watts (2003, p. 8), 'whether or not a participant's behaviour is evaluated as polite or impolite is not merely a matter of the linguistic expressions that s/he uses, but rather depends on the interpretation of that behaviour in the overall social interaction'. This led Locher and Watts (2005, p. 16) to conclude that 'no linguistic expression can be taken to be inherently polite'. The same expression, phrase, or sentence might be judged impolite in some discourse contexts but perfectly acceptable, or even polite in others.

The shift to focus on politeness1 led to a broadening of focus in terms of what is of interest to those working on the pragmatics of interaction. As we have seen, Brown and Levinson's work focused on (mostly) linguistic strategies to mitigate FTAs. Locher and Watts (2005, p. 10) argue that this does not constitute 'a theory of politeness, but rather a theory of facework, dealing only with the mitigation of face-threatening acts'. If, they suggest, we want to investigate how communicators manage social relationships, we should be focusing on the full range of behaviours which constitute what Locher and Watts (2005) call **'relational work'**. Relational work is all 'the "work" individuals invest in negotiating relationships with others' (p. 10) and it 'comprises the entire continuum of verbal behavior from direct, impolite, rude or aggressive interaction through to polite interaction, encompassing both appropriate and inappropriate forms of social behavior' (p. 11).

Many of the examples of polite and impolite behaviours that are discussed in this chapter stand out as designed to either actively enhance or attack face. However, as Locher and Watts (p. 11) discuss, much of the relational work that we do goes unnoticed in everyday interaction. It is simply behaviour that is considered appropriate in the context. Participants will only evaluate something as polite or impolite if it stands out as marked behaviour. For example, Ruytenbeek (2019) analyses conventionalised indirect requests that take the form 'Can you + verb phrase', such as (73).

(73) Can you close the window?

He concludes that this sort of politeness is likely to go unnoticed. When using such an expression, a speaker is more concerned with avoiding impoliteness, rather than trying to appear positively polite. Thus, while the study of relational work includes those interactions which stand out as polite or impolite. It also 'looks at all forms of verbal interaction in their own right' (Locher and Watts, 2005, p. 29).

Finally, what has been referred to as the 'third wave' of politeness research seeks to draw together insights from politeness1 and politeness2. On these approaches, evaluations and perceptions of participants feed into theoretical analyses. A wide range of work falls under this third wave. Some analyses focus more on the perspective of participants (politeness1), while others are more concerned with the analyst's perspective (politeness2). Some focus more on social and cultural aspects of interaction, while others are more pragmatic, adopting, for example, neo-Gricean theoretical perspectives. The wealth of approaches and perspectives encompassed by this third wave of research reflects the ongoing interest in the study of politeness, impoliteness, and relational work more broadly.

221

9.7 Chapter Summary

In this chapter, we have discussed the role that (im)politeness plays in communicative acts. Communication is not just about transferring information. It is also about building, maintaining or, in some cases, damaging social relationships between the interlocutors. It is possible to communicate the same piece of information with different levels of (im)politeness, and we need a way to capture this difference and to understand the strategies that speakers employ. (Im)politeness is also sensitive to the context and is closely tied to the intentions of the speaker. As such, it is a key focus of pragmatics.

We saw how Grice's theory of conversation paved the way for the discussion of politeness and politeness strategies, beginning with work by Robin Lakoff. The notion of face quickly became key to discussions of politeness and led to the development of Brown and Levinson's influential model of politeness. Brown and Levinson's work offers a framework for analysing both face-threatening acts (FTAs) and the strategies that speakers use to mitigate those acts.

In the second half of the chapter, we outlined some of the work that has developed out of, and in response to, Brown and Levinson's model. This includes models of impoliteness, discussions of cross-cultural variation, and moves to adopt a more discursive approach, shifting the focus beyond politeness to the pragmatics of relational work more broadly.

Exercises

9a   Note down some incidents or utterances that you consider to be polite or impolite. Can you use the ideas from this chapter (e.g., Brown and Levinson's notion of FTAs or Culpeper's definition of impoliteness) to analyse these and say why they are polite/impolite?

9b   Consider the scenarios described below. What is the FTA and whose face is being threatened? Is it their positive or negative face? Explain why. Use the social variables (social distance, power, and degree of imposition) discussed in Section 9.3 to discuss each example.

   (i)   A school pupil calls their teacher by their first name
   (ii) A parent tells their child to clean up their bedroom
   (iii) A friend asks you if they can borrow your favourite jacket

(iv) A member of cabin crew on a plane tells a passenger to put their seatbelt on

(v) A friend apologises to you for forgetting your birthday

9c Think of some situations in which you have chosen not to perform an FTA. What made you do so? Can you explain your decision in terms of the FTA that you were trying to avoid and the social variables that were involved?

9d For each of the following scenarios (i)–(v), prepare an utterance using each of the strategies in (a)–(d). Which one do you think you would actually use (if any)?

(a) Off record
(b) Bald on record
(c) Positive politeness
(d) Negative politeness

(i) Your friend has bought a new shirt and you think it looks awful. He asks you if you like it
(ii) Your housemate keeps leaving her dirty dishes in the sink, and you end up washing them up for her. You decide to speak to her about it
(iii) You wish to ask a friend if you can borrow a small sum of money (£10/€10/$10)
(iv) You are sitting on a train, and you notice that a fellow passenger's wallet has fallen out of their bag
(v) You feel ill in the middle of the night and decide to call a friend for help

9e Consider the following ways of asking someone to open the window. Put them in order from most polite to least polite (or most impolite!) based on your own intuitions. Do you think Brown and Levinson would agree with you and why? In which contexts might each be appropriate?

(i) I would love some fresh air
(ii) It's a bit stuffy in here, isn't it?
(iii) Do you think you could possibly open the window?
(iv) Open the window, please
(v) Open that bloody window!
(vi) Why do we have the window closed when it's thirty-eight degrees today?

(vii)   Is there some reason why the window is closed?

(viii) (shouting) Open the window now!

9f   Which of the following are impolite according to Culpeper's definition? Why? Do you agree?

(i)   (Uttered between close friends meeting after a long absence): Get over here, shithead!

(ii)   John asks Charlotte a question. It is obvious to both that she has heard the question. However, she does not respond

(iii)   (Uttered during an intense argument): You bastard!

(iv)   (Uttered by Joan in a sarcastic tone after her boss gives her more work to do): Thanks so much! Just what I needed!

(v)   A police officer shouts at a suspect who is running away, telling them to stop immediately

---

9g   Choose a scene from a television programme or movie where at least two characters interact. What FTAs are being performed? Whose face is being threatened, and is it their positive or negative face? What (if any) politeness (or impoliteness) strategies are used? Why do you think the character has chosen this strategy in the context?

Key Terms Introduced in this Chapter

bald on record, 198
banter, 214
conventionalised indirectness, 211
face, 191
face-threatening acts, 193
hedging, 207
mock impoliteness, 214
negative face, 192
negative impoliteness, 216
negative politeness, 203
off record, 200
on record, 198
positive face, 192
positive impoliteness, 216
positive politeness, 203
redressive action, 198
relational work, 221

Further Reading

Politeness, facework, and relational work are the focus of a wealth of research in pragmatics, and this is a dynamic and evolving field. It is impossible to include everything that an interested reader might possibly and usefully look at in this short section. However, the following should act as starting points, depending on the interests and focus of the reader.

Anyone interested in politeness should refer to Brown and Levinson's (1987) original text. In this they discuss the full range of face-threatening acts and politeness strategies in detail. This is essential reading for anyone wishing to carry out an analysis based on their framework. Much of the subsequent work in the field develops or responds to their original ideas, and so a thorough understanding of Brown and Levinson's approach is recommended for anyone wanting to look at politeness in interaction and communication. Their notion of face draws heavily on the work of Goffman (1967).

Those wishing to explore the second wave of politeness theory may find it useful to read work by Eelen (2001), Mills (2003), Watts (2003), Watts, Ide, and Ehlich (2005), and Lakoff and Ide (2005). Locher and Watts (2005) outline the case for a move to focus on 'relational work' rather than politeness.

As discussed, the third wave of politeness research encompasses a wide variety of work and approaches. However, useful starting points for exploring this area include work by Michael Haugh (2007, 2014, 2018), Dániel Kádár (2017) and Jonathan Culpeper (2011). Those wishing to read more about intercultural and cross-cultural work in politeness might start with Spencer-Oatey (2000) and Spencer-Oatey and Kádár (2021).

Kádár and Haugh (2013), Kádár (2017), and Haugh and Watanabe (2017) provide accessible overviews of the various approaches to (im)politeness theories and are useful as gateways to other work. Readers may also wish to explore articles published in the *Journal of Politeness Research* (De Gruyter Mouton) and chapters in *The Palgrave Handbook of Linguistic Politeness* (Culpeper, Haugh, and Kádár, 2017).

CHAPTER 10

Researching Pragmatics

In This Chapter ...

In this chapter, the focus turns to practical matters as we outline the various ways in which issues and questions in pragmatics can be researched. As we have seen throughout this book, pragmatics is the study of language in context, and it is concerned with (a) the decisions that speakers make when they produce an utterance and (b) the processes that hearers follow to interpret an utterance. How do we advance our understanding of pragmatic processes, and in doing so, learn more about how human communication works? That is, how do we conduct research in pragmatics?

To answer a pragmatics-focused research question or to investigate the pragmatics of an issue or practice we need two things. We need a theory of pragmatics, and we need data. One without the other will only give us half of the picture. Section 10.1 takes a closer look at theoretical frameworks and the role they play in shaping a piece of research. We then move on to look at the different sorts of data that might be collected as part of a pragmatics research project.

Much work in theoretical pragmatics relies, at least initially, on speaker intuitions and, in Section 10.2, we see how constructed examples can be used to test predictions and to fine-tune our understanding. In Section 10.3 the focus turns to experimental pragmatics. We discuss free production tasks where utterances are elicited from speakers in some way, and judgement tasks where participants are asked to judge or interpret an utterance. Section 10.4 describes some examples of pragmatics research that has used transcripts or texts for analysis. We then move on to look at corpus pragmatics in Section 10.5. In Section 10.6 we discuss some of the practicalities of research in pragmatics. We think about how to find a topic to investigate, before discussing the ethical considerations that must be part of any project plan. Finally, we think briefly about the issue of diversity in research and how biases can affect our results.

10.1 Using Theoretical Frameworks

Good research in pragmatics advances our knowledge and understanding of how speakers and hearers communicate. It involves two key activities: working with data and developing theories. Neither theoretical work nor experimental work can stand alone if we are to develop our knowledge and understanding of pragmatic processes and the contributions they make to communication. Experimental work must be underpinned by theoretical predictions, and theoretical predictions must eventually be tested against data.

Later in this chapter, we will see various ways in which we can collect or generate data as part of a research project in pragmatics. However, before we jump into data collection it is important to be precise about what we want to find out and to establish a theoretical context for the research. Various pragmatic theories have been introduced in this book, including speech act theory, relevance theory, and politeness theory. These theories are sometimes referred to as theoretical frameworks because they provide a structure and a framework for conducting research. A theoretical framework provides the researcher with certain principles and assumptions as starting points for their investigations. This means that ideas and **hypotheses** are not developed or tested in a vacuum. Rather they are developed and tested against an existing theory of how communication works.

Theoretical frameworks provide us with a starting point for analysis and they help us to define our parameters as we investigate an issue or question. Suppose for example, I am interested in metaphors, and I am curious to know more about why and how speakers use them. I could collect lots of examples of metaphors from everyday speech, and then I could look for patterns in these data. This might be useful, and I might end up with some interesting observations. However, in this case, the analysis of the data is likely to be fairly unstructured and might also be quite descriptive. I can add structure to my research and move from description to analysis by using a theoretical framework to inform the questions that I ask about the data and the conclusions that I draw.

There are various frameworks that I could use as my starting point. Which one I choose is likely to be determined by what I want to find out. We can focus in on what we want to find out by writing a **research question**. Research questions are key to the success of any research project. They help determine the data collection and analysis methods. A good research question should be focused, well-articulated, and doable. For example, I might focus my general interest in metaphors onto one aspect by asking the question 'What kinds of speech acts do speakers perform when they produce metaphorical utterances?' I now have a much clearer sense of what I want to investigate, and the question helps me to choose an appropriate theoretical framework and to design a methodology. Based on my research question, it seems sensible to use speech act theory as a framework. As we saw in Chapter 3, speech act theory distinguishes between locutionary, illocutionary, and perlocutionary acts, and it provides us with a classification of illocutionary acts. Speech act theory also draws a distinction between direct and indirect speech acts. These categories and distinctions can be used in the analysis of my metaphor data. I can analyse the locutionary, illocutionary, and perlocutionary acts that are performed by the speakers when they produce each metaphor, and I can classify the illocutionary acts as direct or indirect.

In this example, speech act theory also helps me to formulate **predictions** about what I expect to find in my data. Testing these predictions will help me to answer my research question. For example, I might predict that use of metaphorical language is associated with a wider range of perlocutionary effects than literal language use. I might also predict that metaphors are used more frequently to perform indirect speech acts, compared to direct speech acts. Using speech act theory as a theoretical framework provides shape and focus for my analysis and allows me to develop hypotheses to test. This guides me in my data analysis. Each locutionary act in which a metaphor is used can be coded for the illocutionary acts and perlocutionary acts that are being performed and for whether the illocutionary acts are direct or indirect. Patterns can then be identified, and I can assess whether my predictions are correct.

At this point, it is important to keep in mind that disconfirmation of predictions can be as useful as confirmation. Predictions and hypotheses are tools for doing research and for advancing knowledge. A prediction being wrong, or a hypothesis being disconfirmed does not mean that the research has failed. We have still learned something, and we now know something that we did not know before we conducted the study. Similarly, when data aligns with a hypothesis, we talk in terms of the hypothesis being supported, rather than proved. Taking a critical approach to research involves reflecting on other possible explanations for the patterns and behaviours that we observe. Good research asks as many questions as it answers, and researchers think ahead to the questions they can ask and the next project they can undertake to test their predictions and refine their theories.

Different theoretical frameworks help us to answer different questions. Speech act theory will be appropriate for questions relating to speech acts, and politeness theory will be appropriate for pragmatic studies with a more interpersonal focus. Analysing the same data with a different theoretical framework will offer us a different perspective. Imagine that we are still working with metaphors, but perhaps now the research question is 'Why do speakers use metaphors, when literal alternatives are available?' To answer this question, we could analyse metaphors from a relevance-theoretic perspective. As we saw in Chapters 6 and 7, relevance theory assumes that speakers aim to make their utterances optimally relevant. That means that any extra effort to which a hearer is put when processing an utterance must be offset by extra cognitive effects. This leads to the prediction that the extra effort involved in processing metaphors will produce extra effects, and we can use this prediction to guide the analysis. For this project, we can compare each metaphorical example with a literal alternative and ask whether the metaphorical utterance leads the hearer to more effects than the literal version. We might also record what those effects are, using the three categories of cognitive effect identified in relevance theory. Again, the theoretical framework has provided structure for the predictions we make, and for the methods we use to collect and analyse data.

As these examples illustrate, use of a theoretical framework allows us to ask focused and specific questions and guides us in finding answers to these questions. Theories develop and evolve over time as the predictions that they make are tested against data. If the data do not align with the predictions of the theory, we revisit the theory. Crucially, we do not usually reject the theory outright at this point. Rather, we develop it and refine it as we learn more. The process of testing predictions against data is then repeated.

Over the next few sections, we shift our focus to some of the common research and data collection methods that are used in pragmatics research. This is not an exhaustive list, but rather provides some illustrative examples of how data can be used to test the predictions of pragmatic theories and to answer research questions in the field of pragmatics.

10.2 Intuitions and Constructed Data

Many of the examples discussed in this book are **constructed examples**. That is, they have not been collected from **naturally occurring discourse**, but rather have been made up by the researcher. An **informant**, who may be the researcher themselves, then provides their **intuition** as to what the speaker could reasonably have meant. For example, recall the exchange in (1) between Albert and Eileen which we first discussed in Chapter 1.

(1) Albert: Would you like another glass of wine?

     Eileen: I have to get up early in the morning

It is perfectly possible that two people with these names have at some point produced these exact utterances. However, this is really not important. The informant simply has to imagine that they have done so. They then provide an intuition as to what Eileen meant to communicate by her answer.

Constructed examples are used widely within theoretical linguistics and we find studies where participants are asked to provide intuitions in both syntax and semantics, as well as in pragmatics. An advantage of constructed data is that the researcher can carefully control the stimuli that are shown to the informant, and in this way, they can test a very specific hypothesis. For example, as part of my own work on the pragmatics of reference (Scott, 2020), I hypothesised that intonational stress can affect how reference is resolved. I then constructed two utterances which differed only in their stress patterns and asked informants who the speaker was referring to. Examples from this work are given in (2) and (3). Capitalisation of *HE* indicates that this word is pronounced with an added, contrastive stress.

(2) Andrew threw a ball to Ben, and then he threw one to Farooq

(3) Andrew threw a ball to Ben and then HE threw one to Farooq

Most informants agree that *he* in (2) refers to Andrew, while *HE* in (3) refers to Ben or to some other male who is not Andrew. This provides supporting evidence that intonation can indeed affect how reference is assigned.

Different speakers and hearers may, of course, have different intuitions, and indeed, an individual informant may find they have different intuitions on different occasions of asking. The more that intuitions converge, the more confidently we can draw a conclusion from them.

A disadvantage of this approach is that the data is artificial and involves the researcher making assumptions about the sort of things that people say (and don't say). As Noveck and Sperber (2007, pp. 185–6) point out:

> Pragmatic intuitions on hypothetical utterances … are not about how an utterance is interpreted, but about how an utterance *would be* interpreted if it were produced in a specific situation by a speaker addressing a listener, with referring expressions having actual referents, and so on. These intuitions are educated guesses – and, no doubt, generally good ones – about hypothetical pragmatic facts, but are not themselves pragmatic

facts and they may well be in error. That is, we may be wrong about how, in fact, we would interpret a given utterance in a given context.

Constructed examples are also likely to be affected by the linguistic and cultural background of the researcher. Nevertheless, constructed examples can be extremely useful for identifying how a change in language (or a change in the discourse context) can affect interpretation. Intuition-based methods can, of course, be combined with experimental methods or with methods that use naturally occurring data, and we look at some of these in the following sections.

10.3 Experimental Pragmatics

Experiments in pragmatics need not be complicated and they do not necessarily require sophisticated equipment or specialist expertise. In this section, we look at examples of pragmatic experimental studies. These illustrate different ways in which experimental data can be elicited and used to test the predictions of pragmatic theories.

10.3.1 Free Production Tasks

In **free production tasks,** speakers are given some sort of task that prompts them to produce an utterance. This might, for example, involve asking them a question, showing them an image to describe, or asking them to play a game. The responses of the participant(s) are then recorded and analysed. The researcher can vary the task that is set or the discourse context in which the speakers are communicating, and this allows them to study the impact of contextual factors on the utterances that are produced.

As we shall see, a simple, and yet highly effective method of eliciting data was used as part of an experiment that was conducted by Van Der Henst, Carles, and Sperber (2002). This study was designed to test whether, as relevance theory predicts, speakers prioritise relevance over truth in their utterances. The methods and results of this experiment are outlined here in some detail as they provide a clear illustration of how a simple production experiment can be used to test predictions, and how the results can then be analysed to either provide support for hypotheses or to disconfirm them.

As we saw in Chapter 4, according to the Gricean maxims, speakers should try to make their contributions true. Relevance theory, on the other hand, works from the assumption that speakers are striving for relevance, and that literal truth is less important. These two frameworks for understanding utterance interpretation therefore make different predictions about how speakers will behave. According to Grice, speakers will try to make their utterances true. If an utterance is clearly untrue, some true implicature should follow from this (to uphold the cooperative principle). According to relevance theory, speakers need not say things that are true, so long as they say things that are relevant. In Chapter 8, we discussed approximations as a loose use of language, and we saw examples of speakers using rounded numbers (times, prices, distances, temperatures) as part of their utterances. For example, if I ask you how much you paid for the coat that you are wearing, you might reply using the utterance in (4), even though the actual price was €49.95. It would seem unreasonable to accuse you of lying in this case, even though your answer is not strictly and literally the truth.

(4) It cost €50

Rounding is useful as a phenomenon to study because it allows us to compare utterances that are strictly truthful (unrounded) with approximations (rounded). A situation in which speakers often provide rounded answers is when they are telling the time. Van Der Henst et al. elicited utterances of time telling from participants via a series of very simple and easily replicable experiments to investigate several questions about the pragmatics of rounding.

In each experiment, a researcher approached a member of the public in the street and asked them the time. They then noted down the reply that was given. In the first experiment, the researchers wanted to test whether speakers round times to save their own effort. The researchers worked from the assumption that exact times are more easily read from a digital watch than an analogue watch. Most analogue watches provide markers on the clock face at five-minute intervals, and so, they reasoned, it would be easier for speakers to give an answer that was rounded to the nearest of these markers. Digital watches, on the other hand, show a precise time, and so the easiest option for the speaker is to read out exactly what they see on their watch. Therefore Van Der Henst et al. predicted that, if speaker effort is the key driving factor for rounding, those with analogue watches would round to the nearest five minutes, and those with digital watches would not. The researchers noted down which type of watch each respondent was wearing as they gave their answer. Mobile phones obviously provide a digital display of the time. However, these were not so common at the time of this experiment.

Van Der Henst et al. reasoned that if no rounding were taking place, answers would end in either a five or a zero 20 per cent of the time. They compared this with the distribution of answers in the experimental conditions, and from this they calculated the percentage of responders who were rounding (allowing for the fact that in 20 per cent of the cases the precise time would have ended in a five or zero regardless of whether a speaker rounded or not). In this first experiment, they found that 97 per cent of people with analogue watches gave a rounded answer, whereas only 57 per cent of those with a digital watch did so. While speakers are more likely to round when they are using an analogue watch, compared with digital, what is really surprising is the relatively high number of digital watch wearers who chose to give a rounded answer. Rather than simply reading out the time on their watch, these respondents were choosing to go to extra effort to round and thus minimise the hearer's effort. As Van de Henst et al. (2002, p. 461) explain, '[t]his result falsifies the hypothesis that rounding is caused just by the concern of speakers to spare their own effort'. It also provides supporting evidence for the hypothesis that speakers pay attention to their hearer's effort and tend to try to minimise it.

In the second experiment, the researchers wanted to examine what other factors might influence a speaker to round her answer when giving the time. They considered that perhaps the speakers are not confident that their watches are entirely accurate and so round out of prudence. That is, the speaker might be motivated to round because giving an answer that uses the five-minute interval scale makes her less committed to her response being precisely accurate to the minute. To test this hypothesis, the researchers repeated the experiment but changed the procedure slightly to alter the context in which the question was asked. All participants had analogue watches and were approached by a researcher asking for the time. In the control condition, the researcher simply asked for the time, as in the first experiment. However, in a second condition, the researcher held their own watch in their hands and asked the passer-by, 'Hello! My watch is going wrong. Do you have the time please?' These experiments were conducted in Paris and so the original utterances were in French and are translated here. The prediction was that in the second condition the passer-by would be more likely to give an unrounded answer as they would realise that an accurate answer is relevant when setting the time on a watch. While many people did still round in the second condition (49 per cent), this was significantly lower than in the control condition (94 per cent), suggesting that when the context makes clear that an accurate answer is relevant, fewer people will round in their responses.

How relevant it is to provide an accurate answer will, of course, depend on the context. As Van Der Henst et al. point out, if you have an appointment at 3:30 and ask someone for the time, very little extra is likely to follow from it being 3:08 when compared with it being 3:10. The rounded answer will therefore be more relevant as it is easier to process but leads to the same cognitive effects as the accurate answer. However, if the time is 3:28, the difference between an accurate answer and a rounded answer could be very significant. Options that are still available to the hearer if it is 3:28 might be unavailable if it is 3:30. Although 3:28 might be more effortful to process, it is likely to lead to extra effects that justify the effort.

The final experiment tested for whether participants took this difference in relevance into account when giving their answers. Again, passers-by with analogue watches were asked the time. However, in this third experiment, the researchers asked, 'Hello! Do you have the time please? I have an appointment at t', where t was a particular time. The responses were divided into an earlier group and a later group. In the earlier group, there was between sixteen and thirty minutes between the time of the question and the time of the appointment. In the later group there was between fourteen and zero minutes between the time of the question and the time of the appointment. There was a small but significant difference between the rates of rounding in the two groups. In the earlier group 97 per cent of answers were rounded, compared with 75 per cent in the later group. This suggests that at least some respondents were taking the specifics of the context into account and calculating what would be most relevant to their hearer before they gave their answer.

From these three simple experiments, we can draw various conclusions. First, and perhaps most significantly, all three experiments show that rounding is a very common practice, and this suggests that literal truthfulness is perhaps not as important to speakers as Grice's maxims might at first suggest. Second, rates of rounding are significantly lower when the context makes it clear that a literal, accurate answer would be relevant to the hearer (either because they want to set their watch or because an appointment time is drawing near). This suggests that speakers do take the context and the relevance to the hearer into consideration when constructing their answer.

As these experiments illustrate, eliciting utterances from participants can provide a useful data source. The prompts that are used and the context in which the utterance is elicited can be varied to allow for comparative analyses.

10.3.2 Judgement and Interpretation Tasks

In the free production tasks, utterances are elicited from participants. In some other experiments, participants are shown utterances or interactions and asked to provide a judgement or interpretation. Riordan (2017) used this approach to explore the role that emoji play in disambiguation and enrichment in digitally mediated communication. Participants in her study completed an online survey in which they were shown an ambiguous or underspecified message, such as (5) or (6).

(5) Got a shot

(6) Got a ticket

In (5) the word *shot* is ambiguous and could mean an injection or it could mean a short alcoholic drink. In (6), there are various types of tickets that the speaker could be referring to, including a speeding ticket, a travel ticket, or a ticket to see a movie. In some cases, the participants saw only the basic message. In others, an emoji was added, as, for example in (7) and (8).

(7) Got a shot 💉

(8) Got a shot 🥃

Finally, some participants were shown a version with extra text added to disambiguate the meaning, as in (9) and (10).

 (9) Got a shot from the nurse

(10) Got a shot from the bar

All participants were asked to rate how ambiguous the utterance was on a scale of one to seven. Riordan's results suggested that emoji were effective at guiding a reader in the process of disambiguation, and that, in fact, they seemed to work more effectively than adding more words. Again, this was a simple experiment to conduct, but it provided results which can help us understand the pragmatic functions of emoji.

In Chapters 4 and 5, we discussed scalar implicatures. Scalar implicatures arise where the use of scalar terms (such as *some* or *possibly*) leads to an implicature that a more informative term higher up the scale does not apply. The use of *some* implicates that *all* does not apply, and the use of *possibly* implicates that *certainly* does not apply, for example. These scalar implicatures can be cancelled by new information, as in (11).

(11) Some of my friends were invited to the party. … In fact, all of them were!

The information that all the friends were invited is more informative than the initial assertion that *some* were invited. However, it does not make the initial assertion untrue. For Levinson (2000), who takes a neo-Gricean approach, scalar implicatures are default inferences. That is, we draw the inference that *some* implicates *not all* on all occasions of use. That inference may then be cancelled in some cases, such as (11), based on new information. On this analysis, scalar implicatures are GCIs (generalised conversational implicatures). It is assumed that the *not all* inference is intended in most cases, and so deriving this by default is an efficient strategy.

The relevance-theoretic account of scalar implicatures is, however, quite different. As we saw in Chapter 8, the meanings that words communicate are often narrower than the meanings that they encode, and we can understand interpretive narrowing as a process that is driven and guided by relevance. In the case of so-called scalar implicatures, *some*, it is claimed, will be narrowed to mean *not all* in those contexts in which a 'some but not all' interpretation is optimally relevant. However, in other cases, no narrowing will take place, and *some* will communicate 'some and possibly all'. According to this analysis, there is no default inference. The meaning that enters into the explicature of the utterance is either literal ('some and possibly all') or enriched ('some but not all').

Bott and Noveck (2004) conducted a serious of experiments to test the predictions of these two analyses. In the simplest of these experiments, participants were shown a series of sentences and asked to judge them as either true or false. The time taken to make a decision was recorded in each case, and the mean time across participants was calculated for each type of sentence. Examples of these sentences are given in (12) to (17). Before reading on, decide for yourself whether these sentences are true or false.

(12)   Some elephants are mammals

(13)   Some mammals are elephants

(14)   Some elephants are insects

(15)   All elephants are mammals

(16)   All mammals are elephants

(17)   All elephants are insects

Sentences (13) to (17) are control sentences, while (12) is the experimental sentence. If *some* is interpreted as 'some and possibly all', then (12) will be true. Therefore, participants who responded 'true' to sentence (12) were interpreting it literally. If, however, *some* is taken to mean 'some but not all', then (12) is false. Those who judged (12) to be false were, it is assumed, basing this judgement on the enriched, pragmatic interpretation. The study included a range of examples following the same pattern.

In Bott and Noveck's study, there was broad agreement (86–98 per cent) about whether the sentences in (13) to (17) were true or false. However, for sentence (12) ('Some elephants are mammals') 61 per cent of responses marked it as 'false'. The variation in responses to sentence (12) was significantly higher than for the other sentences.

Bott and Noveck then looked at how long it took participants to respond to each sentence. For the experimental sentence (12) there was a difference in the response times for 'true' (literal) versus 'false' (enriched) answers. It is the analysis of these response times that helps us to decide between the two approaches to scalar implicatures outlined above. The GCI analysis treats the enriched interpretation as a default inference. This approach predicts that all participants would have derived the default enriched interpretation. Those who accepted this interpretation and so answered 'false', should have faster response times than those who then decided to cancel the default inference and who therefore answered 'true'. The relevance-based account predicts the opposite pattern. Enrichment is an inferential process. According to relevance theory, those participants who answered 'true' have not undertaken this enrichment process, and so they should have faster response times than those who did enrich the meaning of 'some' to reach the conclusion that sentence (12) is false. In sum, the GCI account predicts that 'false' responses will be faster than 'true' responses, and the relevance account predicts that 'false' responses will be slower than 'true' responses.

Bott and Noveck's results revealed that participants took significantly longer to provide a response ('false') which was based on the enriched interpretation than they did to provide a response ('true') which was based on the literal interpretation. Furthermore, the response times for the literal ('true') interpretation were very similar to the response times for the control sentences. That is, when participants answered 'true', they were performing in much the same way as when they were answering the questions which required no inferential enrichment. Therefore, it seems from this experiment, that deriving the scalar inference of 'some but not all' and answering on that basis takes longer than providing a literal answer. This aligns with the predictions of the relevance-based account.

In this section, two quite different studies have been described. Both asked participants to interpret utterances and provide a judgement of some sort. Those judgements can then help us to understand the interpretive processes that hearers (and readers) are undertaking, and/or how changing the form or content of an utterance might affect how it is interpreted. These methods can be used to test predictions and thus refine theories.

10.4 Transcripts and Texts

Transcripts are textual records of (usually) spoken language, and they can provide a very useful source of data for pragmatic research. A researcher may compile their own transcript or conduct an analysis on an already existing transcript. As part of his work on politeness theory, Culpeper (2009) presents an analysis of a transcript using not only politeness theory, but also speech act theory and Grice's maxims of conversation. The transcript is a record of a conversation between a counsellor and client at a family planning clinic in the United States and was originally used by Candlin and Lucas (1986) for a discourse analysis study of how advice is given. In his analysis, Culpeper classifies the linguistic strategies and type of speech act used by the speakers in terms of Brown and Levinson's politeness strategies. For example, he explains that the counsellor's use of indirect requests can be classified as off record politeness, while her use of hedges, hesitations, and her use of conditionals are negative politeness strategies. These strategies are, Culpeper notes, not very successful at persuading the client to stop smoking. It is only when the counsellor adopts the positive politeness strategy of claiming common ground that the client engages with the conversation. Notice that use of this framework allows us to identify patterns linked to the different strategies, rather than simply describing what each participant said and did.

Literary texts offer an easily accessible source of language data that can be analysed from various perspectives, and the pragmatics of literature is a growing area for analysis and research. One might, for example, analyse the use of metaphor by a particular author or in a particular genre. In my own work on reference and referring expressions (Scott, 2020), I used examples from the first lines of novels to illustrate creative uses of pronouns and other definite referring expressions. Billy Clark has used ideas from relevance theory to analyse the inferential processes that readers go through and the implicatures that they derive as they read. He has conducted analyses of a range of texts including works by Anton Chekhov (Clark, 2014), William Golding (Clark, 2009), and Eimear McBride (Clark, 2019). In my own work, I have used assumptions from relevance theory to analyse misunderstandings in Shakespeare's *Twelfth Night*, linking intentional ambiguity to both plot and character development (Scott, 2019).

10.5 Corpus Pragmatics

A **corpus** is a collection of texts which is usually large and structured in such a way that it can be easily searched. By searching a corpus (plural '**corpora**') a researcher can find instances of words, phrases, or structures as they were produced by speakers in naturalistic and authentic settings. Some corpora collect together texts from a certain dialect and/or time period. The British National Corpus, for example is a collection of texts (both spoken and written) in British English from the late twentieth century. It contains 100 million words. Other corpora may focus on language used within a specific style, genre, or field. For example, the British Academic Spoken English Corpus contains transcribed and tagged lectures and seminars from various British universities. Corpora may be compiled as a general resource for research, or they may be developed for a particular research project. For example, when researching requests and politeness in WhatsApp group chats, Flores-Salgado and Castineira-Benitez (2018) compiled a relatively small corpus of messages. They asked members of two WhatsApp groups to send them chats and then they extracted all instances of requests from the files to form their corpus.

Corpus analysis is particularly useful when we wish to compile a dataset that draws on a wide range of real-life examples. It may be used to establish how words and phrases are used in context, or it might be used to study the frequency of use of different meanings. As part of a wider research project looking at lexical pragmatics, Kolaiti and Wilson (2014) report on how they used corpus analysis to investigate how certain words and phrases are used in context. For example, they used results from a corpus search to establish that non-literal, loose uses of words are not rare or unusual. Their analysis reveals, for example, that the adjective *painless* was found to be used in a strictly literal sense only 20 per cent of the time.

Corpus analysis can also be used to establish whether language is used differently in different contextual conditions. If a corpus includes details of the contextual conditions in which each utterance was produced, we can compare usage across contexts. In my own work on the pragmatics of clickbait (Scott, 2021), I wanted to establish whether there is a difference between the language that is used in headlines on traditional news websites and the language that is used in headlines on websites associated with clickbait. Clickbait is not defined by one or two specific features. Rather, effective clickbait draws on several linguistic and pragmatic techniques. Therefore, analysing individual clickbait headlines would only provide limited insight. However, corpus analysis allowed me to look at a large dataset of clickbait headlines and a large dataset of traditional deadlines and compare the frequencies with which specific words and phrases were used.

10.6 **Practicalities**

10.6.1 Getting Started: Finding a Topic to Research

Many project and research studies develop out of an informal observation about the ways in which we communicate. This then prompts a question about why speakers and hearers (or writers and readers) are behaving in the way they do. For example, we might notice that a speaker uses a metaphor to communicate an idea, and this might lead us to ask ourselves why she would do this. We might wonder what the advantage is of using a metaphor over a literal expression in that discourse context. We might wonder why we find a particular joke funny and begin to think about the interpretation processes that contribute to the humour. We might reflect on our own language choices, and ask ourselves, why, for example, we decided to describe a person or a thing in a particular way, or why we change the way we use language in different discourse contexts. Informal observations and reflections can be useful starting points for a piece of research.

Misunderstandings are another interesting source for pragmatic research and project ideas. While it can be useful to analyse successful interactions, we can learn a lot about how communication works from when things go wrong. To understand why this might be, it can be useful to think about the engine of a car as an analogy. If we look at a smoothly running engine, we might not have much idea about what each part does or about how important each is to the overall running of the vehicle. However, when the engine fails, studying the various components can be enlightening. Testing each part of the engine can help us to diagnose the problem and may well reveal the role that the part plays in the overall running of the machinery. Similarly, when communication is successful, it may be hard to identify precisely what is leading to that success. It can be difficult to reflect on why a particular utterance succeeded in conveying the speaker's meaning. However, when something goes wrong, we can start to identify where the communication has broken down.

We might wonder why or how two interlocutors who speak the same language to a reasonable degree of fluency can misunderstand one another. As we have seen throughout this book, a great degree of speaker's meaning is inferred, rather than encoded. When inference is involved, there are various ways in which the communication can go wrong. A speaker and hearer might have different assumptions. A speaker might assume that her conversational partner has access to certain pieces of information when he does not. A speaker and hearer might have different assumptions about the formality or closeness of the relationship and therefore might have mismatched politeness strategies. All of these can be revealed by carefully designed research into pragmatics.

These are, of course, not the only sources for projects in pragmatics. Issues of interpretation, context, and inference arise wherever we communicate. An alternative approach is to choose a discourse context that interests you (whether that be literary language, sports commentary, comedy, political activism, or any other topic) and ask questions about how communication succeeds (or doesn't succeed) in that context.

10.6.2 Ethics

As we have seen, many sources of data for research projects in pragmatics involve collecting data from other speakers and hearers. As soon as human beings are involved in a project, we must consider the ethics of research, and ethical considerations must be at the heart of any research methodology. If you are conducting your research as part of a programme of study (at a school, college, or university, for example) there is likely to be an ethical approval process that you need to complete before you can collect any data. Ethical processes are in place to ensure that you, as the researcher, and anyone involved in your project is protected from harm. It is crucial that you check with your supervisor, tutor, and/or institution to find out the procedures that you need to follow to ensure your project is ethically sound. Some of the key issues that you are likely to have to consider include **informed consent, anonymity**, and access to data.

Before any participant can be involved in a research project, they must give their informed consent. This means that they must fully understand what they are taking part in, and they must give consent to their participation. They must not only understand how the research will be conducted but they must also understand how the data they provide will be used and shared. This usually involves preparing an information sheet to give to participants that sets out the purpose of the project and the planned procedure, along with details of how the data will be stored, what it will be used for, and whether it will be anonymised or not. The participant then gives their consent, usually by signing a form. It is the responsibility of the researcher to ensure that this information is provided in an accessible and appropriate format so that the consent that the participants give is, indeed, informed. It is also important that participants do not feel pressured to take part and that they are free to withdraw their consent at a later stage if they wish.

In most cases, participants in a research study should be kept anonymous. We should not collect any data that is not needed for the study, and the participants must be aware of, and have agreed to, all the information that is being collected. We cannot, for example, decide to retrospectively record the gender of our participants if that was not part of the original experimental design when ethical approval was given and when informed consent was collected. Anonymity, however, is more complicated than simply omitting names from surveys, interviews, or other responses. The researcher must think about any information that could be used to identify a participant and/or their community. This might include locations, information about work, or details of personal circumstances. In some cases, the data that is collected might be audio or video footage. For obvious reasons, this makes anonymisation more difficult, and it is crucial that the level and means of anonymisation are clearly communicated to the participant as part of the informed consent process.

New researchers often make the mistake of assuming that because data are publicly available, they can be used freely and without ethical consideration. This is an increasing issue as more and more data are easily accessible on webpages and social media sites. Even when material is publicly available, the perspectives of the speakers who produced the content still need to be carefully considered. Even if content is in the public domain, there could be risks to the participants of using it for a purpose for which it was not originally intended. It may be extremely difficult or impossible to obtain informed consent from users of social media sites. However, that does not mean that the data can be used without a full and thorough consideration of ethical issues. Is it appropriate to use the data at all? Is it practical to anonymise it? How sensitive is the subject matter and what are the risks to the participants?

Ultimately, ethical issues are complex and often nuanced, and there is no easy or uniform answer that applies to every scenario or every project. Ethical review procedures are there to protect you and your participants, and it is crucial that you engage with them meaningfully and before you begin your data collection.

10.6.3 Diversity and Bias in Research

Research in pragmatics attempts to answer questions about how we communicate. However, the conclusions that we draw from the research will only be as representative as the diversity of participants and sources in the data that we collect and analyse. We cannot, of course, ask for every speaker's intuition about the meaning of an utterance, and we cannot analyse every instance of a particular speech act. Sampling is a necessary part of research design. It is, however, crucial that we understand the context in which our research occurs and that we interpret results and draw conclusions relative to that context.

If we use participants in a research project, it is highly likely that convenience has played a role in who those participants are. Perhaps you ask friends, family, and classmates to complete your survey or undergo your experiment. Even in larger scale research projects, participants tend to be volunteers, and, for practical reasons, often end up being undergraduate students from universities in 'Western, educated, industrialized, rich and democratic (WEIRD) societies' (Azar, 2010). Research is therefore rarely as diverse as we might want or hope it to be. An awareness of this is important as you plan your project and as you choose your methodology and data collection methods. It is also crucial when you come to analyse your data. It is very easy to fall into the trap of assuming that because all or most of your participants responded in a particular way, everybody else would respond in that same way. It is important to critically reflect on your methods and on the sources of your data. If, for example, you carry out a study using a corpus of written English, you cannot conclude that the patterns that you observe will also be found in spoken data. If you ask participants, all of whom are under twenty-five years of age, to interpret a metaphor, you cannot assume that your results can necessarily be generalised to all age groups.

Throughout this book we have focused on examples and studies in English, and the topics have been selected to support those who are studying or interested in English linguistics and English language studies. Our understanding of pragmatics and interpretive processes can, however, only be enriched by including analyses that cover a more diverse range of languages and cultural contexts.

While it is important to be aware of the potential biases in the data that we analyse, we must also be aware that, as researchers, we are likely to bring our own biases to the interpretation of the data. If you are conducting a study on language data that is in (one of) your first language(s), it is easy to assume that you must be a typical speaker or hearer, and that if you interpret (or misunderstand) an utterance in a particular way, all other speakers must do the same. It is also very easy to be drawn into the trap of deciding what you will find before you conduct the research. **Confirmation bias** is a tendency to search for, interpret, and remember information 'in such a way that it systematically impedes the possibility that the hypothesis could be rejected' (Oswald and Grosjean, 2004).

Carefully designed and planned methodologies can help to minimise the effect of our own biases. However, data must be interpreted and contextualised, and it is highly likely that a researcher's own perspective and ideologies will come into play at some point. As researchers we strive to be objective. However, it is important to also be reflective and to acknowledge the limitations of the research methods that we use and the conclusions that we draw.

10.7 Chapter Summary

Neither theoretical nor experimental work can stand alone if we are to develop our knowledge and understanding of pragmatic processes and of the contributions that they make to communication. Experimental work must be underpinned by theoretical predictions, and theoretical predictions must be tested against data. The chapter opened with a discussion of theoretical frameworks and the role they play in the research process. They help us to frame research questions, and along with those questions, theories help us to design appropriate data collection and analysis methods. Research is an iterative process which leads to new insights but also to new questions.

Data can be drawn from various sources, and we can even use data that we have constructed ourselves. Experimental data can be collected in various ways including eliciting utterances from participants and asking for judgements and interpretations of existing data. Data can be drawn from transcripts of discourse and existing texts of various sorts. Some projects in pragmatics make use of corpus data to identify trends in how language is used to create meaning. The examples and case studies discussed in this chapter represent a variety of experimental methods, many of which are easily accessible and replicable without the need for expensive equipment or specialist expertise.

The chapter ended with a discussion of some of the practicalities of research in pragmatics. We considered some potential sources of inspiration for projects, and we discussed the importance of conducting research ethically. No matter how simple a project might seem, as soon as humans are involved as participants, ethical considerations come into play. We must also be reflective researchers who critically examine the conditions under which the research was conducted, including scrutinising our own limitations and biases. That being said, there are exciting research opportunities available in the field of pragmatics, and I want to end this book by encouraging every reader to be curious about how we communicate, and to explore the fascinating world of language in context.

Exercises

10a What questions do you have about how we communicate? Look back over the previous chapters and think about what you found most interesting. It might be an example, a theory, or a piece of research. What would you like to know more about?

10b Choose one of your questions from 10a and start a project plan to answer it. Think about which theoretical framework you would use, and how you would go about collecting and analysing data. Remember that you will need a clear and focused research question to guide you in your planning.

10c Consider the following scenario and think about what you would do at each stage.

(i) Imagine that you are a completing a project that looks at how people communicate online. You find a really interesting example on Twitter, and you want to use it in your project. The Twitter user who posted the example has a small following of family and friends. Their account is public. What would you do?

(ii) You decide to include the post in your project. What precautions would you take to protect the original user?

(iii) You remove the name and Twitter handle from the post and include the post in your project. You get really positive feedback on your work, and you decide to make your project publicly available. Would you do anything at this stage to further protect the original user?

(iv) You post your project online without any changes. A journalist then notices your work and thinks it would make an interesting article. Your analysis, including the tweet, is referenced in an online newspaper article. Suddenly, a tweet that the user thought had a small audience, is on a website read by millions. Readers can easily identify the author by searching on Twitter. How might the author of the tweet feel? What factors might affect whether they feel positively or negatively about what has happened? How would you feel, as the researcher? What could you have done to reduce the risks to the author of the tweet?

10d Van Der Henst et al.'s (2002) time-telling experiments discussed in Section 10.3.1 collected responses from human participants. What ethical issues would you need to consider when planning such an experiment? What might the risks be to (a) the participants and (b) the researchers?

Key Terms Introduced in this Chapter

Further Reading

There are many excellent books (and other resources) available to help you to plan and conduct a research project. O'Leary (2009) is a good starting point, but any college or university library is likely to have a range of alternatives. Wray and Bloomer (2012) discuss research within the field of language and linguistics. They go into detail about research processes and methodologies, and provide useful sections on data collection and ethics, along with many ideas for possible projects.

Podesva and Sharma (2013) contains more in-depth and special discussions of various data collection and analysis methods in linguistics. Many of these are useful for studies in pragmatics. More recent books which cover research from the perspective of language and linguistics include Sandoval and Denham (2021) and Voelkel and Kretzschmar (2021).

Clark (2013) discusses various research methods that can be used in pragmatics and provides more background on the role played by intuitions. More can be read about experimental approaches to pragmatics in Noveck and Sperber (2004) and Noveck (2018). Wilson (2018) discusses how relevance theory can used to understand the interpretation of literary texts, and two edited volumes by Siobhan Chapman and Billy Clark (2014, 2019) include various applications of pragmatic theories to literature.

The British Association for Applied Linguistics (BAAL) provides ethical resources in their 'Recommendations on Good Practice in Applied Linguistics' (BAAL, 2017). This outlines the responsibilities of the researcher including (but not limited to) ethical considerations. Page et al. (2014) is a good place to start for readers who are specially interested in using online data in their research.

Glossary

ad hoc concepts   Context and occasion specific concepts which are constructed as part of the interpretation process, and which contribute to the explicature of an utterance.

ambiguity   A linguistic expression is ambiguous when its linguistically encoded content is compatible with more that one meaning. Ambiguity may be lexical or structural/syntactic. See *disambiguation*.

approximations   Loose uses of language in which the concept communicated by a word or phrase has been broadened slightly beyond the literal meaning of the encoded concept.

assertives   Illocutionary acts which commit the speaker to something being the case. These include asserting and stating.

assumptions   Beliefs that a person holds to be true. They are sometimes referred to as contextual assumptions.

attributive use   An utterance that is used to represent either a thought or an utterance that is attributed to someone else (or to the speaker at a different time).

cognitive effects   The changes that processing an input (such as an utterance) creates to the assumptions held by an individual. Assumptions can be strengthened, contradicted and eliminated, or they can combine with the input to yield news contextual implications. Along with processing effort, cognitive effects determine the relative relevance of an input in context.

cognitive environment   An individual's cognitive environment is the set of assumptions that are manifest to that individual at a particular time.

commissives   Illocutionary acts which commit the speaker to some future action. These include promises and threats.

communicative intention   The intention to inform an audience of one's informative intention.

concept   A mental representation of something.

constatives   Utterances that can be used to make a statement and which can be evaluated as either true or false.

context   The circumstances in which an utterance is interpreted. In relevance theory terms, the context is the set of assumptions that are used in the interpretation of an utterance or other ostensive stimulus.

conventional implicatures   A Gricean category of implicature which arises because of the use of a particular word or expression. Conventional implicatures do not draw on the cooperative principle or maxims.

conversational implicatures   A Gricean category of implicatures which draw on the workings of the cooperative principle and maxims.

corpus   A collection of texts which is usually large and structured in such a way that it can be easily searched. The plural of corpus is corpora.

declarations   Searle's category of illocutionary acts which perform an action by the very fact they have been produced. Examples include making a bet, apologising, and declaring two people married.

descriptive uses   Uses of language in which the speaker describes a state of affairs in the world.

directives   Illocutionary acts where the speaker is trying to get the hearer to do something. These include invitations, suggestions, requests, and orders.

disambiguation   The process by which a hearer chooses between two or more possible interpretations for an ambiguous word, expression, or structure.

echoic   Attributive uses of language that communicate the speaker's attitude.

explicature   A term used in relevance theory to describe the explicitly communicated proposition. Explicatures are developments (via reference assignment, disambiguation, and pragmatic enrichment) of the linguistically encoded content of the utterance. They can combine with contextual assumptions to yield implicatures.

explicit meaning   The meaning that a speaker asserts and which can be assessed as true or false.

expressives   Illocutionary acts which communicate the emotional reaction or psychological state of the speaker. These include the acts of congratulating and expressing gratitude.

face   A notion first discussed by Goffman and then used by Brown and Levinson in their politeness theory to mean one's public self-image. It consists of two related aspects: positive face and negative face.

face-threatening acts   Acts which threaten the positive and/or negative face of the speaker and/or hearer.

false belief tasks   Experimental tasks designed to test theory of mind (or mindreading) abilities.

felicity conditions   The conditions that must be satisfied for a speech act to be successfully performed.

floutings   A Gricean category of maxim violation in which a maxim is overtly violated at the level of 'what is said', triggering derivation of an implicature to maintain the overall assumption that the speaker is being cooperative.

generalised conversational implicatures (GCIs)   Conversational implicatures which arise without the need for specific or particular contextual information or circumstances.

higher-level explicatures   Explicitly communicated propositions in which the basic level explicature is embedded under a description of the speaker's attitude or emotion, or of the speech act that she is performing.

illocutionary act   The act that the speaker intended to perform when producing an utterance. Illocutionary acts include promising, requesting, apologising, and asserting.

implicature   An intended implication that follows from an utterance by a process of inference. In relevance theory, implicatures may be implicated premises or implicated conclusions.

informative intention   The intention to inform an audience of something.

lexical adjustment   The interpretive process of narrowing and/or broadening the concept that is communicated by a word or expression in line with the speaker's intentions.

locutionary act   The act of producing a sentence with a specific meaning. Locutionary acts have phonetic, syntactic, and semantic features.

manifestness   An assumption is manifest to an individual if that individual is capable of representing the assumption mentally and accepting it as true or probably true.

metarepresentation   The use of a representation (thought or utterance) to represent another representation (thought or utterance). Metarepresentational ability is the ability to have thoughts about thoughts.

negative face   Our desire to act freely and without imposition.

negative impoliteness   Impoliteness strategies which target the hearer's negative face. These include attempts to frighten, mock, and belittle the hearer.

negative politeness   Politeness strategies which mitigate threats to the hearer's or speaker's negative face. These include hedging, as well as impersonalisation and minimisation of the imposition.

neo-Gricean   Approaches to pragmatics which developed directly out of the work of Grice and which, like Grice, propose maxim-like principles.

ostensive communication   Communication in which the communicator has both an informative and a communicative intention. The communicative stimulus is produced openly and intentionally, and the communicator intends for the addressees to recognise that this is the case.

particularised conversational implicatures (PCIs)   Conversational implicatures which arise because an utterance has been produced in a particular context. Specifics from the context play a role in the derivation of PCIs, and if the context changes the implicatures will also change.

performatives   Utterances which can be used to perform an action and which, when produced, bring about a change in the world.

perlocutionary act   An act that is performed as a result of producing an utterance. Perlocutionary acts are acts of achieving an effect on an addressee, and they may be intended or unintended. Perlocutionary acts include amusing, annoying, persuading, and entertaining.

phatic communication   Communication that is intended to establish, maintain, or enhance social relations, rather than to transmit information. Phatic communication is sometimes referred to as 'small talk'.

positive face   Our positive self-image. It is our desire to be liked, admired, and approved of by others.

positive impoliteness   Impoliteness strategies which target the hearer's positive face. These include ignoring or insulting the hearer or signalling a lack of interest in him.

positive politeness   Politeness strategies which mitigate threats to the hearer's or the speaker's positive face. These include strategies to signal agreement, cooperation, and collaboration, and to indicate in-group membership.

pragmatic enrichment   The inferential processes that contribute to the derivation of the proposition expressed aside from reference assignment and disambiguation.

pragmatics   The study of utterance meaning. Pragmatics is concerned with communicative behaviours in context and with what communicators mean by what they say (or do).

procedural meaning   A type of meaning recognised by relevance theory which contributes to the overall meaning of an utterance by guiding the hearer's inferential processes.

processing effort   The mental effort that hearers expend when processing an utterance (or other ostensive stimulus).

proposition   A representation of a state of affairs that can be evaluated as either true or false.

proposition expressed   Also referred to in relevance theory as the 'basic explicature', the proposition expressed by an utterance is the thought that has been explicitly communicated by the speaker.

reference assignment   The inferential process of working out who or what the referring expressions in an utterance refer to.

relational work   The work that speakers do to manage social relationships. This includes work covered by theories of (im)politeness but also covers any work speakers do to ensure their interactions are socially appropriate.

relevance   In relevance theory, relevance is a quality of inputs. An input is relevant if it leads to cognitive effects, and the relative degree of relevance for an input depends both on the cognitive effects produced and on the processing effort that is required to derive those effects.

representatives   An alternative term for assertives.

scalar implicatures   Implicatures that arise from the use of a scalar term (e.g., *some, all, possibly, certainly*). Use of a term that sits lower down on the scale implicates that a higher term does not apply. For example, use of *some*, implicates *not all*.

semantics   The study of encoded linguistic meaning.

sentence   A string of words that is generated by the grammar of a language and which has syntactic and semantic properties. When a sentence is produced by a communicator it becomes an utterance.

speaker's meaning   The overall meaning that the speaker intends to communicate. This includes the intended explicit meaning of the utterance as well as any implicatures.

utterance   The use of a sentence in a discourse context to communicate a speaker's meaning.

what is said   The Gricean notion of explicit meaning. It is arrived at via the processes of decoding, reference assignment, and disambiguation.

References

Austin, J. L. (1962). *How to Do Things with Words*. Oxford University Press.

Azar, B. (2010). Are your findings 'WEIRD'? *Monitor on Psychology*, 41(5). Retrieved 17 August 2022, from www.apa.org/monitor/2010/05/weird

BAAL (British Association for Applied Linguistics). (2017). *Recommendations on Good Practice in Applied Linguistics*. Retrieved 16 April 2021, from https://baal.org.uk/wp-content/uploads/2017/08/goodpractice_full.pdf

Bach, K. (2006). The Top 10 misconceptions about implicature. In B. J. Birner & G. Ward, eds., *Drawing the Boundaries of Meaning: Neo-Gricean Studies in Pragmatics and Semantics in Honor of Laurence R. Horn*. John Benjamins Publishing, pp. 21–30.

Bach, K., & Harnish, R. M. (1979). *Linguistic Communication and Speech Acts*. MIT Press.

Baron-Cohen, S., Leslie, A. M., & Frith, U. (1985). Does the autistic child have a 'theory of mind'? *Cognition*, 21(1), 37–46. DOI: https://doi.org/10.1016/0010-0277(85)90022-8

BBC. (n.d.). 50 hilarious cuttings from The News Quiz. Retrieved 31 March 2020, from BBC News Quiz: www.bbc.co.uk/programmes/articles/4zPVvmSPfsPMV3TjkHg16sD/50-hilarious-cuttings-from-the-news-quiz

Birner, B. J., & Ward, G. (eds.). (2006). *Drawing the Boundaries of Meaning: Neo-Gricean Studies in Pragmatics and Semantics in Honor of Laurence R. Horn*. John Benjamins Publishing.

Blakemore, D. (1992). *Understanding Utterances*. Blackwell.

Blakemore, D. (2002). *Relevance and Linguistic Meaning: The Semantics and Pragmatics of Discourse Markers*. Cambridge University Press.

Bott, L., & Noveck, I. A. (2004). Some utterances are undcrinformative: The onset and time course of scalar inferences. *Journal of Memory and Language*, 51(3), 437–57. DOI: https://doi.org/10.1016/j.jml.2004.05.006

Bousfield, D. (2008). *Impoliteness in Interaction*. John Benjamins Publishing.

Brown, P., & Levinson, S. C. (1987). *Politeness: Some Universals in Language Usage*. Cambridge University Press.

Candlin, C. N., & Lucas, J. (1986). Interpretations and explanations in discourse: Modes of 'advising' in family planning. In T. Ensink, A. van Essen, & T. van der Geest, eds., *Discourse Analysis and Public Life: Papers of the Groningen Conference on Medical and Political Discourse*. Foris Publications, pp. 13–38.

Carston, R. (2002). *Thoughts and Utterances: The Pragmatics of Explicit Communication*. Blackwell.

Carston, R. (2016). The heterogeneity of procedural meaning. *Lingua*, 175–6, 154–66. DOI: https://doi.org/10.1016/j.lingua.2015.12.010

Chapman, S. (2005). *Paul Grice: Philosopher and Linguist*. Palgrave Macmillan.

Chapman, S. (2011). *Pragmatics*. Palgrave Macmillan.

Chapman, S., & Clark, B. (eds.). (2014). *Pragmatic Literary Stylistics*. Palgrave Macmillan.

Chapman, S., & Clark, B. (eds.). (2019). *Pragmatics and Literature*. John Benjamins Publishing.

Clark, B. (2009). Salient inferences: Pragmatics and the inheritors. *Language and Literature*, 18(2), 173–212. DOI: https://doi.org/10.1177/0963947009105343

Clark, B. (2013). *Relevance Theory*. Cambridge University Press.

Clark, B. (2014). Before and after Chekhov: Inference, interpretation and evaluation. In S. Chapman & B. Clark, eds., *Pragmatic Literary Stylistics*. Palgrave Macmillan, pp. 55–69.

Clark, B. (2019). 'Lazy reading' and 'half-formed things': Indeterminacy and responses to Eimear McBride's 'A Girl is a Half-Formed Thing'. In S. Chapman & B. Clark, eds., *Pragmatics and Literature*. John Benjamins Publishing, pp. 139–64.

Clark, B. (2022). *Pragmatics: The Basics*. Routledge.

Clark, E. (2004). Pragmatics and language acquisition. In L. Horn & G. Ward, eds., *The Handbook of Pragmatics*. Blackwell, pp. 562–77.

Clark, H., & Gerrig, R. (1984). On the pretense theory of irony. *Journal of Experimental Psychology: General*, 113(1), 121–6. DOI: https://doi.org/10.1037/0096-3445.113.1.121

Conrad, J. (1902/1994). *Heart of Darkness*. Penguin.

Culpeper, J. (1996). Towards an anatomy of impoliteness. *Journal of Pragmatics*, 25, 349–67. DOI: https://doi.org/10.1016/0378-2166(95)00014-3

Culpeper, J. (2005). Impoliteness and entertainment in the television quiz show: The Weakest Link. *Journal of Politeness Research*, 1, 35–72. DOI: https://doi.org/10.1515/jplr.2005.1.1.35

Culpeper, J. (2009). Politeness in interaction. In J. Culpeper, F. Katamba, P. Kerswill, R. Wodak, & T. McEnery, eds., *English Language: Description, Variation and Context*. Palgrave Macmillan, pp. 523–35.

Culpeper, J. (2011). *Impoliteness: Using Language to Cause Offence*. Cambridge University Press.

Culpeper, J., Haugh, M., & Kádár, D. Z. (eds.). (2017). *The Palgrave Handbook of Linguistic (Im)politeness*. Palgrave Macmillan.

Currie, G. (2006). Why irony is pretence. In S. Nichols, ed., *The Architecture of the Imagination*. Oxford University Press, pp. 111–33.

Eelen, G. (2001). *A Critique of Politeness Theory*. St Jerome Publishing.

Flores-Salgado, E., & Castineira-Benitez, T. (2018). The use of politeness in WhatsApp discourse and move 'requests'. *Journal of Pragmatics*, 133, 79–92. DOI: https://doi.org/10.1016/j.pragma.2018.06.009

Fogal, D., Harris, D. W., & Moss, M. (eds.). (2018). *New Work on Speech Acts*. Oxford University Press.

Fromkin, V. A. (ed.). (2000). *Linguistics: An Introduction to Linguistic Theory*. Blackwell.

Fromkin, V. A., & Rodman, R. (1998). *An Introduction to Language*. Harcourt.

Germanotta, S., Lindsey, H., & Ronson, M. (2016). *Million Reasons*. Interscope Records.

Gibbs, R. (1994). *The Poetics of Mind: Figurative Thought, Language and Understanding*. Cambridge University Press.

Glucksburg, S. (2001). *Understanding Figurative Language*. Oxford University Press.

Goffman, E. (1967). *Interaction Ritual: Essays on Face to Face Behaviour*. Garden City.

Grice, H. P. (1989). *Studies in the Way of Words*. Harvard University Press.

Grigoroglou, M., & Papafragou, A. (2019). The development of pragmatics abilities. In K. Scott, B. Clark, & R. Carston, eds., *Relevance, Pragmatics and Interpretation*. Cambridge University Press, pp. 102–12.

Gu, Y. (1990). Politeness phenomena in modern Chinese. *Journal of Pragmatics*, 14, 237–57. DOI: https://doi.org/10.1016/0378-2166(90)90082-O

Haugh, M. (2007). The discursive challenge to politeness research: An interactional alternative. *Journal of Politeness Research*, 3(2), 295–317. DOI: https://10.1515/PR.2007.013

Haugh, M. (2014). *Im/Politeness Implicatures*. De Gruyter. DOI: https://doi.org/10.1515/9783110240078

Haugh, M. (2018). Linguistic politeness. In Y. Hasegawa, ed., *The Cambridge Handbook of Japanese Linguistics*. Cambridge University Press, pp. 608–27.

Haugh, M., & Watanabe, Y. (2017). (Im)politeness theory. In B. Vine, ed., *The Routledge Handbook of Language in the Workplace*. Routledge, pp. 65–76.

Heider, F., & Simmel, M. (1944). An experimental study of apparent behaviour. *American Journal of Psychology*, 57, 243–59.

Horn, L. R. (1984). Toward a new taxonomy for pragmatic inference: Q-based and R-based implicature. In D. Schriffin, ed., *Meaning, Form, and Use in Context (GURT'84)*. Georgetown University Press, pp. 11–42.

Horn, L. R. (2004). Implicature. In L. Horn, & G. Ward, eds., *The Handbook of Pragmatics*. Blackwell, pp. 3–28.

Horn, L. R. (2007). Neo-Gricean pragmatics: A Manichaean manifesto. In N. Burton-Roberts, ed., *Pragmatics*. Palgrave MacMillan, pp. 158–83.

Iten, C. (2005). *Linguistic Meaning, Truth Conditions and Relevance: The Case of Concessives*. John Benjamins.

Kádár, D. Z. (2017). Politeness in Pragmatics. In M. Aronoff, ed., *Oxford Research Encyclopedia of Linguistics*. Oxford University Press. Retrieved 21 February 2022, from https://oxfordre.com/linguistics/view/10.1093/acrefore/9780199384655.001.0001/acrefore-9780199384655-e-218

Kádár, D. Z., & Haugh, M. (2013). *Understanding Politeness*. Cambridge University Press.

Katz, J. J. (1972). *Semantic Theory*. Harper & Row.

Keenan, E. O. (1976). The universality of conversational postulates. *Language in Society*, 5(1), 67–80. DOI: https://doi.org/10.1017/S0047404500006850

Kissine, M. (2013). *From Utterances to Speech Acts*. Cambridge University Press.

Kolaiti, P., & Wilson, D. (2014). Corpus analysis and lexical pragmatics: An overview. *International Review of Pragmatics*, 6, 211–39. DOI: https://doi.org/10.1163/18773109-00602002

Lakoff, G., & Johnson, M. (1980). *Metaphors We Live By*. University of Chicago Press.

Lakoff, R. (1973). The logic of politeness; or, minding your p's and q's. In C. Corum, T. C. Smith-Stark, & A. Weiser, eds., *Papers from the Ninth Regional Meeting of the Chicago Linguistics Society*. Chicago Linguistics Society, pp. 292–305.

Lakoff, R., & Ide, S., (eds.) (2005). *Broadening the Horizons of Linguistic Politeness*. John Benjamins Publishing.

Levinson, S. C. (1983). *Pragmatics*. Cambridge University Press.

Levinson, S. C. (1987). Minimization and conversational inference. In J. Verchueren, & M. Bertuccelli-Papi, eds., *The Pragmatic Perspective*. John Benjamins, pp. 61–129.

Levinson, S. C. (2000). *Presumptive Meanings: The Theory of Generalized Conversational Implicature*. The MIT Press.

Locher, M. A., & Watts, R. J. (2005). Politeness theory and relational work. *Journal of Politeness Research*, 1, 9–33. DOI: https://doi.org/10.1515/jplr.2005.1.1.9

Matsumoto, Y. (1989). Politeness and conversational universals: observations from Japanese. *Multilingua*, 8(2–3), 207–21. DOI: https://doi.org/10.1515/mult.1989.8.2-3.207

Mey, J. L. (2005). *Pragmatics: An Introduction*. Blackwell Publishing.

Mills, S. (2003). *Gender and Politeness*. Cambridge University Press. DOI: https://doi.org/10.1017/CBO9780511615238

Morrison, T. (1977/1989). *Song of Solomon*. Pan Books.

Noveck, I. (2018). *Experimental Pragmatics: The Making of a Cognitive Science*. Cambridge University Press.

Noveck, I., & Sperber, D. (eds.) (2004). *Experimental Pragmatics*. Palgrave Macmillan.

Noveck, I., & Sperber, D. (2007). The why and how of experimental pragmatics: The case of 'scalar inferences'. In N. Burton-Roberts, ed., *Pragmatics*. Palgrave MacMillan, pp. 184–212.

O'Leary, Z. (2009). *Essential Guide to Doing Your Research Project*. SAGE.

Oswald, M., & Grosjean, S. (2004). Confirmation bias. In F. Pohl Rüdiger, ed., *Cognitive Illusions: A Handbook on Fallacies and Biases in Thinking, Judgement and Memory*. Psychology Press, pp. 79–96.

Page, R., Barton, D., Unger, J. W., & Zappavigna, M. (2014). *Researching Language and Social Media: A Student Guide*. Routledge.

Perry, K., Eriksen, M. S., Hermansen, T., Wilhelm, S., & Dean, E. (2010). *Firework*. Capitol Records, LLC.

Petrus, K. (ed.). (2010). *Meaning and Analysis: New Essays on Grice*. Palgrave Macmillan.

Pilkington, A. (2000). *Poetic Effects: A Relevance Theory Perspective*. John Benjamins.

Podesva, R. J., & Sharma, D. (eds.) (2013). *Research Methods in Linguistics*. Cambridge University Press.

Riordan, M. A. (2017). The communicative role of non-face emojis: Affect and disambiguation. *Computers in Human Behavior*, 76, 75–86. DOI: https://doi.org/10.1016/j.chb.2017.07.009

Rubio-Fernández, P., & Geurts, B. (2013). How to pass the false-belief task before your fourth birthday. *Psychological Science*, 24(1), 27–33. DOI: https://doi.org/10.1177/0956797612447819

Rubio-Fernández, P., & Geurts, B. (2016). Don't mention the marble! The role of attentional processes in false-belief tasks. *Review of Philosophy and Psychology*, 7, 835–50. DOI: https://doi.org/10.1007/s13164-015-0290-z

Ruytenbeek, N. (2017). The comprehension of indirect requests: Previous work and future directions. In I. Depraetere & R. Salkie, eds., *Semantics and Pragmatics: Drawing a Line*. Springer, pp. 293–322.

Ruytenbeek, N. (2019). Indirect requests, relevance, and politeness. *Journal of Pragmatics*, 142, 78–89. DOI: https://doi.org/10.1016/j.pragma.2019.01.007

Ruytenbeek, N. (2021). *Indirect Speech Acts*. Cambridge University Press.

Sandoval, J., & Denham, K. (2021). *Thinking Like a Linguist: An Introduction to the Science of Language*. Cambridge University Press.

Scott, K. (2019). Misleading and relevance in Shakespeare's Twelfth Night. In S. Chapman, & B. Clark, eds., *Pragmatics and Literature*. John Benjamins, pp. 93–114.

Scott, K. (2020). *Referring Expressions, Pragmatics, and Style: Reference and Beyond*. Cambridge University Press.

Scott, K. (2021). You won't believe what's in this paper! Clickbait, relevance and the curiosity gap. *Journal of Pragmatics*, 175, 53–66. DOI: https://doi.org/10.1016/j.pragma.2020.12.023

Scott, K. (2022). *Pragmatics Online*. Routledge.

Searle, J. R. (1965). What is a speech act? In M. Black, ed., *Philosophy in America*. Allen & Unwin, pp. 221–39.

Searle, J. R. (1969). *Speech Acts*. Cambridge University Press.

Searle, J. R. (1979). *Expression and Meaning: Studies in the Theory of Speech Acts*. Cambridge University Press.

Spencer-Oatey, H. (ed.). (2000). *Culturally Speaking: Culture, Communication and Politeness Theory*. Bloomsbury.

Spencer-Oatey, H., & Kádár, D. Z. (2021). *Intercultural Politeness: Managing Relations Across Cultures*. Cambridge University Press.

Sperber, D. (1994). Understanding verbal understanding. In J. Khalfa, ed., *What Is Intelligence?* Cambridge University Press, pp. 179–98.

Sperber, D., & Wilson, D. (1986/95). *Relevance: Communication and Cognition* (2nd ed. with postface). Blackwell.

Valenzuela, J. (2017). *Meaning in English: An Introduction*. Cambridge University Press.

Van Der Henst, J.-B., Carles, L., & Sperber, D. (2002). Truthfulness and relevance in telling the time. *Mind & Language*, 17, 457–66. DOI: https://doi.org/10.1111/1468-0017.00207

Voelkel, S., & Kretzschmar, F. (2021). *Introducing Linguistics Research*. Cambridge University Press.

Watts, R. (2003). *Politeness*. Cambridge University Press.

Watts, R., Ide, S., & Ehlich, K. (eds.). (2005). *Politeness in Language: Studies in Its History, Theory and Practice*. Mouton de Gruyter.

Wharton, T. (2003). Interjections, language, and the showing/saying continuum. *Pragmatics and Cognition*, 11(1), 39–91. DOI: https://doi.org/10.1075/pc.11.1.04wha

Wharton, T. (2009). *Pragmatics and Non-Verbal Communication*. Cambridge University Press.

Williams, P. (2013). *Happy*. Columbia Records.

Wilson, D. (1995). Is there a maxim of truthfulness. *UCL Working Papers in Linguistics*, 7, 197–212.

Wilson, D. (2006). The pragmatics of verbal irony: Echo or pretence? *Lingua*, 116(10), 1722–43. DOI: https://doi.org/10.1016/j.lingua.2006.05.001

Wilson, D. (2013). Irony comprehension: A developmental perspective. *Journal of Pragmatics*, 59A, 40–56. DOI: https://doi.org/10.1016/j.pragma.2012.09.016

Wilson, D. (2016). Reassessing the conceptual-procedural distinction. *Lingua*, 175–6, 5–19.

Wilson, D. (2017). Irony, hyperbole, jokes and banter. In J. Blochowiak, C. Grisot, S. Durriemann, & C. Laenzlinger, eds., *Formal Models in the Study of Language: Applications in Interdisciplinary Contexts*. Springer, pp. 201–20.

Wilson, D. (2018). Relevance theory and literary interpretation. In T. Cave, & D. Wilson, eds., *Reading Beyond the Code: Literature and Relevance*. Oxford University Press, pp. 185–204.

Wilson, D., & Sperber, D. (1981). On Grice's Theory of Conversation. In P. Werth, ed., *Conversation and Discourse*. Croom Helm, pp. 155–78.

Wilson, D., & Sperber, D. (2002). Truthfulness and relevance. *Mind*, 111(443), 583–632. DOI: https://doi.org/10.1093/mind/111.443.583

Wilson, D., & Sperber, D. (2004). Relevance theory. In L. R. Horn, & G. Ward, eds., *The Handbook of Pragmatics*. Blackwell, pp. 607–32.

Wilson, D., & Sperber, D. (2012). *Meaning and Relevance*. Cambridge University Press.

Wray, A., & Bloomer, A. (2012). *Projects in Linguistics and Language Studies: A Practical Guide to Researching Language*. Hodder.

Yanai, I., & Lercher, M. (2020). The two languages of science. *Genome Biology*, 21(147). DOI: https://doi.org/10.1186/s13059-020-02057-5

Yule, G. (2010). *The Study of Language*. Cambridge University Press.

Žegarac, V., & Clark, B. (1999). Phatic interpretations and phatic communication. *Journal of Linguistics*, 35(2), 321–46. DOI: https://doi.org/10.1017/S0022226799007628

Index